More Urban Myths About Learning and Education

More Urban Myths About Learning and Education: Challenging Eduquacks, Extraordinary Claims, and Alternative Facts examines common beliefs about education and learning that are not supported by scientific evidence before using research to reveal the truth about each topic. The book comprises sections on educational approaches, curriculum, educational psychology, and educational policy, concluding with a critical look at evidence-based education itself. Does playing chess improve intelligence? Should tablets and keyboards replace handwriting? Is there any truth to the 10,000-hour rule for expertise? In an engaging, conversational style, authors Pedro De Bruyckere, Paul A. Kirschner, and Casper Hulshof tackle a set of pervasive myths, effectively separating fact from fiction in learning and education.

Pedro De Bruyckere is an education scientist at Artevelde University College Ghent, Belgium, and Postdoctoral Researcher at Leiden University College Leiden, the Netherlands.

Paul A. Kirschner is Distinguished University Professor and Professor of Educational Psychology at the Open University of the Netherlands, as well as Visiting Professor of Education with a special emphasis on Learning and Interaction in Teacher Education at the University of Oulu, Finland.

Casper Hulshof teaches in the Department of Educational Sciences at the University of Utrecht, the Netherlands.

More Urban Myths About Learning and Education

Challenging Eduquacks, Extraordinary Claims, and Alternative Facts

Pedro De Bruyckere,
Paul A. Kirschner, and
Casper Hulshof

NEW YORK AND LONDON

First published 2020
by Routledge
52 Vanderbilt Avenue, New York, NY 10017

and by Routledge
2 Park Square, Milton Park, Abingdon, Oxon, OX14 4RN

Routledge is an imprint of the Taylor & Francis Group, an informa business

Original title: *Jongens zijn slimmer dan meisjes – volume 2.*

www.lannoo.com

Library of Congress Cataloguing-in-Publication Data
A catalog record for this title has been requested

ISBN: 978-0-815-35457-4 (hbk)
ISBN: 978-0-815-35458-1 (pbk)
ISBN: 978-1-351-13243-5 (ebk)

Typeset in Optima
by Swales & Willis, Exeter, Devon, UK

Contents

Acknowledgements

This book would not have been possible without the generous help of our researcher-colleagues and many other critical spirits, from whom we have received tips and advice over the years. Thank you all. Thanks also to Tom Bennett, Jan and Nils Tishauser, Sara Hjelm, Eva Hartell, Eric Kalenze, Dan Willingham, Dylan William, and everyone near and far who is connected in any way with researchED. Your fact-checking and other assistance has been invaluable. We are likewise grateful to the various publishers who have shown great patience with us and in particular to *American Educator* for the interest they showed in our first book.

Pedro would also like to thank Helena and his boys, Clement, Emile, and Remi. All three of them now frequently ask 'Is that really so?' or 'Says who?'. The spirit of Professor Marc Spoelders clearly lives on in them.

Paul thanks above all Catherine, his muse and the anchor in his life, who makes it possible for him to combines projects like this book with all his other crazy ideas. And a special word for grandchildren Elsa and Benjamin, who are now so small and innocent, and deserve to enjoy good education as they grow up.

Casper thanks all the critical online and offline commentators for their feedback, both requested and unrequested. He also thanks his colleagues for their interest and support, and Petra, Myrthe, Benthe, and Jesse for simply being there.

Did We Think We're Done?

This book contains a new series of possible myths about learning and education. Apparently, we were a bit too optimistic in our previous book, when we hoped that we had cleared up these matters once and for all. In fact, it now seems as if we opened a kind of educational Pandora's box! Not only are we still confronted with queries about 'old favorites' like learning pyramids, learning styles, and digital natives, but in recent years all three of us have received lots of new questions about new subjects from readers, from the audiences at our presentations and even from our academic and scientific colleagues, all keen to know whether this story is true or that theory is really correct. It is these questions that have inspired us to write this new volume, which once again involved lots of searching in the sources and lots of weighing up of pros and cons, before finally cutting the knot and coming to a decision in each case: myth or not?

The process of writing this second book was actually much more difficult than the first one. This was not necessarily because most of the most popular and obvious myths and fairy tales had been dealt with first time around, but more because we had been surprised (pleasantly, of course) by the success of our first book. The original Dutch version has sold over 11,000 copies. In addition, translations have appeared in English, Swedish and Chinese, and as we write this introduction negotiations are underway for two further translations. Some of the sections of the English version were also published in *American Educator*, allowing them to be read by millions of teachers, lecturers, and professors, both inside the United States and beyond.

This success made us more aware than ever that we need to get this new book 110 percent right: this means checking, double checking, and even triple checking. In our post-truth society, we have no desire to produce more 'fake news' and 'alternative facts'. This means that, as with our first book, the following ground rules apply:

- If, in spite of all our checking, there are still any errors in the book, these are entirely our own responsibility.
- Everything is based on the knowledge that was available to us at the time of writing.

Of course, in the intervening years we have still kept an eye on the themes dealt with in the first book. Imagine, for example, if evidence had come to light that you really can learn in your sleep![1]

But the most important rule – and one that again we have carried over from the first book – is this: our own opinions do not count. We have tried to record as accurately as possible the current state of the scientific and academic consensus for each of the themes we examine. Which is also why in some cases we will simply admit that we do not know the answer – because nobody else does, either!

New Blocks

This new book is divided into four new chapters of possible myths:

- Myths about 'what' should be covered by education in the curriculum.
- Myths about various didactic approaches and 'how' education should be given.
- Myths about educational psychology.
- Myths about educational policy.

The final chapter of the book will look at a very particular educational myth. True to the old adage that you must be most critical for the things in which you believe most fervently, we will deal with the claim that evidence-based education is ... also a myth.

Are We Done Now?

So have we covered everything this time? That is something we don't dare to say with our hand on our heart. To be honest, we have investigated some themes which, for various reasons, did not find their way into the following pages and new themes are coming to light all the time. This is not the prelude to an announcement about a third book, merely an indication that in education, as in life, you can never be sure what is going to happen next. We will keep our eyes and ears open – and recommend that you do the same.

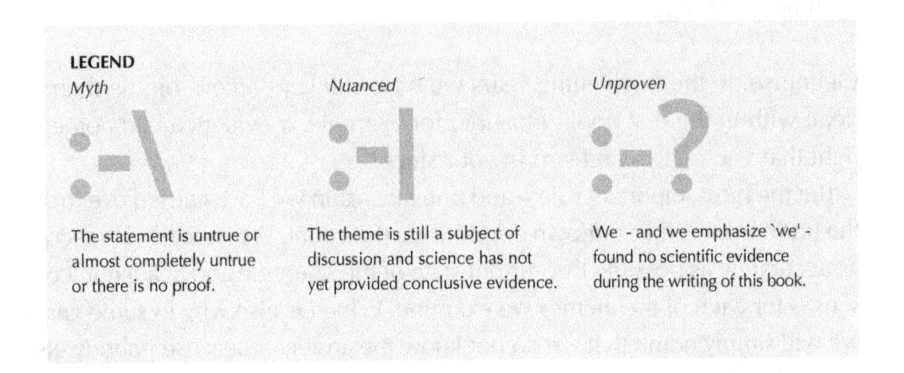

Note

1 Ironically enough, shortly after the publication of the first book it seemed possible that this might happen, but no – it was only a false alarm. See, amongst others: Farthouat, J., Atas, A., Wens, V., De Tiege, X., & Peigneux, P. (2018). Lack of frequency-tagged magnetic responses suggests statistical regularities remain undetected during NREM sleep. *Scientific reports, 8*(1), 11719.

1 Myths about the 'What'

What can possibly happen in the world of education that hasn't already happened? What still needs to be done? People have been thinking about the curriculum for centuries, dating back to at least as far as classical antiquity, with its liberal arts. These liberal arts, which served as the prototypical basis for the western curriculum, were first mentioned by Cicero, but it's not clear when they were actually formulated.[1] It should also be remembered that the model of the seven liberal arts (Grammatica, Dialectica/Logica, Retorica, Aritmetica, Geometria, Musica, and Astronomia), with which we are familiar today, is of more recent origin. These basic educational building blocks remained in the curriculum throughout the Middle Ages (5th to the 15th century) and the Renaissance (between the 14th and 17th centuries), although they each gradually acquired a different content in the process, varying from region to region, particularly as the use of the local language gained in importance.[2] Under the influence of Jean-Jacques Rousseau (1712–1778) and Johann Heinrich Pestalozzi (1746–1827) the curriculum was also extended to include matters that went beyond language and mathematics, with the aim of more closely depicting the world in which the student behind their desk existed. What was that world really like?[3]

Today, there are still frequent discussions about the subjects that should be covered by education. In many countries we have seen an increasing focus on 21st-century skills in the debate surrounding new curriculum initiatives. Such discussions do not necessarily need to be initiated by the government. They can just as easily be activated by anyone who has a particular bee in his or her bonnet about 'something' in society that education needs to solve and who also has access to the media.

Pedro and Casper have kept track of the kinds of things that have been suggested in recent times as being the proper province of education:

- Entrepreneurship
- CPR (cardio-pulmonary resuscitation)
- How people work, and how they can overcome obstacles in their lives
- Learning how to work with drones
- Courtesy and good manners
- Evolutionary theory
- Odd jobs and do-it-yourself
- Dealing with stress and burn-out
- Greater awareness of privacy issues
- Learning about sleep
- Citizenship
- Breastfeeding
- Sign language
- Dealing with laughing gas
- Chess as a miracle aid to mental development (alongside other computational skills)
- ...[4]

Just as in the past where the learning of Latin was seen as an aid to the learning of other languages, nowadays learning to program a computer is seen as an aid to developing problem-solving skills. These 21st-century skills, it's argued, will become increasingly necessary in the decades to come, in a world where futurologists predict that 65% of the jobs that will be carried out by today's students do not yet exist.

In our first book we explained why knowledge is perhaps more important than it has ever been. In this book we'll look at some of the many claims made on behalf of particular subjects and curricula.

Learn A, so that You Are Better Able to Learn B

In our previous book, we discussed how brain apps can help people perform better, but only on those particular brain apps and **not** on anything else. We made clear that brain apps don't transfer from one domain to another[5] whereby 'transfer of learning' is seen as the use of knowledge, skills and/or attitudes that you've learned in one situation in a different situation.[6] This new situation can either be a similar situation (near transfer) or a dissimilar situation (far transfer). In recent years, we've encountered numerous different forms that claim to be examples of far transfer:

- Learn how to program, so that you can easier learn mathematics.
- Learn Latin, so that you can better learn other languages.
- Learn music, so that you can better learn arithmetic.
- Learn chess, so that you can better learn to do just about everything!

But are these claims justified? Are they really examples of far transfer?

Near versus Far Transfer

Imagine that you've learned to drive. You quickly become accustomed to your own car: how the gears work, where to find all the right buttons on the dashboard, etc. If you need to drive a rented car on vacation, some of these things may be different, but your past experience in your own car will soon help you to get the hang of things. It will even help you if you ever need to learn how to drive a bus. This is what we mean by 'near transfer'.[7] Many things from one situation are fairly similar to many things in the new situation, although there may be minor differences here and there.

Far transfer was an idea first described in 1923 by Edward Thorndike.[8] It was Thorndike, for example, who discussed whether or not learning Latin could have a positive effect on logical thinking. Even in those days, it was apparent that this was not the case. According to him, it merely seemed that way because so many of the stronger students and thinkers were automatically encouraged to study Latin. In other words, it was more a question of a correlation than a causal relationship. Consequently, both results were the result of something else, namely smarter students or students from a higher social-economic background.

There is, however, another problem with the delineation of near and far transfer. Perhaps you've come across the following situations in your own classroom. During a geography lesson, students learn how to read a map, but then have difficulty in reading a historical map during a history lesson – which, at first glance, you might think should be an example of relatively near transfer. In a comparable way, mathematics is also used during physics lessons, but here the transfer is much easier to accomplish.

To explain such situations, Thorndike formulated his *Theory of Identical Elements*, which posits that near and far transfer can best be regarded as a continuum. Or to paraphrase his basic conclusion: transfer is easier in relation to the extent that there are more similar or identical elements between what has already been learned and what needs to be learned in the future. Accordingly, he argued that near transfer is, by definition, much easier than far transfer.[9] If we were to take the precepts of this 'old' theory at face value, the outlook for the advocates of far transfer might be fairly pessimistic. But is this really the case? Let's take a closer look at a number of examples.

Is Chess the Key to Success at School and in Life?

In 2011, chess became a compulsory subject in Armenian schools. Armenian authorities are convinced that chess is the key to success at school and in life. By making chess mandatory, they hope to teach children how to think creatively and strategically. As a result, they'll become more intelligent and better able to solve problems. What's more, this does not just mean chess problems, but all problems in all other school subjects, as well as in later life. If true, this is extremely far transfer. There are indeed research studies that demonstrate a link between chess mastery and improved cognitive skills and work performance.[10]

The Advantages of Chess

This section is based on the Armenian curriculum, but it needs to be borne in mind that the idea is not new and is only of limited regional importance. On Chess.com,[11] Tayyab Kahn noted the following benefits of learning to play chess:

- By playing chess regularly from an early age, the learning, thinking and analytical skills of children improve, as does their ability to make decisions.
- Chess teaches children to think strategically about both the game and life in general. In particular, it helps them to realize the importance of thinking ahead and planning.
- By playing chess regularly from an early age, children learn the importance of discipline.
- Chess improves self-confidence, which is an essential element in the growth process of children.

- By playing chess, children learn to investigate, analyze and estimate situations thoroughly before taking decisions. This type of intellectual exercise stimulates mental clarity. Mental clarity and mental agility are essential tools for the solving of problems, the analysis of consequences and the formulation of strategies for the future.
- Children who play chess from an early age develop exceptional powers of memory.
- Chess also helps to improve children's concentration and general academic performance.

Unfortunately, the good Mr. Kahn neglected to quote any evidential sources to back up these impressive claims.

In essence, what the Armenian Ministry of Education is saying is that learning how to play chess is not only the key to developing general skills (in particular, problem solving), but also has a crucial impact on general character traits, such as emotional stability, intellect, memory, alertness and, above all, creativity.

General Character Traits and Creativity

Creativity is not a skill, and it cannot be learned. Creativity is a quality or characteristic that a person possesses. In other words, it's a trait and not a state. Charles Reigeluth explains it as follows: 'Traits are student characteristics that are relatively constant over time ... whereas states are student characteristics that tend to vary during individual learning experiences, such as level of content-specific knowledge.'[12] Viewed in these terms, it's not simply that creativity can't be learned; it's also very difficult to influence. All that teachers can do is to provide a learning climate that offers psychological safety; a climate in which learners feel sufficiently secure, so that they have the courage and the confidence to do things and say things that, at first glance, perhaps seem odd or not completely right. In other words, an environment that encourages them to take risks, safe in the knowledge that mistakes will be tolerated with understanding. We call this psychological safety. Memory is also a trait, so that it, too, cannot be learned. This does not mean that it cannot be trained or improved, but such training needs to be highly focused and demands a huge investment in time. Consequently, this is not something that can be achieved *'en passant'* simply by learning to play chess.

If we look at this in the context of the Armenian claims about chess and creativity, a chess teacher who provides a psychologically safe climate may indeed be able to teach one or more children how to play chess creatively, but the basic starting point is that the child must possess both the necessary chess knowledge (moves, tactics, strategies) and the necessary chess skills (by using that knowledge repeatedly in practice games and competitions). This has been known since 1946, when Adriaan (A.D.) de Groot wrote his famous doctoral thesis *Het denken van den schaker* (Thought and choice in chess).[13]

In our previous book, we discussed the work of Sir Ken Robinson and formulated a number of reservations about his rather narrow definition of creativity (in his book *Creative Schools. The Grassroots Revolution That's Transforming Education*), but even this narrow definition is applicable in this present context. According to Robinson, creativity is: 'the process of having original ideas that have value'. The key word here is 'value'.

Without knowledge and skills it's impossible – except by sheer luck – to create something of value. In fact, if you don't have the requisite knowledge, you are not even in a position to assess the value of what you have done. If you don't know how to play chess, just see how far you get if you are ever asked to develop a creative and valuable solution for a chess problem!

The Effect of Learning to Play Chess on Other Skills

The ability (or otherwise) to change personality traits is still a matter of much discussion, but does chess perhaps have a positive influence on other disciplines and areas of study? This is a subject that has been intensively researched over the years. Some of the resultant studies do indeed suggest a positive effect,[14] whereas others have reached very different conclusions. To help clarify this situation (if we can), it's useful to look at the reviews of the various studies, also bearing in mind the quality of the research methodology used.

Guilermo Gobet and Fernand Campitelli's review on the subject of chess and education came with a painful conclusion: 'Research in psychology and education suggests that cognitive skills acquired in one domain are not easily transferred to another domain. Do the empirical results of chess research undermine this contention? Unfortunately, the answer is: no'.[15] In other words, chess is not an exception to Thorndike's theory of identical elements. A more recent review by Sala, Foley, and Gobet also found very little real evidence for transfer, although their final assessment was somewhat milder.[16] They concluded that the test results show that learning to play chess can sometimes have a positive effect on student learning, but this is confined to arithmetic/mathematics in primary and secondary education. Moreover, this positive effect is only for the short-term; there is nothing to suggest more long-term, permanent benefits. And there is more bad news. They further concluded that there is a correlation between the quality of the research design and the level of the effect identified: the better the design, the smaller the effect. In fact, the most rigorous studies found almost no positive effect whatsoever.[17]

Finally, mention should also be made of the large-scale meta-analysis conducted in 2016 by Burgoyne and colleagues, which investigated the possible link between intelligence and chess.[18] Their conclusion could not be clearer: intelligent players play better chess. This causality follows the same direction that Thorndike established with regard to Latin.

Does Learning How to Program a Computer Encourage Problem-Solving Thinking?

Steve Jobs is supposed to have once said: 'Everyone in this country should learn to program a computer, because it teaches you to think.'[19] But was the Apple boss right? You might be excused for initially thinking that this is an area where very little research has been carried out, so that it's difficult to reach firm conclusions. And you would be right – up to a point. After all, it's only recently that a teaching module for programming was introduced in the UK and computers like the BBC Micro-Bit©, the Arduino© or the Raspberry Pi© are all relatively new in education. That being said, in reality these developments are merely the latest wave in the process of 'programming in education', which actually stretches back over a number of decades and has repeatedly investigated the basic idea that Jobs reformulated. Consider, for example, LOGO, the programming language developed for education as long ago as 1967 by Seymour Papert, with its characteristic 'turtles'. These turtle robots were first invented in the late 1940s by, amongst others, William Grey Walter,[20] but only became widely known in educational circles thanks to Papert, who used them as a means to promote LOGO as a programming language for schools, with the specific aim of stimulating problem-solving capabilities.[21]

The oldest research into such matters was conducted by Richard Mayer and dates from 1975. His work suggested that learning how to program could have a positive effect on problem-solving thinking, although in reality his study focused more on the best way to effectively teach programming.[22]

In contrast, a series of subsequent studies generally concluded that there is no such positive effect. A 1990 study by Van Lengen and Maddux, based on a randomized controlled trial, found no link between programming and the ability to solve problems.[23] This was also the conclusion of a comparable study by Mayer.[24] Research by Clements and Gullo suggested that programming might have a limited beneficial effect on divergent thinking, but this cannot be taken as evidence that it has a major beneficial effect on problem-solving capabilities.[25]

That being said, a review study carried out in 1985 by Douglas Clements which specifically looked at LOGO and its effect on other domains, added an important nuance. Just teaching students how to program with LOGO had little or no effect. If, however, teachers used LOGO for specific tasks with a specific purpose, such as mathematics or problem-solving thinking, a 'moderate' effect could be achieved. But the input of the teacher was crucial to generate this effect; the programming itself played only a marginal role.[26]

Similar conclusions were reached in a 1990 research project by Jho-Ju Tu and John Johnson. They found evidence of a clear benefit for problem-solving thinking as a result of learning how to program. Once again, however, there was an important 'but': their research focused on students in further education who all wanted to learn programming. Moreover, there was no control group.[27] Much the same applies to the study conducted by Joan Littlefield and her colleagues.[28] They, too, found a positive effect, but, like Clements before them, concluded that simply teaching students how to program is not enough to generate this effect. The only effective way that the learning of programming can stimulate problem-solving capabilities is for the teacher to give a clear focus on using those skills in a problem-solving context. And as with Tu and Johnson, there was again no control group to compare, for example, the results of attempts to deal with the same problem-solving content without the benefits of programming skills.

Computational Thinking

Seymour Papert published his conclusions between 1980 and 1996,[29] but it was only after an article by Jeannette Wing in 2006[30] that serious attention was given to the concept of computational thinking and, in particular, to its link with learning to program. Nowadays, this concept is both popular and well-known. Even so, there is still no uniform definition on which everyone can agree.[31] There are, however, four core elements that regularly recur when computational thinking is discussed, for each of which it's easy to see a plausible relationship with 'thinking like a computer', namely: algorithms, decomposition, pattern recognition, and abstraction. Wing herself re-summarized the concept in 2014, using what she calls the three A's:

- Abstraction: formulating problems.
- Automation: articulating solutions.
- Analyses: implementing and evaluating solutions.

Is computational thinking the same as learning how to program? No. According to Wing, it's an approach to the solution of problems, the design of systems, and the understanding of human behavior, based on fundamental insights from the world of computing. In other words, it has nothing to do with programming. It doesn't even necessarily have anything to do with computers! It's simply 'a way' to break down a problem into the different steps that need to be implemented in order to reach the required solution. Consequently, it should be clear that in terms of this semi-definition 'computational thinking' is not a synonym for 'problem-solving thinking', but is one possible approach to such thinking.

Ambiguities of this kind have not made it easy to conduct research into computational thinking. A 2014 review of the work concluded that existing studies vary considerably in their methodology, while the activities for which computational thinking was applied were seldom part of formal lessons; that is, they were additional. Most – but by no means all – of the studies with a control group found a positive effect though this is more or less self-evident, since the kind of step-by-step analysis inherent to a solution-based approach is necessary for effective programming. However, none of the studies offered conclusions about the possible transfer of skills to other domains.[32]

It would be possible to carry on like this for quite some time, but we have probably already quoted enough research to make our point: perhaps the problem is not the teaching of programming; the problem is the idea that it's possible to teach students how to think in a problem-solving manner. Or as Sweller, Clark, and Kirschner concluded in 2010:

> In over a half century, no systematic body of evidence demonstrating the effectiveness of any general problem-solving strategies has emerged [...] There is no body of research based on randomized, controlled experiments indicating that such teaching leads to better problem solving.[33]

Does Music Make You Perform Better in School in General?

Since the three authors of this book are all music-lovers, we need to be wary of possible confirmation bias when it comes to this particular subject: it's sometimes all too easy to search for evidence that confirms what you would like to be true! That being said, a very recent longitudinal study (i.e., a study that follows the same people for a number of years, here also using a randomized design with control group) gives some grounds for optimism.[34] More specifically, Arthur Jaschke and his colleagues examined the effects of learning how to play music on executive functions, the higher cognitive processes that are necessary to plan and direct activities. Over the duration of the study, the scores periodically given to the intervention group for impulse suppression (inhibition), planning and verbal intelligence all improved significantly. It's also possible that the improvements in these three qualities helped account for a similar improvement in general school results. The idea that music can have a positive effect on executive functions is nothing new,[35] although it's still far from clear how long this effect lasts.[36] The Jaschke study attempted to avoid the limitations and shortcomings of many previous studies. Consequently, there is hope that its conclusions will prove more reliable. And this hope is necessary, because, in contrast, a previous meta-analysis found no evidence of far transfer as a result of learning how to play music.[37] Yes, it concluded, musicians are indeed often more intelligent than others (we love you yeah, yeah, yeah), but this is more a correlation than anything else. As far as a possible causal link is concerned, in most studies this is negatively reflected in the quality of the study itself. The better the research, the smaller the link.

But is it actually a good thing to search for far transfer in relation to music? This is the question that the OECD asked in its own review of the influence of art education in general and music education in particular.[38] By asking what value music has for improving performance in other disciplines, there is a risk that this effectively devalues music's worth as a discipline in its own right. This is a fair point: much far transfer thinking is based on the utility principle that makes one discipline subordinate to another. In wider cultural and educational terms, chess is less important than music. But perhaps chess also has the potential to make students better at something else. And perhaps it can do this more effectively than music. What then would be the future of music as an academic subject? And it doesn't just have to be chess. Imagine that something else comes along – the use of classroom rituals, for example -which is proven to have a more significant impact on improved executive functions than music.[39] If music is regarded purely as a means to an end rather than as an end in itself, this might even lead to its removal from the curriculum! It's surprising that this issue should be raised by an economic organization like the OECD, but it's important that someone raises it. In art education, the desire for possible far transfer must remain subordinate to the wider cultural value of artistic disciplines – and not the other way around.

Does Learning Latin Help You to Learn Other Languages Better?

Apart from a huge fortune in the bank, what do Harry Potter author J.K. Rowling and Facebook guru Mark Zuckerberg have in common? They both learned Latin at school.[40] Various universities still use Latin names to add a certain cachet to the study of classics and classical languages. It is as though they seem to say that a knowledge of Latin is the secret to success!

While in many countries (foreign) language education has given way to education based on the so-called STEM subjects (Science, Technology, Engineering, and Mathematics), in the Netherlands and Belgium Latin is still an important part of the curriculum.[41] For centuries, Latin was the language of knowledge and erudition and, consequently, also the language of the elite as it was also an important key to the door that led to university. It was only when education became more readily accessible at the start of the 20th century and Latin gradually disappeared as the language of science and learning, that arguments for its teaching began to change. Latin was now seen as being important for the general education of students, which was effectively the same as saying that that Latin was a good way to teach students how to think. As a subsidiary argument, it was also suggested that learning Latin made it easier to learn other languages, such as French, Spanish, and/or Italian.[42]

But is this true? Does learning Latin teach you anything more than just Latin? During the past century, research has focused primarily on this second argument: Latin as a linguistic facilitator. A review study conducted by Rudolph Masciantonio[43] found evidence supporting a weaker form of this argument, namely that learning Latin helped American children first and foremost learn their own language better. Unfortunately, many of the studies in this field lack reliability as a result of serious methodological shortcomings or due to a failure to properly check out all relevant related factors, such as the socio-economic background of the students (see also Thorndike's conclusions on this matter). One small study that is both relevant and reliable monitored a group of German children learning Spanish. Some of the children also received lessons in Latin, others in French. The results showed that the children benefitted more from first learning French than learning Latin. In fact, the students who also learned Latin made more grammatical errors in Spanish than those who had learned French.[44] Once again, Thorndike's identical elements theory would seem to hold.

As far as the second question is concerned – can learning Latin help you to think better? – very little meaningful research has been conducted, largely because it's so difficult to define what we mean by 'thinking' to everyone's satisfaction. Be that as it may, a study by Joan Carlisle[45] concluded that there was no relationship between the skills needed to learn Latin and the skills needed to learn other languages or mathematics. But that is more or less as far as the research goes at this stage. In other words, there is nothing to suggest a link between 'learning Latin' and 'better thinking'.

If it's unlikely that Latin makes it possible to learn other languages more easily and if Thorndike's theory suggests that far transfer is equally improbable, we can then reasonably ask the same question that we asked of music in the previous section: should Latin still be taught because of any intrinsic value of its own? Up to a point, the answer is 'yes'. There are indications that learning Latin can lead to greater self-confidence and a deeper appreciation for other cultures,[46] although this can just as easily be said for many other foreign languages, such as Chinese. The British classicist-historian Mary Beard offers a more specific reason for learning Latin: it gives young people access to the literary tradition that forms the basis of western culture.[47] Again, this might well be the case, but it's open to discussion as to whether that argument alone is sufficient to merit including Latin in the curriculum. In fact, all the 'old' arguments in favor of Latin – that it has specific characteristics that make it easier to learn other languages and also improves a student's general ability to think – no longer seem relevant or credible in this modern day and age.

Conclusion: Myth

In this section, we investigated four popular examples of claims for far transfer, but in each case the results were disappointing. This is not to say that there is no evidence whatsoever for far transfer, but it's very clear that the level of reliable evidence decreases in relation to the quality of the research: the better the research, the scanter the evidence. One insight – in fact, a slight irritation – that came to light during the investigation and writing of this section is that Thorndike's theory – devised more than 100 years ago – still seems applicable. Throughout the past century, repeated efforts have been made to contradict his claim that the greater the number of identical elements, the greater the likelihood of far transfer. To date, no-one has really succeeded – us included. Even so, it remains clear that far transfer is not the magic remedy for cross-discipline learning that many educationalists once hoped it would be.

Children No Longer Need to Learn How to Write by Hand

When in 2014 Finland announced as the first country in the world that it no longer intended to teach its children how to physically write (i.e., with a pen or pencil), there was a furore in the educational world. As is often the case with such announcements, the way people interpreted this news was not always wholly accurate. A further statement by the Finnish government made clear that Finnish children would still be taught how to write by hand, but that this would be done by using block letters and not, as was traditionally the case, by cursive writing.[48]

Put simply, do we still need to teach children how to write by hand in a world of keyboards, swipes, and smart virtual assistants? The answer is 'yes' – and there are various reasons for this.

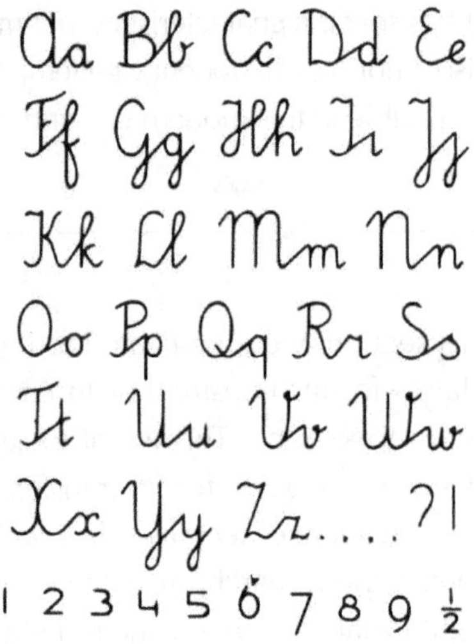

Figure 1.1

The Advantages for Young Children

In 2005, Marieke Longcamp and her colleagues investigated whether it was the typing or the writing of letters that had the most positive effect on letter recognition in children between the ages of 2 years and 9 months and 4 years and 9 months.[49] The results showed that writing was better in this respect, particularly for the 'older' children in the survey. A follow-up study showed that the benefit of writing above typing was not only stable, but was, in fact, at its strongest three weeks after the test training. The researchers concluded that movement plays a key role in letter representation and therefore writing manually contributes significantly to recognising letters visually. According to the researchers the brain receives multiple signals (visual, motor and kinaesthetic) which typing does not do in the same way.

In 2012, Karin James and Laura Engelhardt used fMRI to examine the effects of writing compared to typing on the development of the brains of five-year-old children who could not yet read. They found that writing helped activate parts of the brain that are necessary for learning successfully to read. Consequently, they concluded that 'old-fashioned' handwriting is still important as a means to promote reading ability in young children.[50] This insight was later confirmed by further brain research conducted by Alyssa Kersey and Karin James.[51]

Reading Is Also Important for Writing!

Writing undoubtedly makes an important contribution to learning how to read. But the opposite is also true: the frequency of reading interventions in turn has a positive effect on the quality of writing in students – or this, at least, was the conclusion of a 2017 meta-analysis.[52] Reading more and better texts resulted in writing better texts. Moreover, the positive effect is evident not only in the quality of the text itself, but also in matters such as spelling. Most important of all, these benefits have been demonstrated to be long-term.

In other words, there is little doubt: learning to write by hand is still important for learning to read. Viewed solely in these terms, writing is more an educational means than an educational end. But there is more.

The Benefit of Writing by Hand for Remembering Things

Pam Mueller and Daniel Oppenheimer conducted three studies to determine if there is a difference between keyboarding and simply taking notes on paper.[53] The results of all three studies showed that young people learn or memorize things better – both in the short term (immediately after the lesson) and the long term (after a week or two) – if they take notes with pen and paper. This applied to both the learning of facts and the understanding of content. And it made no difference whether the students re-read what they had written or not. In all cases, handwritten notes were better than typed ones. According to the researchers, the reason for this can be found in the fact that the notes made on the laptop were literal transcriptions of what had been said (most young people nowadays can type faster than they can write and also at the speed of a lecture), whereas the handwritten notes were adaptations of what had been said (paraphrases, summaries, synonyms, ...). In other words, because writing is slower than typing, you need to 'translate' the content into your own words – and as this requires mental processing (!) you learn and remember it better.

These findings were subsequently confirmed by a further study by Annen Mangen and three Norwegian colleagues in *Journal of Writing Research*. They investigated differences in the ability to remember words by test subjects using pen and paper, a keyboard, and an iPad. Their results made clear that there was no difference with regard to the recognition of words, but that there was a significant positive effect for the pen and paper users when it came to the free recall of words.[54]

We also need to remember that taking notes with pen and paper involves much more than just cognitive processes. For example, it requires much greater movement of the hands and arms than is the case with typing. Timothy Smoker and his colleagues conducted research to establish whether or not these movements had an effect on the ability to recognize and remember 'ordinary' words.[55] They concluded that both recognition and memorization were better with pen and paper. This is because the extra cerebral information generated by the additional movement creates a more complex memory trace than typing. Consequently, the researchers further concluded that taking notes by hand is better, because it makes it easier to remember what has been written. This allows writing to become an educational end as the best available means for studying and for committing content to memory.

Last but not least, writing is equally important for the development of fine motor skills. These skills make use of small muscles in the hands and arms to perform manual tasks with precision. This might include fastening a button on your shirt or picking up a dropped coin from the ground. But it also includes writing. And it's not simply that you are doing something with your hands, when you write. It also involves complex eye-hand coordination, muscular control, the development and use of visual memory, and the coordination of both halves of the brain (known in the jargon as 'laterality'). Similarly, learning to write can also stimulate the acquisition of other less mechanical skills, such as a sense of rhythm (particularly with script) and good spatial orientation.[56]

Conclusion: Myth

For the time being, it's better not to remove learning to write from the curriculum. It's not only important as a means for learning to read, but also as an end in terms of better retention.

65% of the Jobs that Our Children Will Do Currently Do Not Exist

The past has (hopefully) taught us that trying to predict the future is tricky. This also applies to trying to predict what jobs there will be in the years ahead. Some jobs have disappeared in our own lifetimes; others have been reduced to the status of 'curiosities'. For example, the sight of milkmen delivering a daily pint of milk to your doorstep is a thing of the past, while wooden clog-making – once a thriving industry in the Netherlands – is now little more than a minor pastime in some historic, open-air museums. This has been counterbalanced by a growing need for (amongst other things) specialists in the areas of social media and online privacy. To a large extent, these and other similar developments have taken many people by surprise. So yes: jobs and their content do change. But how quick and how dramatic is that change likely to be?

How Old Is the 65% Figure?

This is the figure that you nowadays most frequently hear quoted: 65% of the jobs that our children will perform in their futures have not yet been invented. This leads on to the argument that educators must bear this in mind when developing a curriculum for the future. 65% sounds like a lot and it's an interesting claim, but one (in the absence of a crystal ball) that is difficult to prove or disprove. Since the figure is so precise and so frequently quoted, it's not unreasonable to hope that it's based on some kind of reliable scientific evidence.[57] But is this the case?

Apparently so – at least according to the opening paragraph of *The Future of Jobs: Employment, Skills and Workforce Strategy for the Fourth Industrial Revolution*, published by the World Economic Forum:

> Disruptive changes to business models will have a profound impact on the employment landscape over the coming years. Many of the major drivers of transformation currently affecting global industries are expected to have a significant impact on jobs, ranging from significant job creation to equally significant job displacement, and from heightened labor productivity to widening skills gaps. In many industries and countries, the most in-demand occupations or specialties did not exist 10 or even five years ago, and the pace of change is set to accelerate. By one popular estimate, 65% of children entering

> primary school today will ultimately end up working in completely new job types that don't yet exist. In such a rapidly evolving employment landscape, the ability to anticipate and prepare for future skills requirements, job content and the aggregate effect on employment is increasingly critical for businesses, governments and individuals in order to fully seize the opportunities presented by these trends – and to mitigate undesirable outcomes.[58]

In the British media, the figure of 65% is often linked to a 2011 book by Cathy Davidson,[59] who during a subsequent interview in 2017 confessed that she had first read it in a book written as long ago as 2007 by Jim Carroll,[60] who in turn (according to Davidson) had taken it from a study published on an official Australian government website. This website has long since been taken offline, but Carroll still refers to the study in his blog – although a recent request to provide a link to the source has remained unanswered.[61] This is one of the reasons why Carroll no longer uses the 65% figure himself.[62]

Another trace leads to a reference in a text by Debra Kidd,[63] who again claims to have borrowed the figure from a speech given by Paul Collard in 2008.[64] It has not been possible to identify Collard's source, although he has repeated the figure on many occasions, referring to 'a research study conducted by the British government'.[65] From there, this particular trail goes cold.

Various articles on the subject[66] refer to a report prepared by the US Department of Labor[67] in 1999. This report does indeed exist, but there's one small problem: nowhere does it mention the 65% figure.

As you can see, our search has now taken us back to as early as 1999 – which is strange, to say the least, for a key prediction about the future of our children in a rapidly changing world (in the meantime, the young children of 1999 are already the twenty- and even thirty-somethings of today!). But Andrew Smith has found what might possibly be an even older source in a book by Robert Peal,[68] which dates back to 1966.[69] Still not far enough? Benjamin Doxtador[70] refers to a 1958 article by Devereux Josephs,[71] in which he argued that (American) children of the future would do jobs that had not yet been invented. We have been able to trace and read both these texts, and while they do indeed broadly make the same general claim, neither of them cites a specific percentage, nor do they offer any sources to support their arguments.

So what can we can conclude at the end of our search (and, by extension, the past searches of others)? It seems clear that the reported figure of 65% is an arbitrary one, which can vary (from 60% to 85%) depending on the source. It's also significant that the source references are often less than satisfactory, that the sources quoted are not always scientific, and that these sources seldom (if ever) form the basis for quoting a specific percentage figure. Last but not least, the idea is an old one, which many feel has long passed its sell-by date in our high-speed digital age.

How Quickly Do Jobs Really Change?

Carl Frey and Michael Osborne investigated the extent to which jobs are being taken over by robots and computers, and made a summary of the kind of jobs most likely to be at risk.[72] However, they concluded that most jobs do not disappear at a particular location because they have been taken over by robots and computers, but because they have been shifted to a different – and usually cheaper – location. This means that it's not the type but rather the place of the job that changes.[73] Until the end of the 20th century, the automation and later computerization of jobs was largely focused in the first instance on routine, physical tasks, followed in a later phase by the more straightforward and repetitive cognitive tasks (see the left-hand side of Figure 1.2, derived from Frey & Osborne, 2017). Nowadays and for the foreseeable future, the use of computers will also make it possible to take over more non-routine tasks (the right-hand side of Figure 1.2).

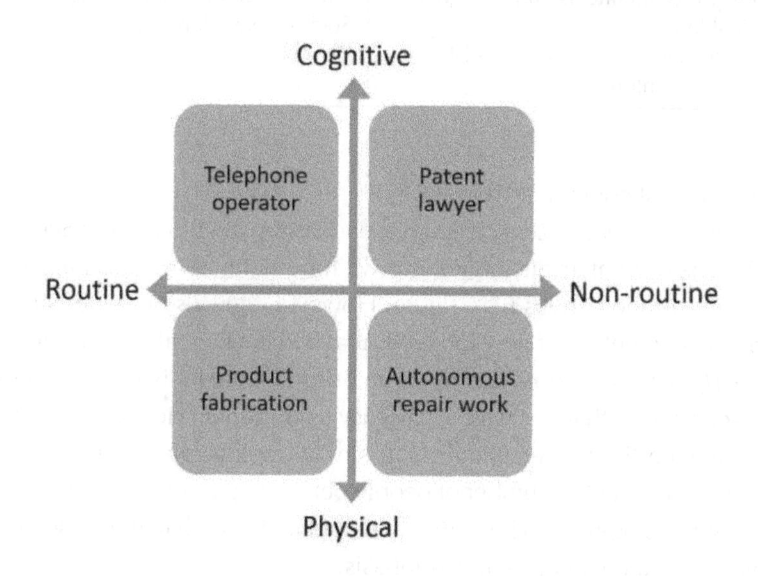

Figure 1.2

Source: Frey & Osborne, 2017.

According to Frey and Osborne, this left to right shift will be made possible by the growth and increasing sophistication of artificial intelligence, the analysis of big data, and machine learning. These developments make it increasingly likely that in the near future, fewer and fewer people will be needed to take jobs requiring non-routine physical and cognitive skills.

Fascinating though this research is, it's difficult to give concrete figures for the scale of these trends. It's also worth noting that Frey and Osborne go no further than to state that some jobs *may be liable* to disappear. Nowhere do they say that this is certain.

Talwar and Hancock took things a stage further and drew up a list of possible new jobs for the future.[74] In their report, they gave a description of the following 20 jobs:

Body part maker Nano-medic Pharmer of genetically engineered crops and livestock Old age wellness manager/consultant specialists Memory augmentation surgeon 'New science' ethicist Space pilots, architects and tour guides Vertical farmers Climate change reversal specialist Quarantine enforcer	Weather modification police Virtual lawyer Avatar manager/devotees – virtual teachers Alternative vehicle developers Narrowcasters Waste data handler Virtual clutter organizer Time broker/time bank trader Social 'networking' worker Personal branders

Their full list contains 110 jobs.

As part of a *More or Less* program broadcast by the BBC World Service in 2017,[75] the presenters attempted – as we have done above – to track down the origins of the famous 65% figure. However, they also tried to calculate the actual percentage of new job types that had been created between 2006 and 2016, using data obtained from the British Office for National Statistics. They soon found that this was not as easy as it sounds. How exactly should you calculate the figure? Should you simply look at the types of job? Or should you look at the number of people performing those jobs? There might still be some clog-makers here and there, but far fewer than there used to be. So where should you place the emphasis?

The data obtained from government sources contained a list of about 600 different jobs, as well as details on the number of people performing those jobs in the UK. The program-makers made two important assumptions. First, if new categories of jobs appeared in the 2016 list, they assumed that these did not exist at all in 2006. Second, if an existing 2006 job category increased in size, they assumed that this was entirely due to new jobs. They realized that both of these assumptions would maximize the number of new jobs in the comparison, but even with this built-in bias they concluded that only a third of the jobs in 2016 had not existed in 2006.

Conclusion: Myth

The source of the 65% figure is not traceable and the only comparable research carried out in recent times resulted in a percentage that was only half as big. In other words, the figure of 65% is not proven and is therefore a myth.

Is There Any Such Thing as '21st-Century Skills'?

The concept of '21st-century skills' has been popular for quite some time. Although there is no clear and universally accepted definition of the concept (as a result of which there are numerous variants),[76] it generally seems to have a lot in common with the supposed importance of generic skills. In a survey of the proposed skill models, Chris Dede[77] pointed (amongst others) to the following organizations who are active in the same field:

- Partnership for 21st-Century Skills[78].
- Metiri Group & NCREL[79].
- American Association of Colleges and Universities.[80]

But what exactly are these 21st-century skills? Within the framework of their own comparative study (2012), Robert Marzano and Tammy Heflebower (2012) identified five different categories:

1. Analysing and utilising information.
2. Addressing complex problems and issues.
3. Creating patterns and mental models.
4. Understanding and controlling yourself.
5. Understanding and interacting with others.[81]

There is a good chance that many of you reading this will complain that the Marzano–Heflebower summary contains almost none of the things in the model with which they are familiar. And that might well be true. Silva argued that there are literally hundreds of different competencies or skills covered by the all-encompassing term '21st-century skills', depending on the nature of the organization arguing for them.

The perceived need for such skills is often linked to a general feeling, not strange to some educational thinkers, namely that education can no longer keep up with the fast pace of worldwide change. These same thinkers fear that an inadequate education system will in turn lead to economic decline, unless greater focus and resources are devoted to more modern skills.[82]

How New Are These 21st-Century Skills?

21st-century skills are nothing new. During the 18th, 19th, and 20th centuries people also needed to solve problems, think critically, be creative, communicate effectively, and collaborate with others. In fact, you can even argue that these skills have been necessary since the dawn of human civilization, perhaps from the moment when the first creative Mesopotamian thinker saw the potential for improving grass to cultivatable wheat, subsequently leading to the development of a stable society with the division of labor that was capable of storing the resulting grain and even trading the surplus.

The stimulation of generic skills was also an important priority in education in previous centuries, and many elements from this tradition can still be found in today's skill models. Creativity was just as vital in the 19th century as it is today. So too was the analysis of new sources of information. Propaganda – nowadays known as fake news – is not a 21st-century invention, nor is the historical criticism it provokes.[83] It seems that the modern world is suffering from a serious bout of chronocentrism: the belief that your own era is somehow 'special'.[84]

Of course, this does not means that skills do not evolve. The consultation and analysis of sources of information is not the same today as it was a hundred years ago. The finding and correct use of internet sources certainly requires an excellent knowledge of the new media, but it also makes use of abilities that have been around for quite some time, as well as a good deal of 'ordinary' knowledge (declarative, conceptual, procedural, and metacognitive, as described in the following section on Bloom). So is this a new skill or is it the evolution of an existing skill? Perhaps, in the final analysis, this is not such an important question. In both instances, further work is required.

Paul Kirschner[85] argues that there are only two new skills that are truly 21st-century skills:

1. Information literacy: the ability to search for, identify, evaluate and effectively use information received.
2. Information management: the ability to store, manage and share information received.

Why are these skills so important? Until the start of the present century, we were able to rely on libraries of 'guaranteed reliable information' as our source of information, which in turn required only limited storage and management. However, since the year 2000 (that is with the large-scale use of the World Wide Web) there has been an explosion of information; some reliable, but also much less reliable, unreliable and even false information. The amount of data that we can store has also grown exponentially, so that nowadays you often hear: 'Yes, I found something useful, but I can't remember where I saved it!'

What Is the Real Discussion About?

Although there's still much discussion about what should and should not be included in the ultimate list of essential competencies for the new century, the real essence of the debate about 21st-century skills focuses on that final word: skills. And this brings us back to the debate that we conducted at some length in our previous book: skills versus knowledge. But here the debate goes deeper. Although some people argue that we no longer need knowledge, it's clear that many present-day skill models still see knowledge as indispensable.[86] The idea that we no longer need (basic) knowledge is a fallacy, a fundamental error. Precisely the opposite is true. Knowledge is becoming increasingly important as a means to assess the value (reliability, validity, usability, etc.) of the tsunami of information available today, which in itself is also often used as an argument in favor of 21st-century skills. Consider, for example, reading comprehension. The (reading) strategy adopted by the reader certainly plays a role in their understanding and analysis of the text or idea concerned, but the importance of this role is open to discussion.[87] Background knowledge about the subject and its associated vocabulary is probably more important, perhaps even essential. The best teacher in the world, with all the very latest reading strategies at her/his disposal, will not be able to understand a text about quantum mechanics, unless (s)he knows something about the subject beforehand.

Many of the popular 21st-century skills are generic; in other words, they're not related to a specific domain. They're not about solving a scientific or mathematical problem, but about problem-solving in general. They're not about analyzing the correctness of a historical source, but about the ability to evaluate all sources. It's this, of course, that makes things so difficult. Skills are domain-specific and not general, just like the knowledge to which they are so inextricably attached.[88] To evaluate the correctness of a source, you need background knowledge about the domain to which that source relates. To solve a mathematical problem, you not only need to know the necessary technical steps (procedural knowledge; the term says it all) to take, but must also be able to properly carry it out (the essence of a skill) and estimate if the outcome is correct. We may know, in theory, how to curl a football (soccer ball for Americans) around a wall of defenders (i.e. the procedure), but that doesn't mean we can actually bend it like Beckham or Messi. In short, you need both mathematical (or football) knowledge *and* skills.

Are All 21st-Century Skills Really Skills?

In some lists of 21st-century skills (see, for example, the list drawn up by the World Economic Forum[89]), we find 'skills' such as initiative, grit, curiosity, creativity, flexibility, agility, and leadership. Unfortunately, these qualities are not skills but are human traits, which cannot be taught or learned (as discussed in the section on personality theories). The most that a school or a teacher can do is to create a situation in which these traits can be stimulated. If you want students to develop creative, out-of-the-box solutions, you need to provide them with an environment in which they feel psychologically safe. This means that they must not be afraid of being reprimanded by the teacher for doing or saying something 'dumb'. If a teacher implies that a proposed solution is 'stupid' or if the student is laughed at or teased by classmates for a response, then that student's creativity will be stifled before it has a chance to develop. Much the same is true for the other traits.

Do Generic Skills Exist and Can They Be Learned?

People who oppose the existence of generic skills usually often cite the celebrated work by André Tricot and John Sweller who put forward numerous arguments to support their contention that generic skills cannot be learned, as opposed to domain-specific skills. To be more precise, Tricot and Sweller do not explicitly state in their article that generic skills do not exist, but instead argue that these skills can never be viewed – or learned – in isolation from domain-specific knowledge and skills. In other words, students can learn something in one domain, but then need to learn anew (although perhaps more quickly) how to apply that something in another domain, for which they must also possess the necessary domain-specific knowledge. Also, the fact that a student might know the right solution or procedure does not mean that (s)he also can implement it. This is in keeping with our conclusions earlier in the book in the section 'Learn A, so that you are better able to learn B'.

So is the development of generic skills really impossible? If, for example, we look at recent work relating to metacognition in schools – often popularly (but too narrowly) known as 'learning how to learn' – it's clear that having separate lessons for the learning of (generic) study skills has hardly any noticeable effect.[90] In the 1970s, much the same reasoning was applied to the learning of (generic) writing skills, which at one time was a popular course at universities. Eventually, however, the same conclusions were reached: you can't learn to write without knowing the domain you are writing about. Students learned a series of heuristics/procedures, but were unable to apply them without the required domain-specific knowledge.

That being said, there are certain techniques that can be used for every subject and would therefore seem to be generic. In order to teach these generic-like study skills (although, in fact, they are really procedures, so that what is being learned is actually procedural knowledge), teachers must refer to the same methods of learning in each separate subject and explicitly highlight similarities with other subjects.[91] In this way – and, admittedly, it's by no means an easy way – the transfer of study skills may become possible, so that it's not unreasonable to speak of a kind of generic skill for the 'best way to study'. Other research shows that (limited) transfer is perhaps also feasible for some other generic-like skills.[92] For example, the 2015 meta-analysis by Philip Abrami and colleagues demonstrated that there are possibilities for learning generic skills in critical thinking,[93] although the authors also indicate that this depends to some extent on how one defines the term 'critical thought', a subject that has been a matter of discussion for more than 70 years! Yet, even bearing this caveat in mind, it seems a bridge too far to say that the acquiring of generic skills is wholly impossible.[94]

Conclusion: Nuanced

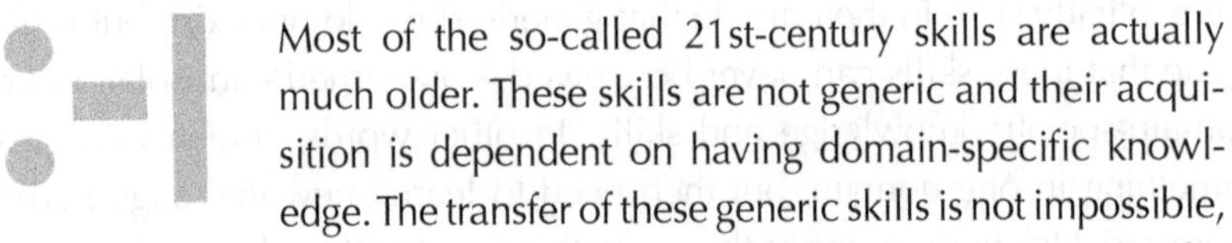

Most of the so-called 21st-century skills are actually much older. These skills are not generic and their acquisition is dependent on having domain-specific knowledge. The transfer of these generic skills is not impossible, but is very difficult to achieve and seldom happens spontaneously. The transfer process can only be initiated by first learning a number of different and very specific applications.

Is Bloom's Taxonomy a Myth?

Following the publication of our first 'myths' book, one of the most frequently asked questions was: what about Benjamin Bloom's taxonomy? As we are now discussing various myths relating to the school curriculum, this might be an appropriate time to assess whether or not this taxonomy is correct – although (as we shall see) this may turn out not to be the right question.

What Is a Taxonomy?

Before we look at Bloom and his work, we need to be clear about what a taxonomy is.

Merriam Webster[95] defines 'taxonomy' as follows:

1. The study of the general principles of scientific classification.
2. Especially: orderly classification of plants and animals according to their presumed natural relationships.

Wikipedia gives the following description:

> Taxonomy is the practice and science of classification. The word is also used as a count noun: a taxonomy, or taxonomic scheme, is a particular classification. The word finds its roots in the Greek language τάξις, taxis (meaning 'order', 'arrangement') and νόμος,

> nomos ('law' or 'science'). Originally, taxonomy referred only to the classification of organisms or a particular classification of organisms. In a wider, more general sense, it may refer to a classification of things or concepts, as well as to the principles underlying such a classification. Taxonomy is different from meronomy which is dealing with the classification of parts of a whole.[96]

Perhaps you once used a taxonomy at school to identify plants or animals (a Chihuahua is a dog, which is a canine, which is a carnivore, which is a mammal, which is a vertebrate, which is an animal). Taxonomies are not specifically confined to one field, but are generally used for the process of systematic classification based on criteria. They, for example, have a role within educational theory and policy where they are used to clarify the nature and type of objectives we wish to achieve in relation to the curriculum. Their most important feature in this respect is that a taxonomy is hierarchical, divided into superordinate, subordinate, and equivalent classification. A Chihuahua and a Labrador retriever are both dogs (and therefore belong to the same equivalent level, sometimes referred to as heterarchic). All mammals are vertebrates (subordinate – superordinate), but not all vertebrates are mammals (a snake is a vertebrate, but is a reptile).

Domain
Kingdom
Phylum
Class
Order
Family
Genus
Species

Figure 1.3

It's also important to realize that taxonomies are seldom carved in stone. A taxonomy (or one of its branches) can be amended on the basis of new developments and insights. This happens quite often in biology when, for example, a new fossil or animal is discovered.

Different classifications and taxonomies can exist alongside each other, simply because people sometimes use different insights or criteria as their starting point. In the educational field, we are familiar with taxonomies by De Block,[97] SOLO,[98] Romiszowski,[99] Miller,[100] and many others. These are all examples of possible classifications that can be imposed on reality to make it more understandable and manageable. Such taxonomies do not summarize educational methods and practices, but group together objectives. In some modified or hybrid versions it may be possible to readily see links with these methods and practices, but in such cases sight of the original work is soon lost.[101]

Bloom?

From 1948 onwards, Benjamin Bloom and his colleagues developed three taxonomies of educational objectives (cognitive, affective, psychomotor), which were finally published in 1956.[102] Their purpose was to serve as a method for the classification of educational objectives, so that student learning and achievement could reliably be evaluated.[103]

Bloom's original intentions were summarized by David Krathwohl[104]:

1. common language about learning goals to facilitate communication across persons, subject matter, and grade levels;
2. basis for determining for a particular course or curriculum the specific meaning of broad educational goals, such as those found in the currently prevalent national, state, and local standards;
3. means for determining the congruence of educational objectives, activities, and assessments in a unit, course, or curriculum; and
4. panorama of the range of educational possibilities against which the limited breadth and depth of any particular educational course or curriculum could be contrasted.

A taxonomy is a classification that can be used to look at reality so to make our thinking about the reality a bit more structured. It shouldn't be an overview of didactical approaches, although the third intention that Krathwohl describes comes pretty close to this idea and some scientists and academics regard this actually as a possible good thing.[105]

Although more than 60 years old, Bloom's taxonomy is still one of the most widely used classification systems used in education. As mentioned, taxonomies can be revised in response to new insights. In Bloom's case, there was an additional reason that made this necessary; the original taxonomy was not really developed based on a proper scientific approach.[106] To counter this criticism, a new version was put forward in 2001, based on more systematic analyses.

Figure 1.4 could be regarded as a summary of both the original and the revised version, but we'll explain how they are both incorrect.[107]

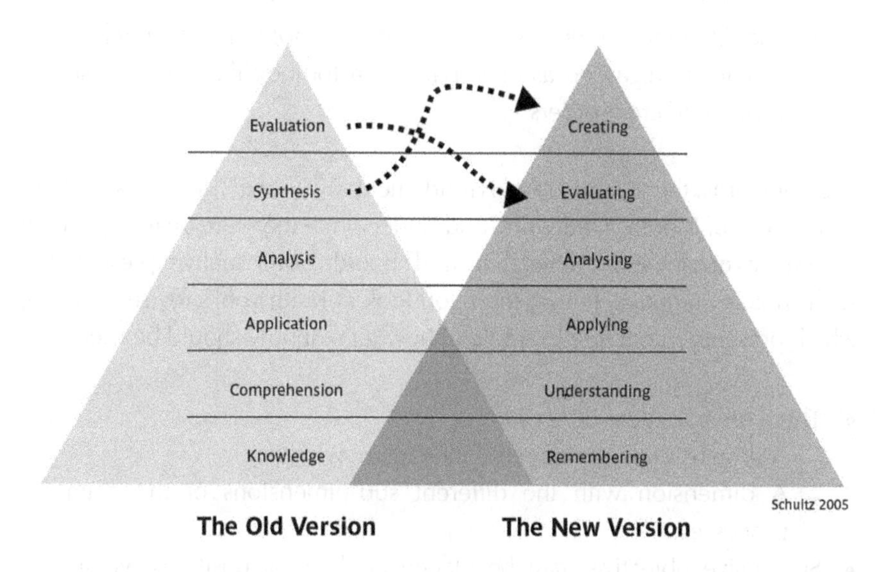

Figure 1.4 The incorrect pyramid-shape versions.
Source: Schultz, 2005.

Even so, a number of problems still remain.

The first problem is that the pyramid form suggests that while knowledge is an important basis for what follows, the other elements are of greater importance and value. In a guest contribution on Larry Ferlazzo's blog, Lorin W. Anderson, co-author of the revised taxonomy along with Krathwohl, dotted the i's and crossed the t's on this point, in a manner that probably caused the writers of many educational manuals to take a deep breath.

1. The pyramid form does not appear in either the original or the revised version of the taxonomy. Anderson thinks that someone probably devised this artificial form in an attempt to make clear that there is a kind of hierarchy between the different levels identified by Bloom.

2. This pyramid form is misleading for a number of reasons:
   - The revised version has two dimensions, and not just one. The authors of the revised version believe that knowledge is so important that it needs to be regarded as a separate dimension, subdivided into different kinds of knowledge: factual, conceptual, procedural and metacognitive.
   - The proper nouns of the original version are replaced by verbs to indicate the cognitive processes involved.
   - The different elements of the taxonomy do *not* form a hierarchy. They should be regarded as aids, parts of a toolbox that can be used in various different orders.

In other words, the pyramid form is fundamentally wrong[108] and runs contrary to the work of Bloom, Krathwohl, and Anderson. It therefore bears repeating: Bloom's taxonomy is *not* a hierarchy and shouldn't be visually represented as such. This is immediately evident if you look at Krathwohl's revised version, which presents a concrete example of how a taxonomy should be used.

- There are two clear dimensions:
  - A dimension with different kinds of knowledge;
  - A dimension with the different sub-dimensions of the cognitive processes.
- Successive objectives can be placed at different positions within this framework, so that one objective is not necessarily 'higher' than another objective, simply because there is no hierarchy in the model.

		Cognitive processes					
		Remembering	*Understanding*	*Applying*	*Analyzing*	*Evaluating*	*Creating*
Knowledge	*Facts*						
	Concepts						
	Procedures						
	Metacognition						

However, there is a second problem that Anderson fails to address in the Ferlazzo blog. It's often the case that only one-third of the complete Bloom taxonomy of educational objectives is discussed, namely the cognitive part.

Bloom's original version consisted of three parts, which together formed his taxonomy as a whole. The other two were:

- *Affective objectives*, in which objectives relating to growth in terms of feelings and emotions, as expressed in attitudes, are central.
- *Psychomotor objectives*, in which physical actions and skills are central.

The affective part, first elucidated by Krathwohl in 1964,[109] can be summarized as follows:

1. *Receiving* – the sensitivity of the learner to stimuli and her/his awareness, receptivity, and selectivity with regard to these stimuli.
2. *Responding* – the attention that the learner actively and consciously devotes to the stimuli and to her/his desire to learn.
3. *Valuing* – the convictions and attitudes of the learner with regard to accepting, preferring, and committing to something.
4. *Organizing* – the internalization of convictions and attitudes, so that the learner can devise her/his own different concepts of possible values and how they relate to each other. Which values are more important than others?
5. *Characterizing* – the highest level of the internalization of convictions and attitudes into values, so that the learner can devise a complete set of values. This translates into a philosophy and vision of the world, which allows the learner to act in accordance with his convictions and values.

The psychomotor part was only elaborated in a similar fashion at a later stage.[110] The following classification is according to Harrow[111]:

1. *Reflex movements* – movements that are inborn or can arise as a result of increasing maturity.
2. *Fundamental movements* – objectives related to walking, running, jumping, pushing, pulling and manual dexterity. They form the basis for more complex actions.
3. *Perceptual abilities* – the absorption of information via the senses and the ability to react in an appropriate manner.

4. *Physical abilities* – endurance, physical flexibility, strength, etc.
5. *Skilled movements* – movements that need to be learned; for example, to participate in sport, games, dance, art, etc.
6. *Non-discursive communication* – objectives related to posture, facial expression and/or creative movement, such as mime or ballet.

So Is Bloom's Taxonomy Right or Not?

There are two aspects to this question:

1. To what extent is the simplification that classification inevitably entails accurate?
2. How usable and useful is the classification?

These are the criteria that need to be used to evaluate any taxonomy, both within the educational field and beyond. In education, all of the taxonomies discussed can serve as a means to encourage educators to reflect on the objectives of their teaching (in particular, whether or not they focus too much on one particular category of objectives at the expense of others). As far as Bloom is concerned, it's certainly true that the most widely spread version of his taxonomy suggests certain matters that do not concur with reality as we know it from cognitive psychology. But as Anderson has described, this is largely the result of the 'corruption' and oversimplification of Bloom's original version. This means that the real question should not be whether or not his taxonomy is a myth, but rather whether or not it's usable and useful in the form in which it has been handed down to us.

Conclusion: Nuanced

It's not really possible to say whether Bloom's taxonomy is a myth or not. However, it's possible to say whether or not it's usable and useful as a means to correctly classify reality. At the same time, we can add that a number of myths have certainly grown up around the taxonomy, largely as a result of its subsequent incorrect depiction as a hierarchical pyramid, which only took account of the cognitive part of his model.

Notes

1 Kimball, 1986.
2 See, amongst others:
- de Rooy, 2018.

3 Beunk, 2014.
4 For the lists, see:
http://komenskypost.nl/?p=3672
https://pedrodebruyckere.blog/2017/12/06/wat-moet-op-school-allemaal-aangeleerd-worden-een-nieuwe-update/
5 See:
- De Bruyckere, Kirschner, & Hulshof, 2015a.

6 Perkins & Salomon, 1992.
Mention is made of transfer or training, whereby the skills trained for in one domain have a positive in another domain.
7 Perkins & Salomon, 1992.
Near transfer and far transfer have meant different things at different times. For example, Royer described the terms as follows: 'I will use the term near transfer to refer to instances in which one classroom learned skill, or bit of knowledge, transfers to another classroom skill or bit of knowledge. I will use the term far transfer to refer to situations in which material learned in the classroom transfers to events or problems encountered outside of the classroom.' See: Royer, 1979.
8 Thorndike, 1923.
9 Woodworth & Thorndike, 1901.
10 See, amongst others:
- Deary, Strand, Smith & Fernandes, 2007.
- Hunter & Hunter, 1984.

11 Check www.chess.com/blog/tayyab/benefits-of-playing-chess-specially-for-children. Own translation.
12 Reigeluth, 1983.
13 de Groot, 1946.
14 There are two Armenian reports mentioning positive effects:
- Aghuzumtsyan & Poghosyan, 2014.
- Mirzakhanyana, Gevorgyana, Sargsyana, & Daveyana, 2017.
- The first study shows correlations; the second illustrates how context plays a role.

15 Gobet & Campitelli, 2006, p. 139.
16 Sala, Foley, & Gobet, 2017.
17 Sala & Gobet, 2017.
18 Burgoyne, Sala, Gobet, Macnamara, Campitelli, & Hambrick, 2016.
19 We searched for and found this video with the comment by Jobs (www.youtube.com/watch?v=mCDkxUbalCw).
20 Matarić, 2007.
21 Papert, 1980.

22 Mayer, 1975.
23 Van Lengen & Maddux, 1990.
24 Mayer, 1975.
25 Clements & Gullo, 1984.
26 Clements, 1985.
27 Tu & Johnson, 1990.
28 Littlefield, Delclos, Lever, Clayton, Bransford, & Franks, 1988.
29 Papert, 1980; 1996
30 Wing, 2006.
31 Tedre & Denning, 2016.
32 Lye & Koh, 2014.
33 Sweller, Clark, & Kirschner, 2010.
34 Jaschke, Honing, & Scherder, 2018.
35 Schmitt, McClelland, Tominey, & Acock, 2015.
36 Jacob & Parkinson, 2015.
37 Sala & Gobet, 2017.
38 Winner, Goldstein, & Vincent-Lancrin, 2013.
39 For how we say things, for example, through rituals, see: Rybanska, McKay, Jong, & Whitehouse, 2018.
40 For an extensive name list, see: https://blogs.transparent.com/latin/famous-people-who-studied-latin/.
41 Bracke & Bradshaw, 2017.
42 We suspect that even if there is a connection it only applies for languages derived from Latin (French, Spanish, Portuguese, Italian) and less for languages like Finnish, Swahili or Chinese. In other words: near transfer!
43 Masciantonio, 1977.
44 Haag & Stern, 2003.
45 Carlisle, 1993.
46 Bracke & Bradshaw, 2017.
47 Beard, 2006.
48 Finnish National Agency for Education, 2015.
49 Longcamp, Boucard, Gilhodes, & Velay, 2006.
50 James & Engelhardt, 2012.
51 Kersey & James, 2013.
52 Graham, Liu, Bartlett, Ng, Harris, Aitken, & Talukdar, 2017.
53 Mueller & Oppenheimer, 2014.
54 Mangen, Anda, Oxborough, & Brønnick, 2015.
55 Smoker, Murphy, & Rockwell, 2009.
56 See, amongst others:
  - Cornhill & Case-Smith, 1996.
  - Kaiser, Albaret, & Doudin, 2009.

57 We are not the first to try and trace this figure to its source. In 2015, Andrew Smith produced a fine summary in a well substantiated blog post. For this book we repeated the process and can confirm that Andrew did his work well. His blog post can be consulted via https://teachingbattleground.wordpress.com/2015/05/27/a-myth-for-teachers-jobs-that-dont-exist-yet/.
58 World Economic Forum, 2016a, p.3.
59 Davidson, 2011.
60 Carroll, 2007.
61 See: https://jimcarroll.com/2008/05/65-of-the-kids-in-preschool-today-will-work-in-jobs-or-careers-that-dont-yet-exist/ (consulted on 8 May 2018).
62 See: www.hastac.org/blogs/cathy-davidson/2017/05/31/65-future-jobs-havent-been-invented-yet-cathy-davidson-responds.
63 Kidd, 2009.
64 The source mentioned by Debra Kidd: Collard, 2008.
65 See, amongst others, the references in:
- Laurie, 2011.
- Daly & Beloglovsky, 2014.

66 See, amongst others:
- www.ideafestival.com/blog/2056
- www.successperformancesolutions.com/65-percent-of-todays-students-will-be-employed-in-jobs-that-dont-exist-yet/

67 Herman, 1999.
68 Peal, 2014.
69 Mauger, 1966.
70 Check his blog post on www.longviewoneducation.org/field-guide-jobs-dont-exist-yet/.
71 Josephs, 1958.
72 Frey & Osborne, 2017.
73 Blinder, 2006.
74 Talwar & Hancock, 2010.
75 BBC World Service, 2017.
76 SLO, 2014.
77 Dede, 2010.
78 Partnership for 21st Century Skills, 2006.
79 Metiri Group & NCREL, 2003.
80 American Association of Colleges & Universities, 2007.
81 Marzano & Heflebower, 2012.
82 Silva, 2009
83 Boone, 2007.
84 Mishra, 2012.
85 Kirschner, 2017.
86 Kereluik, Mishra, Fahnoe, & Terry, 2013.
87 Willingham, 2009.

88 Tricot & Sweller, 2014.
89 World Economic Forum, 2016b.
90 Hattie, Biggs, & Purdie, 1996.
91 De Bruyckere, 2018.
92 Pan & Rickard, 2018.
93 Abrami, Bernard, Borokhovski, Waddington, Wade, & Persson, 2015.
94 Singley & Anderson, 1989.
95 www.merriam-webster.com/
96 Wikipedia (2018). *Taxonomy* (https://en.wikipedia.org/wiki/Taxonomy_(general)).
97 de Block, 1975.
98 Biggs & Collis, 2014.
99 Romiszowski, 2016.
100 Miller, 1990.
101 This is an error. It's one that we have seen often and one, in our opinion, that Bloom initially helped to cause – as will be seen later.
102 Bloom, 1956.
103 Forehand, 2010.
104 Krathwohl, 2002.
105 Valcke (2007) described Bloom's work as a landmark in educational literature, because it provided for the first time a manual to assist with decision taking regarding the composition of didactic activities and actions.
106 Morshead, 1965.
107 Schultz, 2005.
108 Where have we heard this before?
109 Krathwohl, Bloom, & Masia, 1964.
110 See, amongst others:
- Simpson, 1972.
- Dave, 1970.

111 Harrow, 1972.

Myths about the 'How'

There are many things that work in education, but it's seldom that something always works, for everyone, and for every purpose, in all circumstances, and for all students. This will become evident in this second chapter. Homework, for example, is something that we're often asked about. Does it work or doesn't it? As we'll see, it's not always easy to give a single, all-embracing answer to questions of this kind. We're inclined to reply in the same manner as Doug Bernstein, Emeritus Professor at the University of Illinois and Courtesy Professor of Psychology at the University of South Florida, when asked for his opinion on a different subject: 'Does active learning work? That's a good question, but the wrong one.' According to Bernstein, the question should be: 'Which active learning methods, applied by which teachers, in which context or circumstances, lead to significantly better learning outcomes for which students, and are those outcomes significantly better than those of traditional teaching methods?'[1] Some discussions have been dragging on for years and have even led to full-scale academic wars. For example, the evidence about the best way to teach a child to read has been confirmed and reconfirmed time and again over decades, but the debate still refuses to die down.

Another frequently asked question is whether or not it's better to learn with or without music. Once again, the answer is complex. And in searching for the answer we also came into contact with other myths about music and learning that we'd like to share with you.

Of course, possible new myths and discussion are appearing all the time. For example, the 10,000-hour rule has been widely accepted by many people, even though Malcolm Gladwell, who first popularized the rule, is far from sure.

In similar vein, we'll also be looking at the relatively recent philosophy of the universal design for learning (UDL), which was developed, in part at least, as a result of the movement for more inclusive education. It's not our intention to discuss the pros and cons of inclusive education; instead, we'll look at the scientific validity of the UDL concept. In particular, we'll be looking at the blindness (deliberate or otherwise?) of some authors who like to argue against the value of lectures, but who seem to have difficulty in correctly reading the results of research into why and how brain activity falls away during such lectures.

If, after reading the following sections, you still have questions about how best to approach your teaching tasks, you can find further useful guidance in *Ten Steps to Complex Learning* by Jeroen van Merriënboer and Paul A. Kirschner and *The Ingredients for Great Teaching* by Pedro De Bruyckere.

Is Learning to Read Something Natural?

Some myths leave people cold; others give rise to acrimonious debate. One of the most acrimonious and long-standing of all is the debate – if what we see can actually be called a debate – about how children can best learn to read: the so-called Reading Wars.[2]

A War – But About What?

Put at its simplest, this is a confrontation between supporters of learning to read by what is known as the 'whole language' or global reading method and supporters of learning to read via the 'phonics' or structural method.

Math Wars

There is a comparable war in mathematics/arithmetic, which has been raging in the United States since the 1980s; this time between the exponents of the explicit approach to learning maths and realistic methods.[3] What's more, it's a war that has also flared up in other parts of the world; for example, since the turn of the century, the Netherlands has also been engaged in its own version of the same conflict: the *rekenoorlogen* (math wars).[4]

The reasoning behind the whole language or global method is that children in a rich linguistic environment are themselves capable of discovering meaning in texts and can thereby learn how to read. This is how we learn to speak our mother tongue and for proponents of the whole language approach, there is no reason to assume that the same principle cannot apply to learning how to read in that same mother tongue. Goodman calls learning to read a 'psycho-linguistic guessing game', rather than something that requires a deeper analytical approach.[5] Daniel Willingham describes the rationale of this method in the following terms:

> children should be taught to read the way adults read. Adults seem to read entire words or even phrases all at once. (Watch the eyes of someone reading, and you'll see that they do not dwell on each word, but rather stop a few times as they scan each line.) Adults read silently, which is much faster than reading aloud. And adults read what interests them. Children, in contrast, are taught to read sound by sound (not in whole words) aloud (not silently) and out of boring primers (not engaging materials).[6]

This whole language approach is also known as the 'look-say' method. Children are encouraged to learn whole words – and not just separate letters – by heart. For this reason, books for learning to read in this manner only use a limited range of words to make this memorization possible.

With the structural or phonics-based method, reading is taught more explicitly. Children learn how to read by learning how sounds and letters are connected to each other.[7] This is an older method than the global method. In fact, in the Anglo-Saxon world the 'reading debate' goes back more than 200 years to the works of Horace Mann,[8] some of whose arguments are still put forward today. It was Mann who first highlighted the dichotomy between the idea that meaning must be made central in the process of learning to read and the idea that learning to read is best achieved through a more systematic (or, according to its opponents, more mechanical) approach.

The resulting Reading Wars have meant that much (and widely publicized) research has been carried out into this subject in the Anglo-Saxon world. In the Low Countries, an important contribution to the debate was made at the start of the 20th century by Ovide Decroly, who favored the global method of teaching, certainly for reading, where he advocated the use of meaning-rich texts rather than a focus on individual letters and sounds.

More recently, David Geary has analyzed the Reading Wars debate in terms of what he called biologically (or evolutionary) primary and secondary learning.[9] Biologically primary learning occurs seemingly without effort and almost spontaneously; in other words, without explicit teaching. This kind of learning is focused on the things which, in evolutionary terms, have an influence on the availability of social and natural resources and therefore increase the likelihood of the organism's or species' survival. The ability to collaborate, recognize others (for example, to distinguish between friends and enemies on the basis of their facial expressions and posture or who the nurturer is), know which plants are poisonous (by differentiating between pleasant and unpleasant flavors and odors), know the purposes for which you can use a stick (as a tool, as a weapon, etc.), and so on. This was the kind of learning that could quite literally mean the difference between life and death. For example, a child that could not recognize its own mother or was incapable of developing a social bond with her was doomed to die. According to Geary, other examples of the specific knowledge and skills that are needed to survive in any society include learning to speak and understand your mother tongue, learning how to cooperate with others and learning how to solve simple problems. These are things that are evolutionarily important. If you are not nourished as a baby because you cannot bond with your mother, you'll probably die shortly after birth and that gene that caused you not to bond will slowly leave the gene pool. It's just that simple. It's this assumption that the learning of the most important things in life comes naturally which forms the basis of the arguments put forward in favor of the global reading method. But are they right? Biologically secondary learning relates to the things that it's not possible for people to pick up spontaneously. For this reason, it's also referred to as 'cultural knowledge', in the sense of matters that are deemed important from a cultural (as opposed to a survival) perspective and were only developed relatively recently in evolutionary terms. This is the case, for example, with writing, which only came into existence some 10,000 years ago (in evolutionary terms a very short time) and has therefore not had time to have an impact on the evolutionary development of our brains. It's also not something that will determine whether or not you will live long enough to procreate! Consequently, learning to write cannot be regarded as biologically primary learning and therefore this is why it needs to be taught. The transfer of such cultural knowledge is actually the reason for schools. And the same, of course, must also apply to reading. Mustn't it? Or do writing and reading nevertheless somehow share some of the vital 'survival' characteristics of primary learning?

Again and Again and Again ...

These are the arguments that have raged back and forth for decades. This is in some ways very surprising since scientific and academic research have repeatedly shown that there is a very clear winner in this debate:

- In 1961, the Carnegie Corporation asked Jeanne Chall, who was then a professor at the Harvard Graduate School of Education, to conduct an independent comparative study. Her conclusion was clear: phonics is the best method for teaching children how to read.[10]
- In 1997, this research was replicated, since there were still those who challenged the validity of the phonics method. This new research team concluded that Chall had been correct: phonics is best.[11]
- In 2018, Castles and colleagues made yet another attempt to bring the Reading War to a definitive conclusion by going over the same ground again – and with the same result. Final score: phonics 3 – whole language 0.

Even so, the controversy seems likely to persist. The proponents of global reading are like an ageing rock band that keeps on announcing its final farewell tour or a boxer who keeps on getting up every time he is knocked down: they just don't know when to quit.

Does the Global Reading/Whole Language Method have No Value?

The emphasis placed by supporters of the global method on reading pleasure and reading motivation is certainly worthy of consideration and in certain circumstances can enhance the effectiveness – or at least the enjoyment – of the phonics method. Nevertheless, recent research has again demonstrated that at-risk students and students from difficult family backgrounds are most likely to be disadvantaged by a global approach and derive greatest benefit from learning to read via direct instruction based on, among other things, the use of phonemes.[12]

Conclusion: Myth

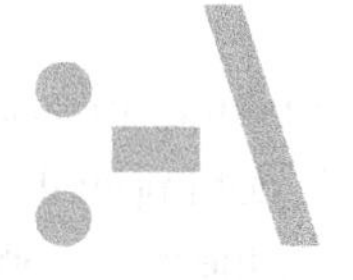

The jury passed judgment on this matter a long time ago, but the discussion unfortunately continues. Of all educational myths, this is perhaps the one that is most difficult to eradicate. To make matters worse, it's also the one that can potentially have the strongest negative effects on the weakest members of society.

Can We Speed Read?

Speed reading seems like a perfect solution to our information overload in an era in which we're swamped by e-mails, posts about breaking news and piles of unread books. It would also have helped us to write this book in less than the three years it has taken …

Ever since the 1960s, various books have been written and many methods have been proposed for assisting us to read more quickly. Some have even claimed that this is the secret behind successful people.[13] And there is no denying that some people can read at lightning speed. In 2016, for example, Anne Jones reportedly read a Harry Potter book in just 27 minutes, whereas back in 2007 she needed a whole 47 minutes to read the new Harry Potter book published that year.[14] In reality, however, this makes her something of a slacker – at least in speed-reading terms. In 1990, Howard Berg was noted in the Guinness Book of World Records with a supposed reading speed of more than 25,000 words per minute.[15] In comparison: in English, an experienced adult reader can read somewhere between 300 and 400 words per minute.[16]

If you've been paying attention, you will probably have noticed the use of the words 'reportedly' and 'supposed' in the preceding paragraph, since the effectiveness (or even the existence) of speed reading is a matter of contention in scientific and academic circles. With this in mind, in 2015 a team of psychologists under the leadership of the late Keith Rayner trawled through the research of recent decades in an attempt to provide a definitive answer to the question of whether speed reading really is possible. And for those of you who don't have the time or the speed to read their conclusions in full, their short answer was: NO.[17]

For Our Slower Readers

The first thing we need to do is distinguish between reading, skimming and speed reading.

According to Rayner's team, reading is the processing of textual information to establish the meaning of each word and sentence. This does not imply that you will immediately understand that meaning, but that, at least, is the intention.

Skimming involves scanning a text to identify specific words or pieces of information, so that you can gain a general impression of the contents. Obviously, skimming is faster than reading – on average, between two and four times faster. The price that you pay for this speed is that you understand and remember less. However, if you first skim through a text to establish its main titles, key words and structure and only then move on to read the text in full, you will normally have a better overall understanding of the content than if you just read without prior skimming. In other words, skimming first is an effective pre-reading strategy. Some speed reading methods are based on skimming.

Speed reading is reading faster than you would normally read but without any loss of understanding. Since the 1959 introduction of the first speed reading program – the Evelyn Wood Reading Dynamics Program – different techniques have been proposed. One such technique, for example, is working with 'meta guides', where you use a finger, pen or other object to point at the words you are reading, so that your eyes will be less inclined to make time-consuming 'jumps' from word to word. What the different methods all have in common is their emphasis on practice, practice, practice.

The idea that repeated eye movement slows down reading speed sounds logical and, up to a point, is true. However, the use of meta guides does little to eradicate the most important speed-retarding factor: our ability to recognize words and understand their meaning.[18] What's more, Rayner and his colleagues argued that eye movement actually serves an important purpose in this respect, since we frequently need to look back at things that we could not immediately understand. In other words, attempting to reduce eye movement

Pronouns

The more a text makes use of pronouns and the greater the distance between the pronoun and the word to which it refers (its antecedent), the more difficult reading the text becomes and the longer it takes to read it. The reason for this is that in these circumstances more reinstatement searches must be performed and the harder it is to find the antecedent. This principle was used in a program – the Unic Writer's Workbench, developed by Bell Laboratories (New Jersey)[20] – which calculated the degree of reading difficulty of a text and helps writers to limit that degree of difficulty.

actually reduces understanding and comprehension! This process of looking back is known as a 'reinstatement search', whereby you search for something you've already read (the so-called antecedent), return to what you are reading now, and then link the two together. This leads to a greater understanding of what you read, but also makes reading slower and more difficult.[19]

Other speed reading methods are based on the idea that people can 'photograph' whole sentences, paragraphs or even pages. Unfortunately, this assumption has absolutely no scientific basis. To begin with, as we already showed in our previous book, the concept of a 'photographic memory' is a myth.[21] Moreover, research makes clear that our peripheral vision is far from clear. In this context, peripheral vision is taken to mean the impressions received by your eyes from the words on either side of the word on which you are focusing. The chance that you can correctly interpret or remember these impressions has been shown to be small.

Another starting point for some methods is the suppression of subvocalization or the use of your inner voice. When we read, we often hear a kind of spoken version of the text in our head. According to some 'experts', this slows down the pace at which we read. In view of what we've already written, it will perhaps not surprise you to learn that there is a plethora of reliable evidence that shows that vocalization – 'hearing' yourself read – actually helps you better understand what you're reading.[22]

Given the digital age in which we live, it was only to be expected that in recent years a number of apps have appeared on the market to help people read more quickly. One technique – used, for example, by the Spritz app – is to show each word individually, rather than in full sentences or pages. The idea is that this makes it easier to focus, in a manner similar to the use of meta guides. Other apps add colors to their texts, so that when your eyes 'jump', they can more easily find their way back to the right place. But as already mentioned, it's precisely this jumping movement that is so important for properly understanding the text.

So What Can We Learn?

Rayner and his colleagues not only established why the theoretical bases for speed reading are incorrect, but also examined research in which the concept was measured in experienced speed readers using the techniques and methods outlined above. A 2009 study compared the performance of accomplished skimmers against ordinary readers. All test subjects were given a short period of time to read the same text. The skimmers generally understood the text better, because they had skimmed it to the end, whereas the slow readers were only halfway through before their time was up.[23] But what also became apparent was that when skimmers came to the most important parts of the text, they also slowed down so that they could understand it better. The use of other techniques almost always leads to a loss in comprehension. This may not become evident during a superficial questioning about the content, but more detailed questioning soon reveals errors or gaps in understanding. The memory retention period is also significantly reduced.[24]

Is There No Hope?

At the start of this section, we already revealed the secret of reading faster and still understanding what you read. Of course, we're not talking about an ability to read 25,000 words a minute. No, we're talking about the need to practice, practice, practice. In due course, this will give you a reading speed which is faster than the average reader. Skimming can also be a useful technique, not necessarily for learning how to read faster, but for extracting information from a text in an efficient manner. And yes, skimming can also be improved by practice.

Conclusion: Myth

For those of you who have had the patience to read through to the end of this section, I am afraid our conclusion remains the same: you will never be able to speed read – at least, not fast enough to get you into the Guinness Book of Records!

Does Homework Work? Or Not?

Is homework a myth, as Alfie Kohn has suggested in the title of his 2006 book *Too Much of a Bad Thing?*[25] If we look at the meta-meta-analysis conducted by John Hattie in 2009, the answer would seem to be: NO. Perhaps homework does not achieve a high score in the eyes of the New Zealand professor, but with an effect size of 0.43 (bearing in mind that the effect of average education is somewhere between 0.15 and 0.40), it's a relatively simple, inexpensive, and effective method.[26] The various analyses carried out by Harris Cooper and his colleagues confirm this.[27]

The reality, however, is more complex. The effect of homework differs with its function and the age of the students. A study conducted by Adam Maltese and colleagues at the University of Indiana revealed that in some cases homework is pointless, in the sense that students who work hard at home achieve no better results than children who invest much less effort.[28] Other researchers have suggested that abolishing homework would have a positive effect in terms of equal opportunities, since some young people receive little help from their parents or else find themselves in home situations that are often far from optimal,[29] although a more recent meta-analysis disputes this.[30]

Given these seeming contradictions, might it not be better to rephrase our question, so that we ask instead: when can homework be effective and when not?

The Purpose of Homework

Homework can be given for roughly four reasons (i.e., learning objectives). The most common reason given is to practise or repeat what was learned or discussed in class. Second, homework can prepare students for what's coming in the following lesson(s). A third reason is what is called extension and is aimed at having the student apply something that was learnt in class in new contexts or situations (i.e., far transfer). Lastly, a possible homework objective is to integrate concepts and skills. This is mostly done through the assignment of essays to write or projects to carry out. According to research from Pedro Rosário and colleagues,[31] extension homework has by far the most positive effect on students' achievements, stating 'when comparing the three homework instructional purposes (Rosário and his colleagues focused on practice, preparation, and extension), students who completed homework that had a purpose of extension had higher grades in mathematics'. NOT doing homework was not part of this research and, thus, it can't be concluded that any of the four is better or worse than no homework. Rosário concludes 'that despite the homework purpose (i.e., practice, preparation or extension), it's always better to do more, compared to less, homework'.

Checking Homework

Even if students are being good kids and doing their homework, the question that then arises is; What does the teacher *do* with it, other than – we assume – 'checking whether it has been done'? Follow-up is critical and this follow-up can have many forms such as providing focussed feedback on the assignment, giving the completed homework a grade, giving small assessments on the homework itself (think about the 'testing effect') and using the homework as the starting point for continued, in-class, discussions.

If teachers give homework and students complete it faithfully, you would or even *should* expect that teachers put a bit more effort into it than just 'checking' whether it was done and if it's complete. The conclusion of many studies is that just giving feedback or grading it has a medium to large significant effect on students' learning. In addition, José Carlos Núñez and his colleagues found that teacher feedback has a positive effect on the amount of homework that students complete and that in turn, again has a positive effect on students' learning.[32]

The Amount of Homework and the Time Spent on It

Ulrich Trautwein and his colleagues have shown in a number of studies that the frequency of doing homework positively affects learning achievements. However, time spent has no or even a slightly negative effect! In other words, it's better to do a little homework regularly than a lot of homework only now and again.[33] This sounds very similar to the proven effective instructional method of distributed practice where, for example, 60 minutes of studying in four separate sessions of 15 minutes works way better than studying the same material for one hour straight.

In general, we know that age (or the grade that the student is in) influences the effect of homework. The relationship between the amount of homework given/done and learning achievement seems to be positive for higher grades within secondary education, but less in the lower grades and sometimes even negative in elementary school. A possible reason is that the attention span of younger children is limited. They can only concentrate for so long.

As to who benefits most from homework with respect to learner characteristics like achievement level, most research reports that better students benefit more from homework than average or slower students, but this doesn't mean that low-achievers don't benefit; research also shows that lower-ability students benefit from spending more time on homework assignments because they need more time to reach the same level as higher-ability students. However, 'grades of low-ability students who did 10 hours of homework or more per week were as good as the grades of high ability students who did no homework'.[34]

This seems to be in line with the well-known rule of thumb (at least well-known in the USA) of '10 minutes per grade'. In other words, in each succeeding grade in school, the amount of homework should increase by 10 minutes. For example, 10 minutes in first grade, 20 in second grade, up to 120 minutes for the last year in secondary school.[35]

Is There Something Wrong with Homework Research?

All research has limitations, but it's worth noting in particular that most research into the effect of homework makes use of self-reports. That means that students (or their parents) need to make their own estimate of how much time is spent on homework tasks. And this, according to a study of trainee engineers by Rawson and colleagues,[36] is where things can go wrong. Instead of using self-report, the Rawson team made use of smart pens, which kept a record of (amongst other things) how much homework was actually done. And what did this reveal? Namely, that there was a greater correlation (.44) between the time the students effectively spent on homework and their school results than the minimal correlation (.16) between the time they thought they spent (and reported spending) on homework and their school results. In this context, it's interesting to note that 88% of the participating students estimated that they spent more time on homework than was really the case. In part, this might be explained by the students counting re-reading as homework time, which is something that might not be picked up in full by the pen – although it's also interesting to note that this would have relatively little real effect.

So what can we conclude from this research in light of our earlier discussions on the homework theme? Well, we can conclude that homework can sometimes benefit older students (the target group in this case), but it says nothing about the wider issue of whether homework in general works or not. And it suggests that much of the homework research carried out previously may suffer from methodological shortcomings ...

To paraphrase Epstein and Voorhis: Doing homework is a daily activity for most students. Each homework assignment requires time and energy from students, teachers, and parents. Given this effort, it's essential that teachers design homework effectively in order to achieve specific objectives. If the design is good, chances are greater that more students will deliver better quality work and, if there is a proper follow-up from the teacher's end as well, the student will benefit more with regard to learning. Only then – perhaps – will the doing homework feel less like a chore (or even a battle) than is often the case.

> *Conclusion: Nuanced*
>
> :-| Homework can be effective, but its effect depends on a number of factors, such as the nature of the tasks and their duration, the age of the students concerned, and what the teacher actually does with the homework. Radical opinions either for or against homework are most likely to be oversimplifications of a complex situation.

Is There Only Minimal Brain Activity in Students during Lectures?

Some research tends to live a life of its own online, appearing, disappearing and reappearing over time. One such example is the study carried out by Poh, Swenson and Picard, using a portable sensor on just a single student (!).[37] This resulted in the graph shown in Figure 2.1.

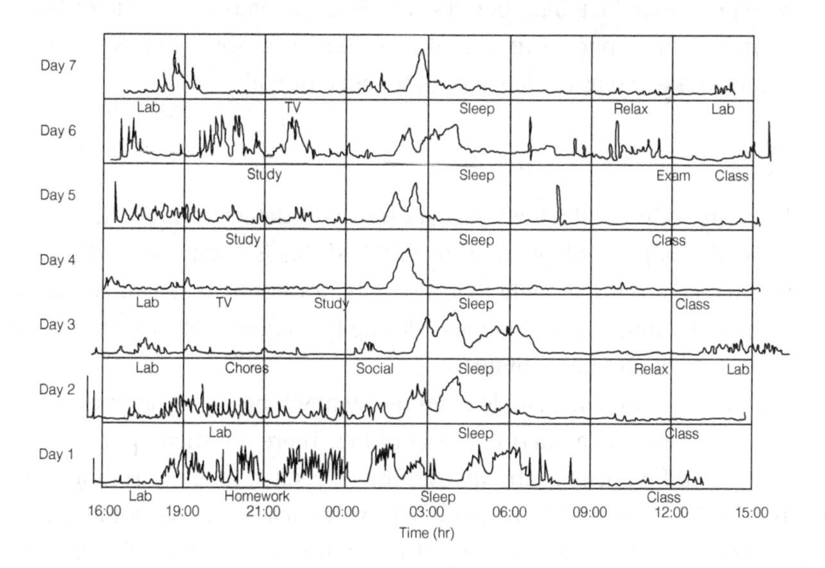

Figure 2.1

Source: *Poh, Swenson and Picard, 2010.*

Poh and colleagues claimed that the sensor registered the brain activity of the student and that this activity was lower – almost flat-lined – during lessons and lectures than when the student was asleep! This kind of eye-catching conclusion soon spread like wildfire on the internet and still occasionally resurfaces. What's more, the idea has even been adopted by a number of scientists.[38]

But is it true? NO. The story was dismantled by Ken Masters in 2014.[39] Poh and his colleagues did not set out to investigate the brain waves of their single test subject. Instead, they measured his Electrodermal Activity (EDA), which is an umbrella term covering all electrical reactions of the skin; for example, how well the skin conducts electricity.

The Lie Detector

Electrodermal Activity (EDA) is the basis of the polygraph or lie detector. The idea is that people perspire when they lie and therefore (perspiration being essentially a combination of moisture and salt) the conductivity of the skin increases. This is a so-called galvanic skin response that you can't consciously suppress. In other words, if the polygraph records a peak in EDA, you're lying. Or that, at least, is the theory. In practice, the lie detector has time and again been discredited as being more fable than fact, although it's still used by some police authorities (mainly in the United States) and is accepted by some courts (again, mainly in the US) as evidence of innocence or guilt.[40]

Measuring skin conductivity is a good way to detect and record changes in physical and psychological arousal.[41] And this is what Poh and his colleagues wanted to do, namely to test whether or not their sensor could give an accurate picture of these changes during the different phases of physical, cognitive and emotional activity.[42]

Can this study of just a single student say anything meaningful about the whole class? Masters argued that it couldn't. There are many possible reasons for the differences in the measurement results, ranging from fear and (sexual) excitement to various stress factors. The research says nothing about the student's brain activity and level of attention, nor about the student's willingness (or otherwise) to think during lessons and lectures.

How Effective are Lectures?

Instruction, and in particular good instruction, plays an important role in education. Lectures are one way of providing this instruction. But is this always the case? Or is it only sometimes? And only for some students? The lecture is a part of the teacher's instructional arsenal for good reasons. Lectures are often very efficient – lots of people are presented with information at the same time by just a single person – and in certain circumstances they can also be very effective. But they are not perfect. Traditional lectures (i.e., when the teacher stands in front of a class and talks) of this kind are highly passive. And what happens? 'Good' students will usually limit themselves to listening and (hopefully) taking some notes, whereas poorer students allow their attention to drift. Moreover, this kind of teaching is not very motivating for many young people, largely because most teachers find it difficult to keep them interested in a manner that appeals to them. With this in mind, a PhD candidate of one of the authors conducted research into the use of podcasts containing epistemic (knowledge developing) questions in the run-up to lectures. The aim was to prompt students to listen in a more focused way and to deal with the content differently than if they just attended the lecture. Questions of this kind often start with how, what, when, where and why. And they do activate thought and reflection.[43]

Another approach to increase the effectiveness of lectures is by using quizzes (testing effect, retrieval practice), which can provide immediate feedback. The need to answer questions that stimulate you to actively retrieve what you have learned, together with timely feedback, strengthens long-term retention of what you've learned. A study conducted by James Pennebaker and his colleagues[44] involved 901 students who were given lessons in this manner and a control group of 935 students who were given the same lessons by the same teacher, but without quizzes. The results revealed that the quiz group scored better on their exams than the control group and also that they scored better in comparison with previous years. This effect also manifested itself in other subjects in that same school year and at the start of the following year. Perhaps even more important was the conclusion that the gap between students from lower and higher socio-economic groups was reduced by 50%, not only for the 'quiz' subject but also for all other subjects, again throughout that same school year and the next. In other words, without disadvantaging one group, the quizzes helped the other group to perform better.

Conclusion: Myth

No, students are not brain dead during lessons and lectures, but it's always a good idea to add new elements that can stimulate their interest and activity.

Is It a Good Idea to Record Lectures and Share Them Online?

Recording lectures and then making them available for students online is something that is done with increasing frequency in higher education: lessons and lectures are recorded so that students can either watch them in advance and/or review them afterwards. To make this possible, universities have invested in the necessary technical infrastructure and have persuaded their professors – some more willingly than others – to give their lectures in front of camera and microphone. But what is the overall effect? Does it help students to learn better?

A number of studies have been published that reveal a possibly undesirable side effect of recording lessons and lectures and making them available. A 2017 study by Eric Bettinger and colleagues showed that not only do online lessons have no positive effect in comparison with offline, but tend, if anything, to have a negative impact.[45] Students are less successful in exams, and not just for the subjects they were able to follow online. As a result, more students drop out and do this more quickly. Once again, there is also an important socio-economic dimension here: the negative effects are more strongly felt by the students from poorer social backgrounds, because it's often more difficult for them to follow the lessons; perhaps, for example, because they need to combine their studies with a job.

A 2018 British study reached much the same conclusions: if you offer lessons and lectures online, participation levels drop and results fall correspondingly.[46] In fact, these are the findings of most of the studies we've examined, although the negative effects seem to be dependent on a number of factors, such as the subject concerned, the interaction between professors and students, how the lecturers and lessons are given, and so on.[47] Given

Does the Flipped Classroom Work?

Thanks (amongst others) to the Khan Academy, the phenomenon of the 'flipped classroom' has become popular. Traditionally, teachers give their lessons in class and students are expected (often via homework) to further apply or extend what they've learnt at home. In a flipped classroom, the students are first brought into contact with new learning material (knowledge, principles, concepts, procedures, theory, etc.) away from the classroom. This can be done in various ways, for example by reading their textbooks, watching videos or internet films (now perhaps the most common method in practice), and so on. The time at school is then spent on mastering and deepening the students' understanding of the learning material first explored at home, above all through discussion and collaborative problem solving.

As a concept, the flipped classroom is not really all that new, but the same cannot be said for the current use of the idea of *flipping* in education. As a result – and notwithstanding its popularity – there is very little evidence to show that flipping is effective and the evidence that there is, is not very consistent. Moreover, the research that has been carried out is not only limited, but often also leaves much to be desired in terms of methodological rigor. Jacob Bishop and Matthew Verleger[50] reported, for example, that there is 'anecdotal evidence [which] suggests that student learning is improved for the flipped compared to traditional classroom. However, there is very little work investigating student learning out-comes objectively.' Recent meta-analyses have demonstrated a possible positive learning effect specifically within the context of medical training, which was one of the first domains to adopt the flipped concept, but the researchers again warned that these findings were based on a very limited amount of research data.[51] In other words, the basic conclusion is that much more (and better quality) research needs to be carried out before reliable conclusions on the value of the flipped classroom can be formulated.[52]

this variability, some studies actually record a positive effect for recorded lessons and lectures, but these studies tend to be in the minority.[48] Research in the Netherlands by Nynke Bos and colleagues revealed yet another nuance: the availability of online lessons and lectures is often used as a reason for not going to the 'real' offline lessons and lectures. However, Bos and colleagues found that students who combined both options – online and offline – scored better in exams than the students who only attended the offline lessons and lectures – although it's possible that this correlation was the result of better students using the online availability to double-check what they had already learnt in the offline setting.[49]

How do the researchers explain these conclusions? Bettinger and colleagues describe how online courses have radically altered the interaction between students and their instructors. Students are free to choose when and what they consult online, but this is a challenge for those with little prior knowledge or who are less proficient in what they are studying.[53] This kind of learning also requires the student to have good self-regulation skills, which, unfortunately, many do not possess. Moreover, because they are less frequently in contact with their instructors 'in the flesh', the pressure to learn is reduced. In addition, other research has shown that distraction is also a problem with this kind of learning: student attention is liable to be disrupted by text messages, social media, emails or the temptation of surfing the web.[54] They attempt to multitask, when this is not realistically possible (see the myth covered in our earlier book *Urban Myths about Learning and Education*).

This brings us to an important point, namely that it's difficult to compare the two. For example, videotaped lessons and lectures without interaction don't seem to be effective. This is not illogical, but we also know that the effectiveness of 'physical' lessons and lectures can also vary, depending on the educational approach used, the quality of the teacher, and so on. When examining available research on this theme, we most often came across case studies that – due to their nature – aren't really suitable in comparing online and offline courses.

In our view, the more relevant research in this domain has made use of the same teachers both online and offline, but even then it's possible to ask whether every teacher is as good in both teaching on and offline. Conclusion? This is not an easy theme to investigate ...

To record or not to record, that is the question. While that is indeed the question, there is no simple and uniform answer. Viewed in overall terms, the disadvantages would seem to outweigh the advantages. The majority of the research still supports the importance of face-to-face lessons, but this conclusion can vary depending on the subject concerned, the approach, the quality of the online lessons, and a whole variety of other factors. What is clear is that online lessons tend to result in reduced participation and this often – but not always – leads to poorer results.

Conclusion: Nuanced

Although more research is certainly needed, the evidence currently available suggests a need to be cautious with online and flipped learning, especially for specific target groups. If in doubt, don't do it.

Do You Have to Study 10,000 Hours to Become an Expert?

The 10,000 hours of practice idea first became really well known through the work of Malcolm Gladwell, who popularized research originally carried out by Anders Ericsson. In *Outliers* (2008), Gladwell described Ericsson's theory, which, through association with the Gladwell name, soon came to be widely accepted. In essence, Ericsson claimed that at least 10,000 hours of study and effort are necessary before you can become really good at something – although it's worth bearing in mind that Gladwell himself did not suggest that this can work for everyone and all subject matter.[55]

But is becoming an expert really as easy as Ericsson argues? No! And if you go back and examine Ericsson's research, this is not what he says.[56] Other subsequent research also confirms that often excellence is harder to achieve than one might think.

Where Does the Idea Come From?

It's self-evident that practice is important in many fields. But how much practice do you need if you wish to excel at something? Gladwell deduced from the work by Ericsson and his colleagues that the best pianists and violinists had practiced for more than 10,000 hours before they reached the age of twenty, and that it was this that made all the difference. Gladwell added – in addition to himself – other examples of the same phenomenon, including The Beatles and Bill Gates.[57] And so the idea was born – and optimistically adopted by many – that you can become whatever you want, if only you practice hard and long enough.

Nature versus Nurture

Anders Ericsson belongs to a school of thought about learning and development that focuses on the importance of environment. This is what we call nurture: what we learn is largely determined by what we get from our parents, teachers, classmates and even society. Ericsson is only willing to accept to a limited degree that natural aptitude can also make an important contribution towards learning performance. He concedes, for example, that being tall is an advantage if you want to play basketball.

Even so, there are sufficient indications that nature – the things we're given genetically through our DNA at birth – can also play an important role in learning. Research involving twins in 2013[58] and 2014[59] concluded that heredity explains more than half of the difference in school results.

There is also a grey area that is described by the term 'epigenetic'. This includes, for example, environmental factors that can affect the development of a fetus. Under the pressure of these factors, the genes of the fetus, while still in the womb, can be turned 'on' or 'off'; in other words, the function of a gene can change without the DNA code being changed. This makes it possible for two people who have an identical genetic make-up (for example, identical twins) to differ from each other epigenetically.

This is not to say that everything is genetically determined. In our view, the following general principles are probably valid:

- The more positive or more stimulating the environment, the greater the influence of aptitude and heredity.
- The more negative or less stimulating the environment, the greater the influence of that environment.

What Does Ericsson Himself Say?

In their book *Peak*, Anders Ericsson and Robert Pool discuss Gladwell's work and his interpretation of the 10,000 hours idea.[60] The authors see four main problems with this.

First, the figure of 10,000 hours is neither magical nor absolute. Gladwell uses that figure, but he could just as easily have used a different one. For example, he might have said 7,400 hours, since that was the average number of hours of practice for the violinists mentioned in Ericsson's original research. But 7,400 doesn't sound as good as 10,000. More importantly, Ericsson said that this was the number of hours practiced by the violinists before the age of twenty, but this did not mean that they had already become experts by that age. In other words, they still had lots of work to do. For example, Ericsson and Pool cite that the winners of international piano competitions often have more than 20,000 hours of practice behind them. The 10,000 hours is, therefore, a random figure, which varies from discipline to discipline.

This leads on to the second problem. The 10,000 (or 7,400) hours is the average number of hours played by the violinists before their 20th birthday, which means that some played more and others fewer hours. This is something that Gladwell failed to understand correctly.

The third problem is probably the most crucial, because it gets to the heart of the theory. According to Ericsson and Pool, it's not per se the number of hours of practice that is important; it's the nature of that practice that makes the difference. They refer to what they call 'deliberate practice', where the practitioner is constantly challenged to push his or her own boundaries within the context of a learning trajectory drawn up by an expert coach or trainer for the purpose of achieving a specific learning goal. Coaches train their top footballers to play better; teachers encourage their students to perform better. Both use feedback to show where things are going wrong, so that the learner can make the necessary corrections and improve. This is very different from 'ordinary' practice or repetition, which, according to Ericsson and Pool, has little real effect. This is why, they argue, the example of The Beatles is not a good one. Yes, they played for hours and hours when they were in Hamburg, but without guidance and without a specific purpose. It was only when they returned to Liverpool and met Brian Epstein and George Martin that things began to change for the better.

The fourth and final problem has already been mentioned: many people expanded the original idea to the belief that anyone can learn anything in

10,000 hours. Gladwell at least recognized that this was not the case and there was one other point where Ericsson and Pool concede that Gladwell was right: forgetting specific figures, you don't become a top talent or a top expert without lots and lots of practice.

What Do Others Say?

How solid is the research by Ericsson and his colleagues? In recent years, various other studies have also examined the importance of practice and the amount that is necessary to become a top performer in different disciplines.

The first clear attack on Ericsson's work was launched in 2013 by Zach Hambrick and colleagues.[61] They went back to examine the same type of experts investigated in the original study: chess players and violinists. But the conclusions they reached were very different: they found that deliberate practice could only account for a third of the difference in performance.

Nor were they alone in this conclusion. A 2014 meta-analysis conducted by Brooke Macnamara and his colleagues[62] at Princeton University agreed that deliberate practice can make an important contribution to achieving a goal, but it is by no means the panacea that is often claimed. They compared 88 studies in widely varying domains, such as music, games, sport, professional development and education. They found that on average just 12% of the difference in the performance of the participants could be attributed to deliberate practice. Moreover – and as earlier pointed out by Ericsson and Pool – this varied considerably from discipline to discipline. For games like chess and draughts/checkers, the figure was 26%; for music, 21%; and for sport, 18%. More significantly, for education the impact of deliberate practice as a differentiating factor plummeted to just 4%, reaching a rock bottom of 1% for professional development. It was also noted that the results declined in relation to the quality with which the practice was measured; the better the measuring, the lower the results.

Hambrick and Macnamara's findings have been backed up by numerous other meta-analyses.[63] So if deliberate practice is not the key differentiating factor, what can explain the difference between people's performance? In chess, for example, intelligence has been shown to play a crucial role,[64] while other research suggests it may have something to do with how efficiently (or not) our brains work.[65]

That being said, we need to bear in mind that all the above-mentioned studies, including Ericsson's initial investigations, suffer from the same basic shortcoming: they all mainly or even exclusively focus on test subjects who have already achieved the status of 'expert'. This leads to a kind of automatic self-selection. As a result, many people who have practiced for thousands of hours *without* achieving expert status remain under the radar. Yet perhaps this is inevitable. It's hardly feasible to set up a study asking test subjects to practice something for thousands of hours over several years, simply to see if deliberate practice really makes a difference! Even so, this means that the research which does exist is far from conclusive.

Conclusion: Myth

The 10,000 hour rule is a myth. Perhaps it seems unfair, but some people can reach the 'expert' level without the need to practice excessively, while others will never reach this level, no matter how hard they practice. As ever, more research is needed to know how to become an expert.

How Scientific Is the Universal Design for Learning (UDL)?

There is a relatively new vision of education that is currently creating something of a furore in educational circles: the Universal Design for Learning (UDL). But what is this, exactly? UDL is a framework based on research about learning, including cognitive neurosciences, for creating a flexible learning environment that will provide optimal learning assistance to each student, irrespective of the many differences that exist between individuals.[66] The idea is closely linked to pleas for a more inclusive form of education and was inspired, in part at least, by the concept of universal design as a guiding principle in architecture.[67]

The UDL framework was first described by the Center for Applied Special Technology (CAST) in 1997, in a document in which (amongst others) David

Rose and Anne Meyer argued in favor of a curriculum which from the design phase onwards would take account of multiple means of:

- *Representation*: learning material should be presented in different ways, so that students can also acquire information and knowledge in different ways.
- *Expression*: students should be offered different ways to show what they know.
- *Engagement*: students should be involved in lessons in different ways, by appealing to their different interests and challenging them in an appropriate and motivating manner to learn.

UDL was added to the US's regulatory lexicon in 1998, where it was described as a philosophy to assist with the design of products and services.[68] But exactly how scientific are UDL's underlying principles? The screen shot of the former CAST website reveals something curious (Figure 2.2).

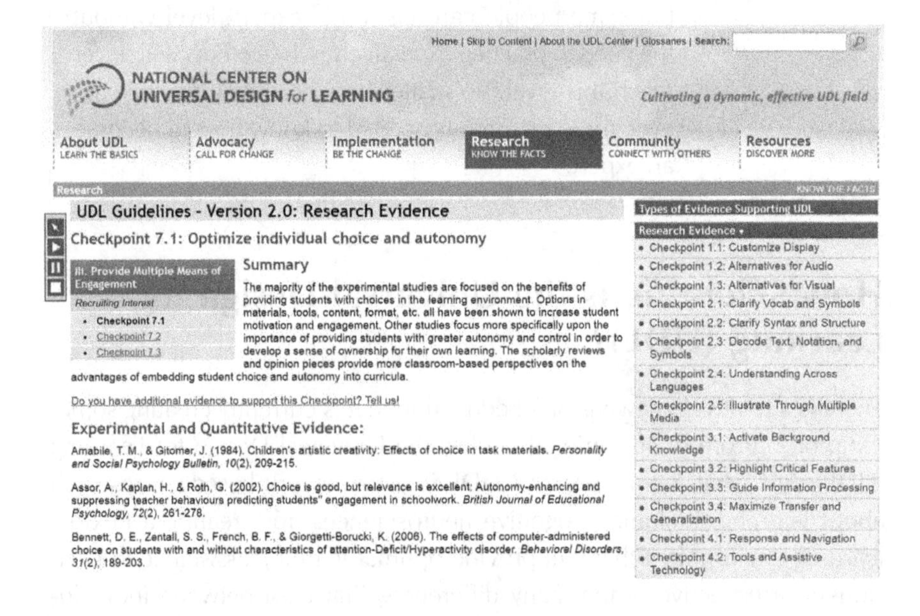

Figure 2.2 The old UDL Guidelines website, 2016 version.

The website made reference to a huge number of articles to support the different elements (or checkpoints) of the UDL framework, but it was accompanied by a highly unusual question: 'Do you have additional evidence to support this checkpoint? Tell us.' This is a very strange way of working. Basically, it amounts to first determining the various basic principles for UDL and then asking others to provide research to confirm the validity of these principles. And it seems to work. If you look at the research cited for each checkpoint, you will see that very little of it has anything to do with UDL, but only with the wider principles of the framework. The main problem with this approach is that it runs contrary to the very principle of scientific investigation, based on Popper, which is generally known as falsification or falsifiability. This requires scientists to make efforts to discover elements that can contradict a theory. If your theory is that all swans are white, the discovery of a black swan will immediately disprove your theory. However, the UDL site turns this methodology on its head: it only seeks confirmation and displays no interest in possible contradiction. Or to express it differently: they've only gone looking for white swans. And not just white swans, but only parts of those swans.

The Mentos Problem

Much of the research mentioned on the UDL site is good quality research, but because it often has little to do with the framework itself, this can lead to a second problem. This is what we call the Mentos® problem.

- Imagine that you are thirsty. You can quench your thirst with a Cola Light.
- Imagine that you have bad breath. You can freshen up your breath with a Mentos® mint.

But what happens if you combine the Cola Light and the Mentos mint together? There are plenty of films on YouTube® to demonstrate the fantastic fountain that this can produce!

Let's now apply this same principle to a lesson you want to give in a class where one of the students has hearing difficulties. You want to use a video and you decide to add subtitles, so that the student with hearing difficulties can also follow it. This sounds logical, but in reality it's counterproductive. Richard Mayer's Cognitive Theory of Multimedia Learning (CTMML) [69] and Allan Paivio's Dual Coding Theory[70] make clear that the learning ability of the other children in the class will suffer, because their working memory will be overloaded when required to process a combination of spoken text and written text – a phenomenon known as the redundancy effect in both John Sweller's cognitive load theory[71] and in the CTMML.[72]

If you only ask for research that supports your pre-determined principles, you will never discover how these principles interact with each other in either a positive or a negative way. Or might it be that the proponents of UDL feel they've no alternative? After all, they are putting forward a model and a philosophy that they intend to be all-encompassing, which does make UDL potentially difficult to investigate. That being said, a number of efforts have been undertaken. For example, a 2013 study compared a control group against a test group that was given lessons by teachers who had been trained for five hours in UDL principles.[73] What were the conclusions? Over a full school year, the engagement of the teachers in both groups improved and the students in the test group were better able to recognize UDL principles, but – and it's a big 'but' – no effort was made to see if any more had been learned. And as we know, engagement is a notoriously poor proxy for learning!

In 2017, Matthew James Capp published a meta-analysis of 18 studies that explicitly had one or more principles of UDL as their subject and also contained both a pre-test and a post-test. On the basis of this research, Capp concluded that UDL can be effective.[74] On closer examination, however, it again became apparent that only 2 of the 18 studies had worked with a control group[75]: the motivation study by Erdogan Halat and Fatih Karakus, and the study by Davies and colleagues into the ability of UDL principles to improve the educational process, for which they used an intervention group of six teachers and a control group of three others. Similarly, only 2 of the 18 examined the effect of UDL principles on the learning performance of students,[76] one of which – by Mavrou and colleagues – also used a control group, although the authors admitted that it was only a small group involving very young children. Some of the remaining studies – such as the one conducted by Kennedy and colleagues – not only failed to use a control group but also displayed a number of other significant limitations. Perhaps this helps explain why Capp, at the end of the day, concluded that the positive effects he had recorded in his analysis needed to be tempered by the fact that relatively little research into UDL had been carried out.

Learning Styles and Inclusive Education

In 2016, the United Nations published its General Comment No. 4[77] about the right to inclusive education. To avoid any misunderstandings, two extracts from the text are reproduced below.[78]

A 'whole person' approach: recognition is given to the capacity of every person to learn, and high expectations are established for all learners, including learners with disabilities. Inclusive education offers flexible curricula, teaching and learning methods adapted to different strengths, requirements and learning styles. This approach implies the provision of support and reasonable accommodation and early intervention so that they are able to fulfill their potential. The focus is on learners' capacities and aspirations rather than on content when planning teaching activities. The 'whole person' approach aims at ending segregation within educational settings by ensuring inclusive classroom teaching in accessible learning environments with appropriate supports. The education system must provide a personalized educational response, rather than expecting the student to fit the system.

[...]

A process of educating all teachers at pre-school, primary, secondary, tertiary and vocational education levels must be initiated to provide them with the necessary core competencies and values to work in inclusive educational environments. This requires adaptations to both pre and in-service training to develop appropriate skill levels in the shortest time possible to facilitate the transition to an inclusive education system. All teachers must be provided with dedicated units/modules to prepare them to work in inclusive settings, as well as practical experiential learning, where they can build the skills and confidence to problem-solve through diverse inclusion challenges. The core content of teacher education must address a basic understanding of human diversity, growth and development, the human rights model of disability, and inclusive pedagogy including how to identify students' functional abilities – strengths, abilities and learning styles – to ensure their participation in inclusive educational environments. Teacher education should include learning about the use of appropriate augmentative and alternative modes, means and formats of communication, such as Braille, large print, accessible multimedia, easy read, plain language, sign language and deaf culture, education techniques and materials to support persons with disabilities. In addition, teachers need practical guidance and support in, among others: the provision of individualized instruction; teaching the same content using varied teaching methods to respond to the learning styles and unique abilities of each person; the development and use of individual educational plans to support specific learning requirements; and the introduction of a pedagogy centered around students' educational objectives.

Just to be clear on this point: since the publication of our previous book about educational myths, no evidence has been found that supports the existence of learning styles.

Conclusion: Unproven

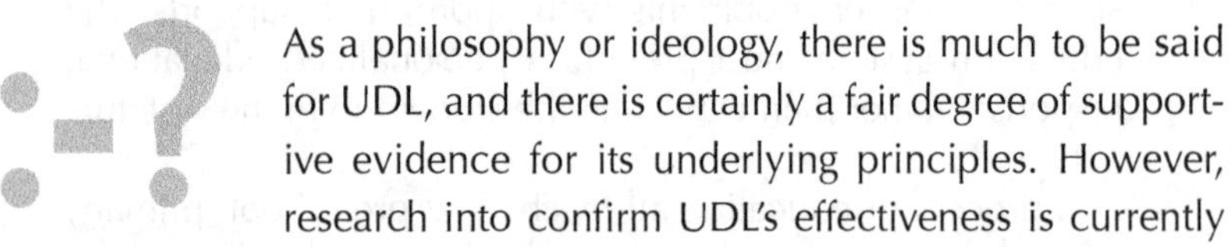

As a philosophy or ideology, there is much to be said for UDL, and there is certainly a fair degree of supportive evidence for its underlying principles. However, research into confirm UDL's effectiveness is currently limited, in part because it's open to question whether or not the concept as a whole is actually capable of investigation.

Myths about Music and Education

In our previous book we discussed the so-called 'Mozart' effect, which incorrectly supposes that unborn and newborn children can benefit from listening to/hearing classical music. Elsewhere in this book, we'll also look at the role that some people claim music can play in transfer. But there are still plenty of other myths about music and education, the most prevalent of which have been addressed by Nina Düvel and her colleagues[79]– although in the following survey we've also added a few more of our own. It wasn't easy to decide where exactly to categorize this subject, since there are elements that are connected both to Chapter 1 on the curriculum and to Chapter 3 on educational psychology. But because the first of the following myths is the one we're questioned about most frequently, we decided to put it in this second chapter on the 'how'.

Passive Listening to Music Can Help Students Study

:-| It's true that there is a link between studying and listening to music, but this link is fairly complex (see the box below). However, one thing is clear: it doesn't make much difference if the music is classical or not.[80]

Is It Better to Listen to Music while You are Studying or Not?

Some people seem to be able to study better while listening to music. Others – very often parents – find it impossible to believe that someone can study with all that noise! In reality, this question is more complex to answer than you might think.

If music distracts your attention, studying to music is not a good idea.[81] In particular, listening to music with lyrics in the same language as you are studying can work counterproductively.[82] There is evidence to support both of these conclusions, but this does not mean that all research suggests that music has a negative effect on studying. For example, music can be used to mask other more distracting sounds, although in these circumstances it's better to use 'neutral' music that you neither love nor hate.[83] This implies, of course, that the key factor as far as study effectiveness is concerned is whether or not you actively listen to the music. If the music is nothing more than background or a means to block out other noise, it can be a good thing. For example, if you want to study or work on a train where everyone else is talking and telephoning, a soothing piece of Bach in your earphones will allow you to concentrate better. In other words, music can help you to study because it first makes it possible for you to study. This is not a consequence of the music itself, but of its ability to eliminate other interference in your environment that would otherwise make studying more difficult, if not impossible. You can achieve the same effect with good earplugs or noise-cancelling headphones, or perhaps even headphones playing white noise.

If, however, you start actively listening to the music, this will have a negative impact on your studying, since we human beings are simply not capable of multitasking (see our first book). If you are devoting your cognitive attention to the music (What chords is the guitarist playing?) or its lyrics (What is Bob Dylan saying here?), you will not be able to concentrate on what you are reading or writing. It's one thing or the other, not both.

It's also indisputable that music can affect your mood. Some songs make you sad and melancholy; others pep you up and give you a lift. Of course, this can differ from person to person and even moment to moment. Research into the concentration levels of employees has shown that it's music that people hate which is most likely to distract them. Music that people like tends to assist concentration.[84]

That being said, it's not simply a question of musical likes and dislikes that plays a role. The task that you are attempting to carry out also helps to determine the effectiveness of the music. For example, it's known that upbeat music can help with the performance of more creative tasks.[85] And, last but not least, there is also a link between how well your working memory functions and the extent to which music can help you to study better.[86]

So to summarize: is it a good idea to study while listening to music or not? Sadly, there is no 'one-size-fits-all' answer. It depends on the nature of the person, the task and the music, which all have an impact on each other.

Different Music Genres Require Different Ways of Listening

:-\ Some people say, for example, that listening to classical music demands an intellectual mindset. This is, however, nonsense. Music does not speak exclusively to the intelligence. The way a person responds to music is also dictated by how well (s)he knows the genre, which emotions and memories (s) he attaches to it, and a whole variety of other factors that have little to do with mindset.[87]

The Ability to Improvise Is Largely Determined by the Right Half of the Brain.

:-\ Is it possible to stimulate the right half of your brain through mental exercises? As discussed in our previous book, this is not the case. Not for music, not for anything else.[88]

Some Music Genres Encourage Violence and Criminality

:-| In 2013, research was conducted in the Netherlands to see if a connection exists between the music you listen to during the early years of your youth and the likelihood that you will commit criminal acts in later life. What conclusions were reached? It seems that young people who listened to rap or rock music had a slightly higher chance of committing crime as adults, such as shoplifting, vandalism, getting involved in fights, etc. This was not the case for twelve-year-olds who listened to pop or jazz. It's true that these types of music are good predictors, irrespective of the social background of the test subjects, but the study was unable to conclude that music was the cause of this phenomenon. In fact, it still seems more likely – according to the researchers – that music is a kind of safety valve for letting off steam, rather than a cause of problematic behavior.[89]

I Have No Feel for Music

:-| There is certainly such a thing as tone deafness. This is the situation where children pick up very little or no feeling for music from their environment. However, research by Cuddy and colleagues has shown that more people say they are tone deaf than is actually the case. It's often said that around 4% of the population is tone deaf (although some experts argue that this estimate is on the high side[90]), but in surveys some 27% of people say that they are afflicted in this way! In other words, there are many people who say they've no affinity for music, but who could most probably develop such an affinity through proper training.[91]

Outstanding Classical Musicians are More Intelligent (Myth)

:-\ It may sound logical to assume that people who play classical music to a high standard are more intelligent, although the section on transfer earlier in the book may cast doubt on this conclusion. The bad news – for the musicians, at least – is that no such correlation exists.[92]

Summary

There are lots of myths relating to music and learning, and in many ways that is good news. It means, for example, that we can all listen to classical music (if we want to), that you don't need to be super-intelligent to play an instrument well, and that the likelihood you are tone deaf is much smaller than you might have thought!

Notes

1 https://onderzoekonderwijs.net/2017/12/06/werkt-actief-leren-goede-vraag-maar-de-verkeerde/.
2 Castles, Rastle, & Nation, 2018.
3 Klein, 2007.
4 Wisman, 2018.

5 Goodman, 1967.
6 Willingham & De Bruyckere, 2016.
7 See, amongst others:
  - Chall, 1967.
  - Flesch, 1955.
8 Castles, Rastle, & Nation, 2018.
9 Geary, 2007.
10 Chall, 1967.
11 National Institute of Child Health and Human Development, 2000.
12 See, amongst others:
  - Hempenstall, 1997.
  - Hempenstall, 2016.
13 www.forbes.com/sites/brettnelson/2012/06/04/do-you-read-fast-enough-to-be-successful/#4615a87e462e
14 https://news.sky.com/video/reading-harry-potter-in-27-minutes-10518667. While Anne Jones can apparently read at great speed, she chose to remain a housewife.
15 www.toptenreviews.com/software/articles/who-is-the-fastest-reader-in-the-world/.
16 Rayner, Schotter, Masson, Potter, & Treiman, 2016.
17 Rayner, Schotter, Masson, Potter, & Treiman, 2016.
18 Miellet, O'Donnell, & Sereno, 2009.
19 O'Brien, Albrecht, Hakala, & Rizzella, 1995.
20 See also:
  - Cherry & Macdonald, 1983.
  - Frase, Keenan, & Dever, 1980.
  - Smith, 1983.
21 See also:
  - Lilienfeld, 2010.
22 Forrin & MacLeod, 2018.
23 Duggan and Payne, 2009.
24 This conclusion was also reached in:
  - Just, Masson, & Carpenter, 1980.
  - Just & Carpenter, 1987.
25 Kohn, 2006.
26 Hattie, 2009.
27 Also see:
  - Cooper, 1989.
  - Cooper, Robinson, & Patall, 2006.
28 Maltese, Tai, & Fan, 2012.
29 See, amongst others:
  - Lea Theodore, quoted in Weir, 2016.
  - Van Den Branden, 2011.
30 Fan, Xu, Cai, He, & Fan, 2017.
31 Rosário, Núñez, Vallejo, Cunha, Nunes, Mourão, & Pinto, 2015.

32 Núñez, Suárez, Rosário, Vallejo, Cerezo, & Valle, 2014.
33 Trautwein, Köller, Schmitz, & Baumert, 2002.
34 Epstein, J. L. and Van Voorhis, F. L. (2001).
35 Fernández-Alonso, Suárez-Álvarez, & Muñiz, 2015.
36 Rawson, Stahovich, & Mayer, 2017.
37 Poh, Swenson, & Picard, 2010.
38 See, amongst others:
- Lancaster, 2013.
- Mazur, 2011.
- Neve, Livingstone, Hunter, & Alsop, 2013.
- van der Vleuten, 2013.

39 Masters, 2014.
40 See, amongst others:
- National Research Council, 2003.
- Saxe, 1991

41 Dawson, Schell, & Filion, 2007.
42 See:
- Poh, Swenson, & Picard, 2010.

43 See also:
- Popova, Kirschner, & Joiner, 2013.
- Popova, Kirschner, & Joiner, 2014.

44 Pennebaker, Gosling, & Ferrell, 2013.
45 Bettinger, Fox, Loeb, & Taylor, 2017.
46 Edwards and Clinton, 2018.
47 See also, for example:
- Bacolod, Mehay, & Pema, 2018.
- Fernandes, Maley, & Cruickshank, 2008.
- Jaggars & Xu, 2016.
- Joyce, Crockett, Jaeger, Altindag, & O'Connell, 2014.
- Xu & Jaggars, 2013.
- Xu & Jaggars, 2014.

48 Traphagan, Kucsera, & Kishi, 2010.
49 Bos, Groeneveld, Van Bruggen, & Brand-Gruwel, 2016.
50 Bishop & Verleger, 2013.
51 See also:
- Gillette, Rudolph, Kimble, Rockich-Winston, Smith, & Broedel-Zaugg, 2018.
- Hew & Lo, 2018.

52 Abeysekera & Dawson, 2015.
53 Chevalier, Dolton, & Luhrmann, 2014.
54 Szpunar, Khan, & Schacter, 2013.
55 Baer, 2014.
56 Ericsson & Pool, 2016b.
57 Gladwell, 2008; Ericsson & Pool, 2016a.
58 Shakeshaft, Trzaskowski, McMillan, Rimfeld, Krapohl, Haworth, & Plomin, 2013.
59 Davis, Band, Pirinen, Haworth, Meaburn, Kovas, & Curtis, 2014.
60 Ericsson & Pool, 2016b.

61 Hambrick, Altmann, Oswald, Meinz, Gobet, & Campitelli, 2014.
62 Macnamara, Hambrick, & Oswald, 2014.
63 Macnamara, Moreau, & Hambrick, 2016.
64 Burgoyne, Sala, Gobet, Macnamara, Campitelli, & Hambrick, 2016.
65 Bassett, Yang, Wymbs, & Grafton, 2015.
66 Rose & Meyer, 2002.
67 Burgstahler, 2007.
68 Assistive Technology Act of 1998, Pub. L. 105–394, §§ 2 & 3.
69 Mayer, 2009.
70 See, amongst others:
- Paivio, 1986.
- Clark & Paivio, 1991.

71 Sweller, 2005.
72 Mayer & Moreno, 2003.
73 Davies, Schelly, & Spooner, 2013.
74 Capp, 2017.
75 Namely:
- Davies, Schelly, & Spooner, 2013.
- Halat & Karakus, 2014.

76 Namely:
- Kennedy, Thomas, Meyer, Alves, & Lloyd, 2014.
- Mavrou, Charalampous, & Michaelides, 2013.

77 UN CRPD Committee, 2016.
78 Ibid., pp. 4 & 19.
79 Düvel, Wolf, & Kopiez, 2017.
80 Jäncke, 2008a.
81 Hughes, 2014.
82 Perham & Currie, 2014.
83 Middlebrooks, Kerr, & Castel, 2017.
84 See, amongst others:
- Gold, Frank, Bogert, & Brattico, 2013.
- Huang & Shih, 2011.

85 Ferguson, 2017.
86 Lehmann & Seufert, 2017.
87 Jancke, 2008a.
88 See also:
- De Bruyckere, Kirschner, & Hulshof, 2015a.
- Wiedemann, 1985.

89 Ter Bogt, Keijsers, & Meeus, 2013.
90 Henry & McAuley, 2010.
91 Cuddy, Balkwill, Peretz, & Holden, 2005.
92 See also:
- Altenmüller, 2006.
- Jäncke, 2008b.
- Schellenberg, 2004.

3 Myths about (Educational) Psychology

In education, we not only make use of insights from the field of cognitive psychology (the branch of psychology that explores the operation of mental processes related to perceiving, attending, thinking, language, and memory, mainly through inferences from behavior[1]; in other words, the science of how people learn), but we also make use of insights from – among many others – the fields of neuropsychology, personality theory, and group dynamics. In recent years, we see that various incorrect insights that have become popular in the domains of human resources and therapy have also gradually gained credence in the world of education. Of course, it's a good thing if you, as a teacher, want to try to find the best way to gain access to the personality of the person(s) you're teaching, but this inevitably leads to the following problem: Which of the models put forward to achieve better teaching are real and which ones are pseudoscience?

For example, neurolinguistic programming (NLP) has found its way into education and teaching. While it may sound scientific and is, indeed, to a limited extent based on scientific insights (albeit from decades ago), there is now a consensus that NLP is more pseudoscience than the real thing.

Some concepts from (educational) psychology seem so simple and so easy to apply that they're adopted quickly in educational practice, often much to the dismay of the original researchers. Many teachers and schools are now familiar with concepts such as growth mindset and grit, but are the effects of these concepts as significant as they think? More importantly, are they replicable?

The Replication Crisis in Psychology

What do the following research studies have in common?

- The Stanford prison experiment carried out by Philip Zimbardo;
- The obedience experiments by Stanley Milgram;
- The bystander effect of John Darley and Bibb Latané;
- The marshmallow test by Walter Mischel; and
- The pencil-in-the-mouth research by Fritz Strack and colleagues.[2]

Apart from the fact that they were all studies that enjoyed a high degree of fame – or perhaps even notoriety – among the wider general public, they are all studies whose conclusions have come under increasing pressure in recent times. Sometimes, this is because we have come to know that the research that was carried out developed in a way not originally expected or intended, as was the case with Zimbardo[3] or Milgram.[4] Sometimes, it's because new ideas made it necessary to replicate the original experiments to see if the same results can be obtained. Only then can we, as scientists and general public, be 'sure' that the results were reliable. And, if this isn't the case, the original insight comes into question or might even be considered invalid, as happened with the pencil-in-the-mouth study.[5] Of course, it might also be the case that the experiment is replicated and identical/similar results are achieved.[6]

What we've seen however is more the former than the latter and has been labelled the replication crisis. While this replication crisis had led to a good deal of controversy, this isn't necessarily a bad thing. Perhaps it even has more pros than cons. Successful replications make research results more credible, while even failed replications can help us to further refine our knowledge.

Though the use of things coming from various pseudosciences is often embraced by teachers, administrators, politicians and the general public, it can just as easily happen that a concept like IQ is dismissed in educational circles. In this chapter, we investigate whether this is justified.

Can You Think Yourself into Being Smarter?

It sometimes happens at the start of a school year that a student says to a teacher: 'There's no point explaining that to me; I'll never be able to understand it'. What is going on here? More importantly, can you do anything about it? Is it enough if you simply say: 'Just do your best; it will all work out in the end'? Does this student have a fundamental motivation problem or are there other elements at play? Is this situation capable of being corrected and, if so, how? These questions have been central to the research carried out in recent decades by the American professor Carol Dweck, who has sought to identify the factors that explain why some children are successful in their education and others are not. This led to the introduction of the concept of mindset.

A Macabre History

Mindset might seem like a relatively new concept, but Professor Dweck has been studying it for more than 40 years and its history goes back even further. What's more, it's a history that in some ways is as macabre as it's fascinating. It all started back in the 1960s, when the American psychologist Martin Seligman first published his ideas about 'learned helplessness', which, in its way, is a type of mindset. In essence, it's a phenomenon by which animals and people who learn that they can have no influence on what happens to them in a given situation lapse into a state of passivity. This could also be regarded as a form of acceptance, and is associated with the development of various psychological disorders, including depression.

Learned Helplessness in Rats

As long ago as 1957, the biologist Curt Richter first demonstrated this effect in a series of lugubrious experiments. He put a succession of rats into a water tank from which the rodents – not famed for their swimming ability – could not escape. He then timed how long it took for them to drown. The results showed that there was a significant difference between the behavior of tame rats and wild rats. Most of the tame rats swam for as long as they could (sometimes literally for days on end) before giving up and accepting the inevitable. The wild rats gave up the fight for survival after just a few minutes. This suggested that the wild rats more quickly appreciated that they had no control over the situation and therefore could do nothing to change the outcome. This was confirmed by a follow-up experiment, in which wild rats were periodically removed from the water, faster at first, but less quickly as time progressed. In this way, the rats 'learned' that their situation was not necessarily hopeless and they then kept swimming for as long as the tame rats in the initial experiment. Richter contended that this effect also exists in people: if the situation is hopeless, they soon accept their fate. But as long as there is a grain of hope, they'll continue to struggle in the belief that eventual release and recovery is still possible.[7]

The Introduction of the Term 'Mindset'

The term 'mindset' (in the sense of a state of mind or mentality) first became widely known following Dweck's publication of her book *Mindset: The New Psychology of Success* in 2006. In this book she defined mindset on the basis of a number of examples that included both success and failure, and came to the conclusion that the attitude people adopt towards success and failure to a large extent determines the way they live their lives.[8] According to her, there are two ways you can look at these things: (1) you can think that your talents have been permanently defined and cannot be changed: the fixed mindset; or (2) you can think that your talents are changeable and capable of improvement with the necessary effort: the growth mindset.

The discussion about the potential changeability of cognitive characteristics is almost as old as the concept of intelligence itself. Alfred Binet who, together with his colleague Théodore Simon, developed the first intelligence test, did not regard intelligence as something fixed. On the contrary, he regarded such a view as 'regrettable'.[9]

Dweck's experiments showed that the level of belief that people have in their own changeability – what she called their 'implicit intelligence theory' – can influence their behavior, especially in terms of the causes to which they attribute their success or failure with regard to a particular task.[10] This implicit theory gradually acquired the status of a belief in one's own ability, founded on research which demonstrated that praising the performance of children on the basis of their intelligence – 'You're so clever!' – had a negative impact on their subsequent motivation and performance.[11] The implicit conclusion is that if you perform well because you are so clever (a static quality), this leaves little room for improvement (growth). In other words, you can follow one of two pathways: a path that presupposes the presence of a fixed intelligence which is not capable of change; or a path that believes there is always a possibility for further intellectual growth. It was not long after the completion of this research that Dweck first began to refer to this dual pathway in terms of different 'mindsets'.[12]

Mindset Today

The term 'mindset' is widely known and a lucrative commercial market has been built up around the concept. There are dozens of informative, self-help books on the subject and there is mindset training available for teachers and students. This even includes nursery school-age children, for whom a broad range of educational materials is available, including a series of picture books intended to 'promote a growth mindset'.[13] There seems to be a general assumption that transforming a fixed mindset into a growth mindset is both possible and beneficial. However, research post-Dweck has shown that things are not as simple as they might seem.

The Effects of Mindset Interventions

A number of studies has been carried out to investigate the effect of mindsets in education. In nearly every case they involved research into interventions designed to teach students about the changeability of their intellectual skills; in other words, teach them how to develop a growth mindset. This research was a logical consequence of the earlier conclusion reached by Dweck that children who attribute their failure to complete a given task to their own shortcomings eventually develop 'helpless' behavior.[14] Dweck herself was one of the first to conduct further investigations to confirm this,[15] but the study in question was focused on a specific group; namely, children who had already displayed extreme helpless behavior. The test subjects were referred to Dweck by the school psychologist and the numbers involved were very small: just six in the intervention group and six in the control group. However, more recent larger scale and more realistic intervention studies have recorded only minimal effects or even no effect at all. For example, a correlation study conducted by the Czech researchers Št pán Bahník and Marek

Vranka with 5,653 prospective students found no relationship between the degree of growth mindset[16] and the outcomes of various skill tests[17] (although the value of the limited instrument used to measure mindset is open to question). Another study by Teresa De Backer and colleagues[18] investigated the long-term effect of a one-off mindset training session on a group of 14- and 15-year-olds. The only noteworthy effect was the students said that they felt less worried about appearing stupid in class. Moreover, even limited successes of this kind are not always long lasting – as Gábor Orosz and his colleagues have demonstrated.[19] They looked at an intervention designed to promote a growth mindset that had some initial success, but found that this effect faded over time, so that the situation eventually returned to what it had originally been. In other words, mindset interventions can sometimes change things, but it's hard to know if the change will be permanent.

A recent mega-research project involving 12,542 participants spread over 65 randomly chosen American schools was conducted by David Yeager to assess the effect of a relatively short lesson about growth mindset.[20] After this training, the number of students who failed to complete their course of studies at school in time fell by 3%. This was a small but nonetheless significant result. If the result could be generalized to all American schools, this 3% figure would mean that almost 100,000 students would be kept on the right path towards achieving their secondary school diploma. Just as importantly, if not more so, the effect was most noticeable in the students with the greatest learning difficulties. Yet while an improvement of 3% is nothing to be sneezed at, it's nonetheless much more modest than many of the mindset propagandists are wont to claim. If you were to believe some of their claims, you might expect to see a positive effect in almost every student! What's more, it's far from clear precisely what effect this mindset training generates. Does it really create a new mindset in the students concerned? Or is it more an effect of the message that 'hard work is rewarded'? If the latter is the case, this means that 'belief in your own ability' is irrelevant to explain the effects of mindset.

Even more extensive than Yeager et al.'s study, and in some ways more convincing in terms of outcome, was the meta-analysis carried out by Victoria Sisk and her colleagues into the effect of mindset interventions on academic performance.[21] The first striking conclusion was the dearth of reliable, high-quality research. They applied a set of research criteria to the more than 15,000 available studies and found that just 29 met the required standard. In other words, fewer than 1 in every 500 studies (0.2%) was able to satisfy the criteria for reliability and quality! The 29 quality studies reported a total of

43 effect sizes. In 37 of the 43 cases there was no effect whatsoever. In the six cases where there was an effect, five were significantly positive, but the sixth was just as significantly negative (in other words, the students who had received mindset training subsequently performed worse than the control group). The overall effect size *d* was 0.08, which is hardly earth-shattering. Mindset interventions are relatively cheap, and easy to implement, but the evidence suggests that their effect is minimal or even non-existent.

Problems with Mindset Theory

The American education expert Alfie Kohn recognizes the scientific basis of mindset theory, but is skeptical about the concept as a whole.[22] Yes, it's useful if, as a student, you can see that your efforts will be rewarded. Effort, however, is not the only factor that determines success or failure. Mindset theory is not an educational or pedagogic theory. This means, for example, that no account is taken of the quality of education. The theory, therefore, places the entire responsibility for success or failure squarely on the shoulders of the student. Your results are poor? You need to adjust your mindset. Your results are still poor? Your mindset must have been wrong. By focusing on mindset in this way, it's not possible to predict results, but only to explain them retrospectively. In scientific terms, this means that the theory is not falsifiable.

A further problem is that the theory frowns upon the praising of characteristics ('My you're clever!') and argues that praise of effort is the only effective way to improve performance. For young children, this strategy can be effective and a large part of Dweck's early research concentrated specifically on this age group. But it can also have the opposite effect.[23] A study by Jamie Amemiya and Ming-Te Wang reported negative effects in a group of teenagers.[24] They explained the theory's failure to work as predicted by arguing that while praising effort does get across to the students the message that greater effort will lead to better performance, it also implies that this greater effort is necessary because the students have a lack of natural (that is to say genetically determined) intelligence. In this way, the message effectively becomes: 'Even though you are naturally stupid, you can still achieve something if you work hard enough'. This interpretation of the message can be highly demotivating and Amemiya and Wang noted that it was this interpretation that the teenagers tended to apply to their own circumstances.

Comparable results were obtained in a study by Rachael Reavis and colleagues with adult participants.[25] One group was asked to carry out a difficult task and was told afterwards that they had failed to complete it successfully, although it was emphasized that they were 'hard workers'. According to mindset theory, this kind of praise should have had a positive effect. Instead, the participants found the task to be less enjoyable and attributed their failure to their lack of intelligence. The Reavis team concluded that the previously recorded effects of mindset interventions are not replicable in older children and adults. In broad terms, this conclusion was confirmed by the research of Melody Chao and her colleagues.[26] They discovered that placing too much emphasis on a growth mindset had a negative impact on good performing students from a low socio-economic background. In fact, these students seem to be irritated by the growth mindset. Why? These children regard themselves as special, because they have managed to do what many others from their socio-economic group have not been able to do. But if they are then told that this success was only possible because they work so hard, this has a demotivating rather than a motivating effect. Findings of this kind have important consequences for interventions in schools designed to alter the mindset of students and probably also explains the general lack of success recorded in empirical research into mindset, as described above.

This allows us to draw two tentative conclusions. First, there is a difference in the way young children and adolescents/adults respond to praise. This means that the focus on learning how to develop a growth mindset should be confined to the former. Even then, the tendency to concentrate exclusively on praising effort can have a negative effect. Dweck sees this tendency as an incorrect interpretation of the theory and refers in such cases to what she calls a 'false growth mindset'.[27] In an interview with the online magazine *Education Week*, she said that she sometimes lies awake at night, worrying that some people interpret her theory simplistically as: 'praising effort is enough to ensure success'.[28] Children, she maintains, are not so easily fooled! Moreover, in some cases (she argues) a static mindset can be better than a growth mindset. Dweck cites sexual orientation as an example and, in so doing, also gives us an insight into her own mindset and the subjectivity that underlies any such judgment.

Second, although mindset theory is both elegant and easily understandable, in many respects it's just too simple. It could be described as typically American, with its clear emphasis on the individual's control over his/her own success or failure, relegating all other factors to a subsidiary role. Kohn identifies a perverse incentive in this approach. For example, if you want to explain why fewer girls than boys opt to study the exact sciences, the advocates of mindset theory would argue that this is simply a question of mindset. But in this way, the sexism inherent in the academic community is quietly and conveniently swept under the carpet because it's the girl's own fault. They have the wrong mindset!

Mindset is not a cure-all for all of society's problems – although the popularity of Dweck's books and the huge availability of mindset workshops and training courses certainly show that interest in the subject is huge. However, in some ways the concept has also started to live a life of its own, which goes far beyond its original conception. For example, Dweck has even tried to apply her theory to the current political problems in the Middle East.[29] According to her, a focus on growth could help to solve the conflict between the Israelis and the Palestinians. At the same time, Dweck attempts in her interviews and articles to put forward the 'correct' explanation of the concept and recognizes that it needs to be more firmly embedded in personality and motivation theory.[30]

Conclusion: Nuanced

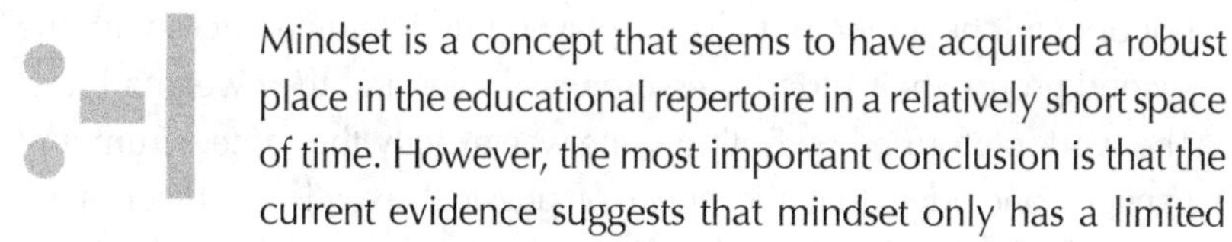

Mindset is a concept that seems to have acquired a robust place in the educational repertoire in a relatively short space of time. However, the most important conclusion is that the current evidence suggests that mindset only has a limited effect on those who are taught its methods and purpose. It's certainly not a miracle remedy to turn poorly performing students into model students.

The Placebo Effect: A Possible Explanation for Mindset Effects?

In medicine, a placebo is something that performs like a medicine, even though it contains none of a medicine's active ingredients. A wide-ranging meta-analysis conducted in 1998 concluded that the treatment for more than half of the patients suffering from depression was based on a placebo effect. In this context, belief in the effect of the treatment plays an important role, as confirmed in an interesting experiment using poison ivy. People who were persuaded that they had come into contact with the plant developed the characteristic itchy rash and lumps, even though in reality they had only handled a harmless substitute form of ivy.[31]

The remarkable thing about the placebo effect is the wide number of fields in which it can be found. It goes far beyond the use of medication and even plays a role in education. As always, belief in the effect is crucial. As part of a study by Barry Blackwell, Saul Bloomfield and Ralph Buncher, students were asked before going into a lecture to take either one or two pink or blue pills, which would have either a stimulating or a soporific effect.[32] The results of the experiment were very clear: students who took the blue pills felt drowsy, students who took the pink pills felt stimulated, and in both cases two pills had a much greater effect than one. In reality, of course, all the pills were just sugar pills; in other words, placebos. Even more remarkable results were obtained by Alia Crum and Ellen Langer. In their study they told one group of hotel cleaners that their work was actually good exercise, almost like a form of sport. They told a second group of cleaners – the control group – nothing. Four weeks later, the cleaners in the first group not only felt healthier, but also displayed physical differences with the second group: their blood pressure was lower and they weighed less. The work performed by both groups was exactly the same. Crum and Langer concluded that the effect of physical exercise is determined to a significant degree by the placebo effect, in which context they talked appropriately about the role of mindset on health.[33] In short, the way that we think about ourselves can affect our physical condition. However, this does not mean that you can automatically improve your health by changing your mindset, nor that the possible effects on physical condition can have a similar impact on learning behavior.

How Important Is Grit in Education and Can You Learn It?

According to the dictionary, the word 'grit', in addition to meaning 'sand or gravel', also means 'courage, determination and strength of character'. Think, for example, of John Wayne in the film *True Grit* and you will soon get the idea. In a school context, working with grit means working very hard to achieve success. This concept of grit in education has become highly popular in recent years, thanks to the work of Angela Lee Duckworth, the Christopher H. Browne Distinguished Professor of Psychology at the University of Pennsylvania. But what exactly is it, this magical quality? Although it sounds tangibly powerful, when you actually try to define it you soon find that it has very little real substance, other than as a vague composite concept of different elements.

What Is Grit?

According to Duckworth, in the context of learning grit is 'the passion and perseverance' that is necessary to achieve long-terms goals.[34] For her, grit is more than mere resilience. It means being so passionately driven to achieve your goal that you never give up but keep on fighting to overcome all the obstacles that stand between you and your objective. In short, it's a combination of persistence, dedication, diligence and resilience. In her original study involving military cadets at West Point (an elite military academy in the United States), Duckworth concluded that grit was a better predictor for successfully completing the training course than 'conscientiousness',[35] which had a strong correlation with grit, regardless of intelligence. She based these conclusions on research into two separate classes at West Point and on the further analysis of children participating in a spelling bee. Together with her colleagues, she used the results to develop the so-called 'grit scale', an instrument that allows students to assess for themselves just how much grit they possess.

In this way, grit can be regarded as a higher order (and therefore composite) concept. As such, it's made up of various layers of meaning, like 'maintaining effort' and 'persisting in showing interest'. In an interview for a Freakonomics®[36] podcast, Duckworth even went a step further, by saying that grit is actually a combination of interest, practice, determination, and hope.[37]

Credé, Tynan and Harms[38] had their doubts on this score. In an attempt to create clarity about what grit might or might not be and to assess whether or not it added anything new as an independent concept, they analyzed 88 independent samples involving 66,807 test subjects and 584 research outcomes. They first looked to see if grit is something new or if it's simply a new name for something we've known about for a long time. Their meta-analysis revealed that grit, as a factor influencing learning and performance, adds little or nothing to existing factors, such as determination and conscientiousness. They then examined the relationship between grit and learning performance, remembering what had been learned, and cognitive capacity. They concluded that there is hardly any correlation between grit and learning and grit and remembering, although there is a correlation for cognitive capacity (IQ) and other study habits and skills. Even the factor 'determination' has a higher correlation with learning than grit does! In other words, it's open to serious question whether the concept adds anything at all to better learning.

How New Is Grit?

While we nowadays associate grit with the work of Angela Lee Duckworth, she was not the first to develop the concept. According to a longitudinal discourse analysis by Ethan W. Ris,[39] grit has been a subject of discussion and even controversy in American educational circles for more than a century – although in a manner very different from what we are used to today. Whereas grit is now put forward as a way to encourage better performance, as a result of which there are pleas to make efforts to develop more grit in children from disadvantaged backgrounds, Ris's historical analysis shows that in the past it was assumed that poor children had more grit, which he describes as 'a type of character-building that privilege prevents'. In other words, until recently it was believed (on the basis of a somewhat romantic reasoning) that children who grow up in luxury are all wimps, because they have never had to struggle for anything and therefore need no grit to overcome the challenges of life!

Can Children Learn How to Have More Grit?

This, of course, is the most important question. As with personality and intelligence, there is a hope that through the stimulation of certain elements or characteristics it may be possible for children to achieve better results at school and, ultimately, greater success in life. But can grit be learned? If, to a significant degree, conscientiousness is determined genetically (as we shall later see in the section on personality characteristics), and if there is a close link between conscientiousness and grit, the likelihood of grit being teachable is either minimal or non-existent. At best, it will be difficult. Even Angela Duckworth is no longer certain on this point. She hopes that grit is learnable, but says there is too little evidence. As a result, she is irritated by those who argue in favor of measuring grit in education or, worse still, suggest that schools should be judged on the basis of whether their students have built up enough grit.[40]

So can grit be learned? To assess this, we first need to know whether determination and passion are fixed, non-pliant, innate traits or, in contrast, are fluid and pliant states. We know, for example, that it's possible to create environments that can either stimulate or inhibit certain characteristics, but this is not the same as learning something. Take creativity, for example. We can create an environment in which creative, out-of-the-box solutions to problem situations are either discouraged (think of a teacher or parent who belittles or pokes fun at a child who comes up with such solutions) or encouraged (teachers and parents who praise such solutions, even if they are wrong).

In an interesting and illuminating study involving 2,321 pairs of twins, Rimfeld and her colleagues[41] demonstrated that grit, like most other personality traits, seems largely determined by genetics. In other words, it is innate and not learned, and therefore not (or only minimally) susceptible to environmental influences. The researchers also concluded, like Credé and colleagues, that while certain personality traits like conscientiousness can influence people's learning performance, grit – as an independent personality factor – adds very little to the learning process.

As mentioned, Duckworth herself is also starting to have doubts on this matter, as is clear from her comments in an interview given to *The New Yorker*,[42] in which she expressed concern that her research was being taken over by the hype:

> I think the misunderstanding – or, at least, one of them – is that it's only the perseverance part that matters. But I think that the passion piece is at least as important. I mean, if you are really, really tenacious and dogged about a goal that's not meaningful to you, and not interesting to you – then that's just drudgery. It's not just determination.

Yes, but if there is one thing that cannot be learned, it's passion! A person can have it and develop it, but learn it? Sadly, not.

Is Teaching Grit a Danger for Democracy?

In 2016, Nicholas Tampio[43] wrote an essay with the catchy title 'Teaching "grit" is bad for children, and bad for democracy.' In this essay, Tampio explains why he believes that the stimulation of grit can be harmful for society, basing many of his arguments on examples cited by Duckworth in her books and lectures. What to think, for example, of business leaders who are praised for their grit, but who use every means at their disposal, not matter how ruthless, to achieve their goal? And what about Martin Seligman, Duckworth's mentor, who achieved fame with his concept of learned helplessness? It was his experiments with dogs that inspired Duckworth's vision of grit, but these experiments are now regarded as extremely cruel and would no longer be possible today. Not that this bothered Seligman and Duckworth at the time. The dogs were strapped into a harness and given electric shocks. Some of the dogs could avoid the shocks by pressing on a panel with their nose. The following day the dogs were confined in a pen and again given electric shocks. This time all the dogs could avoid the shock by jumping over a barrier. What happened? The dogs that were able to avoid the shocks on the first day also avoided them on the second day, whereas the dogs that could not avoid the shocks on the first day also made no effort to avoid them on the second day, even though this was now possible. They had learned how to be helpless.

Tampio argues that the pursuit of 'grit' often induces people to do stupid and cruel things, often blindly. 'Not giving in' is all that counts, whereas democracy – and good performance at school – requires people who can think for themselves and are willing to question authority when they think it's wrong.

Conclusion: Myth

:-\

Apart from the fact that it's nothing new and seems to have little or no impact on student performance, grit also can't effectively be taught or learned. But as is so often the case in education, this does not prevent companies from wanting to exploit the concept commercially; for example, by developing lesson and computer programs which – according to the companies – can alter the mentality of children.

Can Personality be Divided up on the Basis of Letters and Colors?

One person is introvert, the other is extrovert. One person is intuitive and acts on gut feelings, the other reasons and thinks everything through before acting. These may seem to be self-evident truths. But are they? That's what we are about to find out in this section.

An analysis of articles about learning via computers and learning styles published in 2016 and 2017[44] revealed that, in addition to the popular VAK (Visual-Auditory-Kinesthetic) and Kolb learning style theories, increasing reference was being made to another theory that does not really fit in well with the learning styles concept. This theory is based on the MBTI (Myers-Briggs Type Indicator), which classifies people on the basis of their personality traits. Donna Dunning attempted to translate this personality theory in a way that would allow it to fit into a learning style framework, but there are a number of fundamental problems with this approach.[45]

As with learning styles, the idea behind MBTI is that people's personalities have different characteristics and that the optimal way to learn is by adjusting the learning situation to reflect those characteristics. But bearing in mind that MBTI first gained popularity as a tool in HR circles, the question is whether a theory that divides personality into different types is suitable for use in education.

The MB in MBTI

The Myers–Briggs Type Indicator is an introspective questionnaire (or, if you prefer, test) developed by Katharine Cook Briggs (the B) and her daughter Isabel Briggs Myers (the M) in the 1940s, based on the theories put forward two decades earlier by Carl Gustav Jung. Their intention was to create a personality-based method to help select the right people for the right jobs. In particular, Myers thought that differences in personality can predict how and why a particular person might not be suitable for a particular job. She also suspected that there were different kinds of jobs that required different kinds of personalities to do them well. The mother–daughter team was attracted by Jung's ideas, but in reality their test deviates significantly from the famous psychoanalyst's original theory.[46]

Between 1943 and 1957, Myers experimented with the test on different groups and made changes accordingly. In 1957, she was recruited by the Educational Testing Service (ETS) to promote the test as a possible research instrument. The ETS also provided the necessary technical support for the test's further evaluation. An internal review later concluded that the test was not satisfactory,[47] so the ETS withdrew its investment. It was not until 1975 that the Consulting Psychologists Press acquired the rights to MBTI and it was from this point onwards that the theory's success story begins.[48]

The TI in MBTI: A Story of Extremes

The basic theory developed by Myers is that people can be classified on the basis of four dimensions:

1. *Extraversion* (E: you derive energy and inspiration primarily from the external world around you) versus *Introversion* (I: you derive energy and inspiration primarily from your own inner world of experience).
2. *Sensing* (S: you assimilate information directly for the world around you) versus *Intuition* (N: you are intuitive and make implicit connections between the things you encounter).
3. *Thinking* (T: you take thoughtful decisions based on logic) versus *Feeling* (F: you take impulsive decisions based on emotions).
4. *Judging* (J: you assess things and make a value judgment) versus *Perceiving* (P: you observe in a way that allows you to see things as they are, without making a direct conclusion).

Only the first three dimensions are based on Jung; Judging versus Perceiving was added by Myers.[49] It was essential for the test in its original form that people are either one thing or the other on each of the four dimensions; in other words, E or I, S or N, T or F, J or P. This leads to sixteen (2x2x2x2) possible types. For example, you might be ISTJ, which means that you are an introvert, sensing, thinking and judging person.

This immediately brings us to the first problem with the test. Working with mutually exclusive pairs of dichotomous characteristics does not correspond with what we now know today about how people's personalities are made up.

- Thinking and feeling may seem like opposites, but they are, in fact, separate factors that can occur together and independently of each other, to a greater or lesser degree.[50]

- According to MBTI theory, you are more T (a thinker) if, for example, you recognize yourself in a phrase like 'I enjoy technical and scientific fields, where logic is important' and more F (a feeler) if you recognize yourself in 'I look for what is important to others and express concern for others'. However, it's perfectly possible to be good with facts and reasoning, while still being concerned with the people around you (something that, hopefully, the partners of the present authors can confirm!). In other words, MBTI compares apples with oranges – and is therefore of little value.
- Of course, it's also perfectly possible that you might indeed be more of a thinker than a feeler – but this highlights a further defect in the MBTI methodology: it only works with extremes. For MBTI, you are either all thinker or all feeler. In reality, most people are somewhere in between – and this applies for all four dimensions.[51] In recent years, the original test has been modified to take account of this, but in essence it still remains an 'either / or' dichotomy.
- This dichotomous method of classification doesn't take account of emotional stability – the personality characteristic that describes the extent to which a person will remain calm under pressure in stressful circumstances.[52] Emotional stability is a good predictor of how people will function in certain situations.

The Big Five or HEXACO

Another method of personality classification for which validity and reliability has been established is the HEXACO model, based on five key factors known as 'The Big Five'.[53] In contrast to MBTI, this theory does not require dichotomous choices to be made but instead makes use of scales upon which people can be graded.[54] The Big Five factors are:

1. Extraversion (outgoing/energetic versus solitary/reserved).
2. Agreeableness (friendly/compassionate versus challenging/detached).
3. Conscientiousness (efficient/organized versus easy-going/careless).
4. Neuroticism (sensitive/nervous versus secure/confident).
5. Openness to experience (inventive/curious versus consistent/cautious).

This classification system is often used in research, but in recent years it has undergone an evolution, as the five scales appeared not to be able to cover all the different personality traits of people. As a result, a sixth scale was added, leading to the HEXACO model:

H. Honesty-Humility
E. Emotionality
X. eXtraversion
A. Agreeableness
C. Conscientiousness
O. Openness to experience[55]

Bearing these problems in mind – most of which were identified a long time ago by the ETS – various studies have been carried out during the past few decades to investigate to what extent the MBTI classification is accurate and, consequently, whether or not it's a good predictor.

Following from earlier work by Pittenger, Carskadon and Cook[56] and Kuipers and colleagues,[57] a 2002 meta-analysis looked specifically at the reliability of the test, focusing on the extent to which it produced the same results over time (if, for example, it was carried out again in the same circumstances two weeks later; test-retest reliability). In other words, the study looked at repeat measurements that should in theory have produced the same, or at least very comparable, results. You can think of it like weighing yourself. If you weigh yourself on a set of scales and what you weigh today is roughly the same as what you weighed a week and a fortnight ago, you can conclude that the scales are more or less reliable. If, however, there are significant variations, you would probably say that the scales are not reliable. When the researchers attempted to compare MBTI results in this way, one of the first things they noticed was that most past studies had paid very little or no attention to reliability, so that their results were of minimal value. In contrast, the studies that took reliability into account generally produced reliable results, although even here some of the outcomes were not acceptable by normal standards.[58] A more recent meta-analysis from 2015 also confirmed that reliability issues exist, mainly due to the normative nature of the test which requires people to position themselves within each of the different factors, even though they might not necessarily 'belong' in this or that factor.[59]

A Pyramid Game

In a 2015 blog post, Donald Clark explained why he thought MBTI has so many uncritical admirers. He described MBTI as a 'Ponzi scheme' or pyramid game.[60] In the business world, this is essentially a form of fraud which lures new investors and pays profits to earlier investors by using funds obtained from the newer investors. A comparable technique is often used in commercial approaches to theoretical methods and models. In terms of MBTI, you first have to pay a trainer in order to take the test yourself. Later, you can also become a trainer, so that you in turn can earn money by giving the test to others. However, you have to pay some of the money to the person at the level above yours, just as the person at the level below yours will later have to pay money to you. Viewed purely from the perspective of commercial logic, this system is perhaps understandable. But it makes internal criticism that much more difficult.

MBTI Is Not Alone

In recent years, we've received various questions about models similar to MBTI, some of which have been praised as being as good as or even better than the original! With this in mind, we offer the following tips to these trusting souls:

- If a model is based on an (introspective) self-report – in other words it's based on what the subject her-/himself thinks about how (s)he thinks and acts – there is a strong likelihood that the results will not be reliable so don't use them.
- If a model is normative in nature, which seeks to 'pigeon-hole' people in sharply defined boxes, don't use it. When people are placed in boxes, they are often treated and act accordingly.
- If a model is part of a pyramid-like structure, don't use it.
- If a model does not include emotional stability as a dimension, don't use it.

Is There Then No Link between Personality and Learning?

As a teacher, you've probably noticed that some students are better at paying attention, some are quicker on the uptake, some are more determined to see a task through to the end, etc. Surely these are recognizable personality characteristics that can perhaps be linked to success at school!

During the past decade, various research studies have been conducted to determine whether or not a correlation exists between a high score on one or more of the Big Five dimensions and good performance at school. These studies have concluded that there is indeed such a link, particularly for Conscientiousness, but also, for example, for Openness.[61] But these are only correlations. What's more, the results suggest that they are largely determined by genetics, which means that it's questionable as to what extent it is possible to do anything effective to further improve the situation.[62]

Conclusion: Myth

Several currently popular models have fundamental weaknesses and, consequently, are not good instruments. Yes, there are correlations between the scores for certain personality traits and good school performance, but it's doubtful if these correlations can be exploited in any meaningful way, never mind that a child's entire education should be geared to them.

Is NLP (Neuro-Linguistic Programming) Science?

In the mid-1970s, Richard Bandler, a psychology and philosophy graduate, working together with linguist John Grinder, developed the first system for neurolinguistic programming (usually abbreviated to NLP, but not to be confused with natural language processing from the world of artificial intelligence). The basis of their theory was originally a combination of observations made during therapy with the work of Noam Chomsky, the American linguist and philosopher. In fact, you could say that Bandler and Grinder synthesized many different ideas from many different areas.

The Central Premise of NLP

The central premise of NLP can be summarized as 'The Map is not the Territory'.[63] This means that each of us acts on the basis of how we see or internally represent the world (that is the 'map'), which conversely means that we do not act on the basis of the way the world really is (that is the 'territory').

In order to communicate with others (or if a therapist wants to help a patient in treatment), it's crucial to be able to uncover and read that internal map.

According to Bandler and Grinder, the map is constructed by the five senses, but everyone has a preferred sense or Preferred Representational System (PRS).[64] Tapping into that preference is therefore necessary for someone else – an outsider – who wants to understand the map and, where possible, to help the map's creator.[65] One of the ways to do this is by monitoring eye-movement,[66] although the use of certain words and certain types of non-verbal behavior can also give access to the map.[67]

And Where Does All This Lead?

This makes it possible to thoroughly re-program your personality. In short, you can become a different person. Or so says the theory. This immediately explains the title of one of Bandler and Grinder's books: *Frogs into Princes*. By altering your use of language, you can help yourself and help others – although it's sometimes suggested that it's more a question of manipulating than helping.[68]

Do Eye Movements Betray that You are Lying?

This is one of the propositions that is very popular in NLP: eye movements can show whether or not you are lying. For example, in NLP a right-handed person who looks repeatedly to the right is probably lying, whereas if (s)he looks consistently to the left (s)he's probably telling the truth. In 2012, this theory was tested in a series of experiments by Richard Wiseman and his colleagues.[69] In their first study, a number of the test subjects were filmed while they were telling the truth (or not) and their eye movement was noted. The results did not match the pattern predicted by NLP. In a second study, one group of participants were given an explanation of the NLP theory about lying and eye-movement, whereas this information was withheld from the control group. Both groups were then asked to undergo a lie-detector test. There was no difference in the results of the two groups. In a third and final study, the researchers examined known lies and truths expressed during important press conferences. Once again, there was no difference.

There was once an old Belgian song called: 'I see the lies in your eyes'. We suspect the writers of the song also must have been lying.

Popularity and Research

NLP became increasingly popular during the 1970s. As a result, during the 1980s a number of scientists decided to investigate the theory's basic premises and approach. It soon became clear that there was almost no scientific basis for the claims made by Bandler and Grinder. A 1988 report comparing NLP as a therapy against more standard therapies was devastating in its criticism.[70] Even so, the popularity of NLP continued to grow throughout the 1990s. In 2010, a non-peer-reviewed research paper[71] was published, in which a series of case studies were presented as positive proof for NLP, although Bailey and colleagues were quick to point out that the authors had ignored all the standard rules that generally apply to such a paper. Mayne also observed that the review was written by an NLP coach,[72] which obviously had implications for its impartiality. A further review was conducted by Witkowski, this time more in keeping with accepted practice, but perhaps for this reason it failed to find any empirical basis for the claims of NLP.[73] In short, there is no substantiation for NLP's theoretical premises and no evidence for its effectiveness. In 2006, the majority of a panel of 101 psychology experts expressed their opinion that NLP belonged to the category of approaches in science that are no longer valid.[74]

NLP and Language Education

NLP continues to be popular in language education, and particularly in English language education.[75] Once again, however, there is no scientific basis to back up its use.[76] A number of elements in the method of teaching may seem familiar and can indeed be effective, but this is only because they are also used outside of NLP. These include:

- Searching for differences.
- Guiding a 'blind' fellow student.
- Making mind maps which is a visual representation of hierarchical information with a central idea surrounded by connected branches of related topics.
- Playing 'telephone' where students send messages to each other.
- Using the jigsaw technique, a method of organizing classroom activity that makes students dependent on each other to succeed by splitting the tasks in different pieces for different teams to work on.[77]

We know that jigsaw can be a very effective method for collaborative learning,[78] but we also know that trying to link this to learning styles – such as those that appear in Millrood and are closely related under the surface with the PRS thinking of NLP – is one of the most persistent educational myths.[79] According to Mayne, there is absolutely no proof for the effectiveness of NLP in education. More recently, other authors – some of them pro-NLP – have admitted the same thing, although their argument then becomes that if, as teacher, you think NLP works, it works.[80]

Conclusion: Myth

While NLP still has it followers, there is little to no substantiation for its basic premises and no reliable empirical evidence to confirm its effectiveness.

Do the Internet and Computer Screens Make Children Autistic, Narcissistic, Depressive, Etc.?

In 2009, Baroness Susan Greenfield offered the following thought to the British House of Lords:

> *Firstly, the human brain adapts to the environment;*
> *secondly, the environment is changing in an unprecedented way;*
> *so thirdly, the brain may also be changing in an unprecedented way.*[81]

This thought provoked a good deal of controversy. Greenfield is not just anybody. The baroness is a professor and one of the few scientists in the House of Lords. On top of this, her specialty is neurology. In other words, she should know what she is talking about. The baroness had already formulated this opinion in her book *Mind Change*, but in her speech to the House of Lords she went much further (as recorded in the official minutes):

> Perhaps we should therefore not be surprised that those within the spectrum of autism are particularly comfortable in the cyber world. The internet has even been linked to sign language, considered as beneficial for autistic people as sign language proved for the deaf. Of course, we do not know whether the current increase in autism is due more to increased awareness and diagnosis of autism, or

whether it can – if there is a true increase – be in any way linked to an increased prevalence among people of spending time in screen relationships. Surely it's a point worth considering.[82]

In other words, we here have a neuroscientist who is making a possible link between internet use and autism. In the same speech she also mentioned ADHD and internet use in the same context. What's more, she repeated these claims in 2011.[83]

Baroness Greenfield is not alone. In an article in *The Telegraph* Iain McGilchrist argued – as a psychiatrist – that smartphones and tablets are making our children more narcissistic and less empathic, referring to American research which showed how far this trend has already come. Closer to home (at least for the present authors), on 8 September 2014 a well-known Flemish psychiatrist stated on national television that in his opinion very young children playing with tablets run the risk of later becoming what he called 'screen zombies'.[84]

This is a subject that has repeatedly made the headlines in recent years. Greenfield reiterated her arguments on her website in 2014, this time citing a list of 500 peer-reviewed papers to support her case.[85] Dorothy Bishop, a fellow neuroscientist, decided to examine both the claim and the sources. She looked at all 500 papers and what did she find? Of the 395 unique articles (not 500), 234 had indeed undergone peer review (in addition to newspaper articles and pressure group reports), some 168 of which dealt specifically with the possible effects of technology, of which in turn just 15 dealt specifically with the brain, but only in the broadest possible sense. Not surprisingly, Bishop concluded that the 'smoking gun' – the hard proof from different sources that Greenfield had cited – was lacking.[86]

Vaccinations Do Not Lead to Autism

This is a claim that you will often come across if you look up information about vaccination. There is a body of research which supposedly shows that vaccination can sometimes lead to autism in the vaccinated children. And in 1998 there was indeed a study published in *The Lancet*[87] that seemed to show a correlation, but this was later withdrawn from the respected scientific journal when more information about the nature of the study became available. What is the case?

- The study was extremely small-scale (it involved just 12 children) and there was no control group.
- No other research was able to show a similar correlation.[88]
- The data in the study had been manipulated to achieve the 'desired' results.[89]
- The researcher in question, Andrew Wakefield, was asked to perform this manipulation by the parents of children with autism, who wanted to sue the makers of the vaccines.[90]

In other words, the so-called evidence in this case is simply one of the more well-known and more flagrant examples of scientific fraud,[91] whose author was struck off the medical register for the gross misconduct this involved.[92]

Much of this debate centered on the diagnosis of autism, which had increased significantly during the previous decades. But this increase began before everyone was glued to the internet and their smartphones and can probably be accounted for by changes in the criteria that were used to make the diagnosis.[93] In a post on this theme, Bishop commented (correctly) that nowadays autism is often diagnosed as early as the child's second or third year.[94] Of course, it's true that many toddlers do now play with tablets, but is this the real reason for the changing pattern? As already mentioned, the initial claims made by Baroness Greenfield date from before the period when the use of the iPad first spread like wildfire amongst young children, just as the increase in autism predates the massive explosion of interest in the internet.

So what about the idea that technology can also make children less empathic? The research cited by McGilchrist in his *Telegraph* interview was conducted by Jean Twenge, who used it as a basis for a book she co-wrote with W. Keith Campbell: *The Narcissism Epidemic*.[95] Unfortunately for the modern-day Luddites, the study conducted by Twenge and colleagues in 2012 showed that the growth in narcissism actually took place during the 1980s; in other words, again long before the breakthrough of the internet.[96] What's more, recent research has concluded that the prevalence of narcissism[97] among young people to some extent decreased between 1990 and 2010,[98] a period during which their media use, if anything, moved in the opposite direction.

It was the same Jean Twenge who in 2018 put forward the idea that smartphones not only make our young people narcissistic, but also depressive.[99] She based this new claim on data gathered between 2010 and 2015 from 506,820 American adolescents between the ages of 13 and 18, arguing that there was a marked rise in feelings of depression among young people from 2012 onwards. She saw a clear link between this trend and a corresponding increase in average screen time. But this is not a link; it's a correlation.[100] An earlier meta-analysis had already shown, for example, that people who feel lonely are more likely to seek solace on social media.[101] This brings us back to Greenfield, who at best also only found a correlation. Rather than causing autism, is it not possible that people who suffer from the condition, and therefore have difficulty with forms of social contact and verbal interaction with others, can actually overcome (or at least reduce) these difficulties through the use of a machine or some other instrument? A correlation (for example, between clouds and rain) does not mean that there is a causal relationship (the rain does not cause the clouds).

New technology usually provokes an initial negative reaction. People are afraid of change and of the unknown. This is known as 'moral panic'.[102] Moral panic is a disproportionate, hostile and media-generated response to a situation, technology, person or group that seems to threaten existing values and norms.[103] Consider, for example, the phenomenon of *radiotismus*; a label given to men who made a hobby of the new medium of radio in the 1920s. These men were supposed to be 'possessed' by the voices they heard from the radio, which 'forced' them to spend hours listening in the attic rather than being with their families. This diagnosis of the 'disease' as something specifically affecting men disappeared when the radio came down from the attic and was given a place in the living room. From then on, the same diagnostic label was also stuck on women. Their nerves could not cope with the sensory experience of mediated voices, as a result of which they increasingly neglected their household duties! This example is taken from the work of Carolyn Birdsall and Senta Siewert,[104] and shows all too clearly that the supposed link between madness and media is nothing new: it simply changes through time in keeping with new societal and technological trends. During the 1950s, rock and roll was the new social evil. In the 1960s and 1970s, it was the possible negative influence of televisions and violent films. Today, it's social media and shooter games.[105]

Does all this mean that social media and excessive screen use have no negative effects? No, of course not. But we need to be careful about making spectacular claims, certainly when they are linked to other matters that have a longer recent history, like autism and depression. These kinds of unfounded claims, with no real substantiation other than inconclusive correlational research, can unnecessarily increase the level of guilt often felt by the family of the sufferers of these and other conditions.

But let us return to the (possibly genuine) negative effects. In 2018, a group of researchers published the results of a large-scale longitudinal study in the *Journal of the American Medical Association*, in which they came very close to establishing a clear link between screen use and the symptoms of ADHD in adolescents. However, as the researchers themselves were honest enough to point out, the nature and purpose of their research was such that it's still not possible to make a causal connection between screens and ADHD, no matter how suggestive the results might be.[106] In other words, this cannot be regarded as proof that excessive screen use leads to ADHD; all it demonstrates is that such use can result in the development of certain symptoms in adolescents, while at the same time confirming that average screen use should not generally result in problems of this kind.[107]

Other recent research has revealed a clear correlation between intensive screen use and short-sightedness, especially during the period when the eyes of young people are still developing and changing. The Erasmus Medical Center in Rotterdam, the Netherlands concludes: 'It's suspected that the changing lifestyle of children is harmful for their eyes.' Orthoptist Jan Roelof Polling adds:

> Children are no longer playing outside enough, but instead do too much 'close-up' work indoors, including reading and being on the computer. The popularity of tablets is making this problem much worse. Children are now sitting in front of a screen almost all day and play games that require them to view things at close range.[108]

What Is the Optimal Screen Time?

This is a discussion that has been going on for quite some time: how many hours a day should young people be allowed to sit in front of a screen? In an age in which we all have smartphones and tablets and in which technology also plays an increasingly large role in education, this is an important question. One of the most frequently cited 'rules' is a maximum 2 hours a day for children younger than twelve and no screen time during the first two years of life.[109] The source for this rule was the American Academy of Pediatrics (AAP), but in 2015 the academy realized that its views – first drawn up at a time when 'media' largely meant television – needed revision.[110] In the meantime, other European researchers, including Patti Valkenburg and Sonia Livingstone, had also made similar pronouncements. The existing rules were withdrawn and while awaiting the completion of research that would allow new recommendations to be made, parents were simply advised to monitor their children closely and act accordingly.

New guidelines were finally issued in 2016.[111] Once again, they were fairly conservative and although the conclusions were inspired by research, the actual guidelines themselves were not specifically investigated.[112] As a result, they must be seen for what they are: inconclusive recommendations:

- No screen time during the first 18 months of a child's life and no screen activity for the mother if she is busy with her child. 'The noise and activity of a screen are distracting for a child. Even if the baby isn't directly looking at the screen – for example, if a mother is nursing her child on the couch while watching TV – the baby can be overstimulated by the lights and sounds, which may cause distress and sleep problems.' Even more striking is the link made with bonding. Yolanda Reid Chassiakos – the author of the report – explained to CNN: 'When a mother is breast-feeding, that is a crucial bonding time. The more face-to-face interaction children have with mothers and other adults, especially eye contact, the better for the brain development of infants.'[113]
- 2 to 5 years: a maximum of 1 hour of screen time per day. The AAP recommends 'creative, unplugged playtime' for toddlers and infants, and argues in favor of quality programs like Sesame Street®, rather than other types of programs, especially with advertisements/commercials. Other beneficial screen time includes the use of Skype® and other face-to-face apps, which can be used, for example, to encourage contact with grandparents.

- 6 years and older: limited screen time. It's noteworthy that (compulsory) screen time at school and for homework is no longer included in the calculation of total screen time. Instead of setting a fixed limit in hours, the AAP now emphasizes the importance of children and teenagers getting enough sleep, physical exercise and offline social interaction.
- For children of all ages (bearing in mind the potentially negative impact of staring at screens on eyesight): do not continuously look at the screen for long periods. Your eyes need to make a significant effort it you want a close-range object to be fixed on your retina in focus and in detail. This is known as accommodation. During this process, your eye expands backwards in an attempt to relieve the pressure and avoid becoming overtired. The more your eye expands backwards, the worse your long-distance sight will eventually become.
- Alternate screen use with other activities. Use the 20-minute guideline as a good rule of thumb.

Conclusion: Nuanced

There is no evidence that the internet, social media or screen use lead to autism. This does not mean that screen use cannot have negative consequences, but we need to be aware about spectacular claims that link technology and medical or psychological conditions which we know are innate.

Develop Your Talent!

There is a nice idea behind the thinking about talent: everyone can do something well! Hence the popular appeal that the talent residing in every child should be stimulated. But there is sometimes more to this than meets the eye. You could just as easily say that if talents are not developed, the value of those talents is thrown away – which then immediately transforms the appeal into more of an economic story. However, there is just one tiny problem with all this: what exactly is talent? Talent seems to be a concept that everyone understands, but as soon as you try to define it you quickly get stuck. Even scientists cannot agree what it is![114] At a superficial level, we can perhaps say that having a talent means that someone does something or shows something that is regarded as being better than that which others do or show.

But this is where the real questions start, as summarized by Henk Sligte and colleagues[115]:

- If we say that someone has a talent or excels in something, *in what* exactly do they excel?
- Is talent a question of intelligence, insight, creativity, a special aptitude or moral judgment, or is it a combination of all these things?
- What is the most important talent?
- What kinds of ability need to be encouraged?
- Is everyone blessed with one or more talents?

Then there is the question of how you measure talent:

- Does talent need to be measured and, if so, why?
- If we measure, do we need to use standardized tests so that we'll have absolute data and knowledge, or should the intention be to simply acquire indications that will make it possible for the student and her/his environment to better anticipate and deal with the situation?
- If we measure talent in specific ways, some individuals with talents not picked up by that way of measuring will be overlooked. If we only look at what people have done, this effectively means that talent is determined retrospectively.
- Which measuring procedures are valid and reliable?
- What kind of measuring can identify students with special potential?

Which in turn leads on to questions about quantifying the measurements:

- To what extent must a student excel to have talent?
- Must the student do better than 50, 80 or 99% of the group with which (s)he is being compared?
- What is the nature of the comparison group? Should it consist of all students from the same school, or all students of the same gender, ethnic group, social economic background, etc.?

And finally:

- Why do students with talent need to be identified?
- Does this have social and/or cultural benefits?
- Or is it an economic question?
- Does 'talent spotting' help to maintain an elite or even create one?
- Or is it simply a way to provide a more meritocratic basis for education?

These are all valid questions, but there are far too many to answer in this short section. Moreover, because all of the answers relate to what we generally understand by the term 'talent', this will soon lead to a focus on the old discussion between nature (innate talents) and nurture (learned or acquired talents). Perhaps a different approach will yield more useful insights.

Strengths?

Related to talent but still different is the concept of 'strengths'. Strengths are certain positive qualities or characteristics that a person possesses. This can be seen, for example, in the work of Peterson and Seligman,[116] who refer to character strengths that are more innate than learned, but can nevertheless be influenced, or in the work of Park and colleagues, who regard these strengths as biological in origin.[117] In a more economic-commercial context, the translation of Daniel Ofman's idea of core qualities,[118] as interpreted (amongst others) by Fred Korthagen, sees a strength as something that is already present, but needs to be recognized and possibly further developed.[119] This is a vision that can potentially clash with another theme we've discussed earlier in the book; namely, the idea of a growth mindset. If you do not have a particular strength, this means that there is nothing you can do about it – a vision that, to say the least, has been subject to considerable criticism.[120] Researchers like Anders Ericsson, who is a strong advocate of the nurture vision, have been vehement in their opposition. For example, Ericsson and Pool noted that top performers often do not possess special qualities that allow them to excel in their profession, but have achieved their success more by targeted training and hard work – which, according to Ericsson and Pool, are the only real talents.[121]

Intelligences?

We've already discussed another vision of talent in our previous book and will do so again in the next section on IQ. This vision is based on Howard Gardner's idea of multiple intelligences. While Gardner himself might not be keen on the use of the word 'talent' in this context, in practice his theory is often reduced to a discussion of talents. This is perhaps understandable when he talks about mathematical intelligence, musical intelligence, interpersonal intelligence and so on, because this is the basis of his theory: intelligences are equivalent to knowledge domains. You are better at maths, I am better at music, he is better at languages. This suggests that Gardner leans more towards nature than nurture, but this begs the question of whether his classification system covers all the things that people are good at.

It's also possible to regard talents as skills, which are not per se innate, but which can be developed to a high level. If you do something better than someone else, this is not necessarily the result of an innate ability; it may simply be the result of your own hard work, as Ericsson believes. In that case, a number of other ideas fall away, such as the argument that you need to go in search of your talents or that teachers must help their students to discover their innate gifts. At the same time, this also brings us back to the age-old question: is it possible for people to become anything they want through training and hard work alone?

Is It Better to Just Follow Your Passion?

The advice 'Follow your passion' is often given on the basis of the assumption that the things you like to do, you will do better and for longer. It's sometimes suggested that passion is the same as talent, although there are enough talent shows on television (of the 'Idol' variety) to show that this is not necessarily the case. But what does science have to say on the matter?

It all depends on how you view a passion – or that, at least, is the opinion of O'Keefe, Dweck and Walton, who have carried out a number of experiments in this field.[122] You can regard passion either as something you are born with or as something that can grow as you develop as a person. This brings us back to the distinction mentioned earlier in the book between a fixed mindset and a growth mindset. So what did the results of the experiments show? People who think that a passion is something that is naturally present from the moment of birth tend to give up on their passion when the going gets tough. This approach also results in a greater lack of interest for things outside of the supposed passion, so that people who think this way effectively put all their eggs in one basket. This was the conclusion of the first experiment conducted by O'Keefe and his colleagues, a successful replication of an earlier study. The second and third experiments confirmed the same findings. The fourth experiment investigated the level of resilience displayed in dealing with complexity and challenge, and revealed that people with a growth mindset respond better. However, the test population for this study was fairly small, so that the results were underpowered. For this reason, the researchers decided to do a fifth experiment with a larger sample. This final experiment confirmed the result of the previous one. Based on these findings, it might well be that 'Develop your passion' is better advice than 'Follow your passion'.

But how do these experiments fit in with the replication crisis that we discussed earlier with regard to growth mindset? The answer is that they don't. These experiments were not really focused on stimulating a growth mindset and how this stimulation might lead to better performance. In this approach, it was more a question of investigating an implicit theory that a person may or may not possess and seeing what effect that implicit theory has on her/his actions.

Conclusion: Unproven

:-?

It's impossible for us to declare talent to be a myth. As a concept there is no single scientific definition on which everyone can agree. This is one of the reasons why researching the subject is so difficult. Of course, this does not prevent questions about the concept from being asked, one of the most important of which is whether or not talent is innate, and what consequences this has. A major pitfall when dealing with talent is that the subdivisions into which it is classified are too narrow, so that they do not cover all the things that a child or adult might be good at doing.

Myths about IQ

Back to basics: the intelligence quotient – the most popular and widespread instrument for the measurement of human intelligence – is a total score obtained in a number of standardized tests. Usually, the IQ score is determined by that total score (known as the mental score) divided by the age of the person being measured in years and months and then multiplied by 100. A 'normal' IQ is somewhere between 85 and 115 (1 standard deviation from the 'norm' of 100) and this range contains roughly 68% of the population. A person with an IQ of more than 130 is very intelligent; a person with an IQ of less than 70 is mentally weak or even retarded. Both categories contain 2.2% of the population.

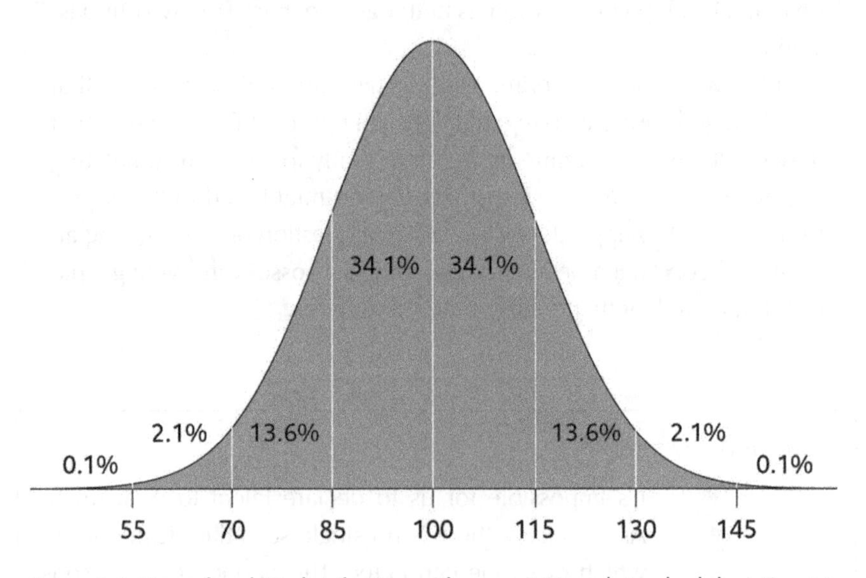

Figure 3.1 Normalized IQ distribution with mean 100 and standard deviation 15. *Source*: Wikimedia Commons, by Dmcq.

Intelligence and IQ have increasingly become subjects for discussion in education in recent years. The most important voice raised against too strong a focus on IQ was probably Howard Gardner, whose theory of multiple intelligences was discussed in our previous book (and also mentioned in the preceding chapter). We concluded that his theory has no solid foundation. Although people naturally differ in their levels of intelligence, these differences do not necessarily match the classifications devised by Gardner. Other frequently made criticisms made against IQ are that it's racist, is not a good predictor, and that an overly exaggerated IQ thinking is deterministic. According to this last argument, IQ is something innate, so that your ability to be a success or failure is fixed at birth. Other IQ detractors contend that this form of 'intelligence' is nothing more than the things the tester decides to include in the test. If you put other things in the test, you get other results.

Gardner on His Own Theory of Multiple Intelligences

In 2016, Gardner wrote a short essay reviewing his career, in which his theory of multiple intelligences played a central role. In his essay, he mentioned three things casting doubt on his theory that go much further than the criticisms we made in our previous book. Gardner claimed that:

- his theory had never really been properly researched;
- his theory is now out of date;
- he used intelligence as a concept to make sure his work would get published.[123]

Viewed historically, some of these criticisms contain an element of truth. At the same time, however, the critics are often not aware of the most current nuances of thinking on IQ and intelligence, so that many of their criticisms evolve into misleading myths. For this reason, we'll now discuss four of the most prevalent myths surrounding IQ.

What Is Intelligence?

The most original definition that we've ever heard is that 'intelligence is what you measure in an intelligence test'. This definition may seem to border on the ridiculous, but the 'definition issue' is nonetheless a criticism that is often aimed at the advocates of IQ tests: there is no clear understanding of what exactly is being measured. Legg and Hutter collected numerous definitions of intelligence from different domains and came to the conclusion that intelligence:

- is a property that an individual agent has as it interacts with its environment or environments;
- is related to the agent's ability to succeed or profit with respect to some goal or objective; and
- depends on the agent's ability to adapt to different objectives and environments.[124]

Stuart Ritchie argued that it's important to realize that intelligence can vary from person to person,[125] which falls within the third element of Legg and Hutter's findings. And it's precisely because intelligence can vary in this manner that so much interest and energy is devoted to the desire to measure it. Viewed historically, there has been an important predictive element in this desire right from the very beginning. The first usable IQ test was developed for the French government in 1904 by Alfred Binet and Theodore Simon. With the introduction of compulsory education, the test was intended to ascertain which students were weaker, so that their weaknesses could be remedied.[126] In the first instance, Binet used words like *imbecile* and *idiot* to categorize the results, the aim being to indicate a level of mental handicap based on the measurement of IQ.[127] Later, Binet came to the insight that it was more appropriate to make a comparison with age, so that students were classified as being ahead of or behind the average development of their age contemporaries.

The original intention of both the French government and Binet and Simon was reasonable: they wanted to provide each child with education that was appropriate to its abilities.[128] The scope of this book is too narrow to include a full history of intelligence research. We'll therefore confine ourselves to dealing with the most important criticisms and the most common myths.

Is IQ Purely Genetic?

There is a strong genetic basis for intelligence. This has been established many times in many different ways.[129] Some of the most important research material has been gleaned from the so-called 'twin studies', in which identical (monozygotic) twins, fraternal (dizygotic) twins and ordinary brothers and sisters are compared with each other. The most well-known institute in this field in the Benelux (and perhaps even in the world) is the Netherlands Twin Register,[130] founded in 1987 by the Vrije Universiteit Amsterdam. The twins of one of the authors were recorded in the register at their birth in 1988 and have been followed ever since. It's important to note that not all aspects of intelligence are fixed at birth. The influence of heredity evolves over time, from roughly 20% at birth to roughly 80% in later life.[131] In other words, the bad news is that the older you get, the more you become like your parents. The good news is that you will never turn out to be exactly the same, in part because you do, of course, have two different parents.

Don't Be Deceived by the Seeming Harshness of the Terminology

Although Binet's classifications seem harsh today, at the time they did not have a pejorative meaning, but were simply clinical classifications. It was only when the public began to use these same words as terms of insult that they were replaced by new and less hurtful classifications, which then in turn also became terms of abuse, and so on. We can see this, for example, with a word like 'invalid', which later became 'handicapped person' and has now been transformed to the more politically correct 'person with a limitation'. Yet even this can give cause for criticism; some deaf people regard their hearing difficulties as a gift, rather than a limitation.

There are plenty of other indications that environment can play an important role in intelligence. The most famous of these is probably the Flynn effect, which shows that the average score of a particular population in intelligence tests increases over time. The test battery of questions in IQ tests is regularly re-calibrated: some questions become outdated, society continues to evolve, etc. James Flynn asked himself whether an average IQ of 100 could be maintained or even increased over a period of many years. The results suggest that it can. Since the 1930s, there has been an enormous increase in IQ levels in the western world.[132] The causes of this increase are far from clear and many possibilities have been suggested:

more challenging television, the amount of lead in the air, better guessing, improved access to education, etc. It should be noted, however, that the Flynn effect is now slowing down or even stopping in many European countries. At the same time, recent research has also shown a sharp rise in rapidly developing countries, like China.[133] What do all these factors that can potentially influence intelligence have in common? They are all clearly environmental factors.

The influence of the environment becomes even more apparent if you look at the effect that adoption can have on intelligence.[134] Imagine that you are a child from a poor social or socio-economic background and you are adopted by a richer and more highly educated family. This can increase your IQ by between 12 and 18 points in comparison with children who remain in the same social class. There are even environmental effects in the womb, where epigenetic changes can occur, as a result of which even identical twins can be genetically different.

One of the best ways to increase a person's IQ is … let them attend school. Each extra year that a person spends at school boosts their IQ by between 1 and 5 points.[135]

On the flip side of the coin, there are also things that cannot increase a person's IQ, such as brain games and playing classical music to unborn babies. We explored these myths (and others) at length in our previous book.[136]

Are IQ Tests Racist?

One of the most damning criticisms of IQ tests is that they are racist. It's certainly true that intelligence tests were quickly adopted by advocates of eugenics.[137] Eugenics is the idea that racial improvement is possible by excluding certain genetic groups deemed to be less desirable. The concept was first developed by Francis Galton, a distant relative of Charles Darwin, who also played an important role in intelligence research. The link with Darwin probably explains why Galton sought to improve the human race via a process of natural selection, with intelligence as one of the criteria.[138] The distinction between innate and acquired intelligence also had its origin with Galton. Unfortunately, eugenic thinking also had a huge influence on the Nazis, as a result of which it has become inextricably associated with the Holocaust, so that it's now very much a taboo subject.[139] This has also cast a shadow over intelligence and its significance.

But while eugenics as a subject for research has been scientifically out-of-bounds ever since World War II, the IQ test has survived and thrived. Even so, various books in recent decades have argued that this instrument, like eugenics, is also essentially racist. In 1969, Arthur Jensen published a much quoted but highly controversial article with the title 'How much can we boost IQ and scholastic achievement?'[140] Jensen described at length how various programs to improve the academic performance of children from socially deprived backgrounds had failed in the United States, according to him because 80% of intelligence is innate. This was interpreted as saying people of color are (more) stupid. A similar situation based on a similar argument and resulting in similar public and academic outrage arose following the publication in 1994 of the book *The Bell Curve* by Richard Herrnstein and Charles Murray.[141] Ritchie commented that in the prevailing atmosphere of disapproval it's becoming difficult to conduct meaningful research into such matters. We've also noticed in our own discussions of these two controversial works that it's difficult to express certain opinions – even as possibilities – without making people angry.

So what is going on here? We've already made clear that intelligence has a genetic basis. But heredity at a personal level says nothing about heredity at a group level. There are indeed intelligence differences between countries, as Ritchie pointed out, but here also there is nothing to say that heredity plays a role. It might just as easily be the case that environment is once again the key factor.

This brings us on to the younger sister of racism: cultural discrimination. The argument goes that since time immemorial IQ tests have been designed and calibrated with a certain culture in mind: usually a white, wealthy (or at least middle class) culture. This means that some questions will not be understood by or are not suitable for other cultures, so that people belonging to these cultures will achieve a lower score. To eliminate this possibility, from the mid-20th century onwards what was known as the Culture Fair Intelligence Test (CFIT) was introduced. This test was developed by Raymond Cattell and was meant to provide a measure for cognitive capacity that was not dependent on socio-cultural and environmental influences.[142] Because language is probably the main carrier of culture, the CFIT consists of three scales with non-verbal, visual puzzles (such as following a maze, copying symbols, identifying similar figures, etc.) and other non-verbal tasks.

Do IQ Tests Demonstrate a Particular Preference or Bias?

When intelligence tests are compiled, a whole series of questions is formulated and then put to a wide range of people. If you can complete the same number of questions correctly in the same amount of time as your age contemporaries, you will have an average IQ of 100. If you can answer more (or fewer) questions or the same number of questions faster (or more slowly), you will have a higher (or lower) IQ.

Of course, it's not unthinkable that if the original list of questions is completed by, for example, a largely white, middle-class population that this can have an influence if the same test is later completed by people from a different background. This is what we call a bias, and helps explain some of the differences found by researchers, as mentioned in the previous paragraphs. For example, Anne Anastasi and Susana Urbani have argued that IQ tests favor white men from the middle class.[143]

This is obviously an important matter and it would be regrettable if its sensitivity resulted in a lack of proper research. Fortunately, this is not the case. In 1978 and again in 1994, on the occasion of the publication of *The Bell Curve*, two multi-disciplinary teams were put together to investigate precisely this question. Both teams concluded that IQ tests as a whole have no bias against women and/or minority groups.[144] In this instance, however, each word in the previous sentence is important: we've deliberately written 'as a whole'. It's also possible to investigate whether or not there is bias at the level of individual questions or tasks. Certain questions or tasks in certain IQ tests may indeed be easier or harder for particular groups. But even if particular questions and tasks display a bias (and both research teams found this to be the case), this does not mean that the test in its entirety is biased. It was shown that the biased questions favored different groups (and not always the same group), so that any possible overall bias was avoided.[145] This fallacy was also discussed in the book *50 Great Myths of Popular Psychology* by Scott Lilienfeld and colleagues. Their warning bears repeating: the fact that today's IQ tests no longer display a bias does not means that there will be no differences between the results of different groups taking the test. In this respect, shooting the IQ test is rather like shooting the piano player: it's not the test's fault. As a result, you don't need to think too hard to find the reasons for these differences, which, according to Lilienfeld and his colleagues, are to be found in environmental factors.[146]

Are IQ Tests Good Predictors?

A higher IQ is associated (amongst other things) with:

- better health and a longer life;
- the extent to which a person is religious or not;
- political engagement;
- higher income; and
- school results.[147]

It's possible to extend this list, but the essence can be made clearest by reference to school results. The correlation between the results of an IQ test and school results is .50, which in concrete terms means that about 25% of the difference between children in school results can be explained by their IQ. Let's be clear on this point: that's a lot. But let's be equally clear: it does not say everything.[148]

The correlation of .50 is also an average. Different studies have shown different results and there can also be differences between different school subjects (for example, mathematics is more heavily influenced by intelligence than languages).[149] And don't forget: schooling itself also has an influence on IQ.

So what can we conclude? In general, IQ is a good predictor, but not an absolute one. An absolute predictor would mean that with a single test we could predict how someone's life – for example, in terms of school results or career prospects – would develop. But this is certainly not the case, because many other factors also play a role, such as personality traits and socio-economic status. That being said, IQ nonetheless remains a relatively good predictor that is quick and easy to use, allowing it to provide useful input that can form the basis for appropriate action (educational or otherwise). In reality, the original intention behind Binet and Simon's development of an IQ test remains valid, namely to determine who needs extra help – and what help – to make them improve.

Are Girls Smarter than Boys?

Average intelligence does not vary according to gender, but this average conceals a further difference that is repeatedly revealed by research; namely, that there is a larger IQ spread within males in comparison with females. In concrete terms, this means that you will often find more boys with a low IQ than girls, but you will also find relatively more boys with a high IQ than girls.[150] There also seem to be subtle differences between men and women within some sub-aspects of intelligence research. The important question is why this should be the case. Regrettably, the answer is far from clear. In some respects, finding more lower IQs amongst boys is not wholly illogical, since the incidence of certain mental disabilities is also higher amongst boys. But there is, as yet, no uniform explanation that can account for the larger variance in high IQ scores, nor for the differences in the aforementioned sub-aspects.[151]

Conclusion: Nuanced

Intelligence and intelligence tests are contentious subjects both inside and outside education, in part because of unfortunate historical associations from the past. Even so, intelligence tests are useful and generally reliable instruments that display little bias and are good (though not absolute) predictors for certain (but not all) matters.

Notes

1 https://dictionary.apa.org/cognitive-psychology
2 See:
- Haney, Banks, & Zimbardo, 1972.
- Milgram, 1963.
- Milgram 1974.
- Darley & Latané, 1968.
- Mischel, 2014.
- Strack, Martin, & Stepper, 1988.

3 See, amongst others:
- Blum, 2018.

4 For a summary, consult the post by BPS Digest: https://digest.bps.org.uk/2015/10/13/social-psychology-textbooks-ignore-all-modern-criticisms-of-milgrams-obedience-experiments/.

5 Wagenmakers, Beek, Dijkhoff, Gronau, Acosta, Adams, & Bulnes, 2016.
6 Doliński, Grzyb, Folwarczny, Grzybała, Krzyszycha, Martynowska, & Trojanowski, 2017.
7 Richter, 1957.
8 Dweck, 2006.
9 Binet said the following on this matter: 'Never! What a strong word! A few modern philosophers seem to lend their moral approval to these deplorable verdicts when they assert that an individual's intelligence is a fixed quantity, a quantity that cannot be increased. We must protest and react against this brutal pessimism. We shall attempt to prove that it's without foundation.
Binet, 1975.
10 Dweck & Leggett, 1988.
11 Mueller & Dweck, 1998.
12 Dweck, 1999.
13 On https://voluit.be/prentenboeken-groeimindset-stimuleren/ you can find a summary of mindset picture books.
14 Dweck & Reppucci, 1973.
15 Dweck, 1975.
16 Bahník & Vranka, 2017.
17 Also see http://onderwijskunde.blogspot.com/2017/06/got-my-mindset-on-you.html.
18 DeBacker, Heddy, Kershen, Crowson, Looney, & Goldman, 2018.
19 Orosz, Péter-Szarka, Bőthe, Tóth-Király, & Berger, 2017.
20 Yeager, Hanselman, Paunesku, Hulleman, Dweck, Muller, & Duckworth, 2018.
21 Sisk, Burgoyne, Sun, Butler, & Macnamara, 2018.
22 Kohn, 2015.
23 Dweck, 1975.
24 Amemiya & Wang, 2018.
25 Reavis, Miller, Grimes, & Fomukong, 2018.
26 Chao, Visaria, Mukhopadhyay, & Dehejia, 2017.
27 Dweck, in Gross-Loh, 2016.
28 Dweck, 2015.
29 Dweck, 2012.
30 Dweck, 2017.
31 Blakeslee, 1998.
32 Blackwell, Bloomfield, & Buncher, 1972.
33 Crum & Langer, 2007.
34 Duckworth, Peterson, Matthews, & Kelly, 2007.
35 See the section in this book about personality and learning.
36 http://freakonomics.com/podcast/grit/
37 Dubner, 2016.
38 Credé, Tynan, & Harms, 2017.
39 Ris, 2015.
40 Duckworth, 2016.
41 Rimfeld, Kovas, Dale, & Plomin, 2016.
42 Dahl, 2016.
43 Tampio, 2016.

44 De Bruyckere, in prep.
45 Dunning, 2008.
46 Pittenger, 1993.
47 Strieker & Ross, 1962.
48 Pittenger, 1993.
49 Myers, McCaulley, Quenk, & Hammer, 1998.
50 Grant, 2013.
51 See, amongst others:
- Bess & Harvey, 2002.
- Pittenger, 2005.

52 Le, Oh, Robbins, Ilies, Holland, & Westrick, 2011.
53 Bell, 2007.
54 Digman, 1990.
55 Lee & Ashton, 2014.
56 Carskadon & Cook, 1982.
57 Kuipers, Higgs, Tolkacheva, & de Witte, 2009.
58 Capraro & Capraro, 2002.
59 Salgado, Anderson, & Tauriz, 2015.
60 http://donaldclarkplanb.blogspot.com/2015/04/myers-briggs-useless-ponzi-scheme.html.
61 Poropat, 2014.
62 Tucker-Drob, Briley, Engelhardt, Mann, & Harden, 2016.
63 Lankton, 1980.
64 Did we hear someone shout 'learning style'?
65 Grinder & Bandler, 1976.
66 Witkowski, 2010.
67 Bandler & Grinder, 1979.
68 Vermeren, 2007.
69 These paragraphs are based on:
- Wiseman, Watt, Ten Brinke, Porter, Couper, & Rankin, 2012.

But for the sake of completeness, it should be noted that much previous research had also shown that this was probably not the case:
- Beck & Beck, 1984.
- Elich, Thompson, & Miller, 1985.
- Thomason, Arbuckle, & Cady, 1980.

70 Druckman & Swets, 1988.
71 Carey, Churches, Hutchinson, Jones, & Tosey, 2010.
72 Bailey, Madigan, Cope, & Nicholls, 2018.
73 Witkowski, 2010.
74 Norcross, Koocher, & Garofalo, 2006.
75 Pishghadam & Shayesteh, 2014.
76 Mayne, 2017.
77 See, amongst others:
- Millrood, 2004.
- Revell & Norman, 1999.
- Rosenberg, 2013.

78 See, amongst others:
  - Hattie, 2009
79 See the first myth in our previous book *Urban Myths About Learning and Education*.
80 See, amongst others:
  - Harris, 2002.
  - Tosey & Mathison, 2009.
81 Greenfield, 2015.
82 The official minutes can be consulted at: https://publications.parliament.uk/pa/ld200809/ldhansrd/text/90212-0010.htm.
83 Swain, 2011.
84 Theo Compernolle, in the *Ter Zake* program on Canvas, a Flemish television station.
85 The list was originally posted here: www.susangreenfield.com/science/screen-technologies/.
86 http://deevybee.blogspot.com/2014/09/why-most-scientists-dont-take-susan.html.
87 Wakefield, Murch, Anthony, Linnell, Casson, Malik, & Valentine, 1998.
88 See, amongst others:
  - De Stefano, 2007.
  - Stehr-Green, Tull, Stellfeld, Mortenson, & Simpson, 2003.
  - Taylor, Swerdfeger, & Eslick, 2014.
89 Deer, 2011.
90 Horton, 2004.
91 Godlee, Smith, & Marcovitch, 2011.
92 Meikle & Boseley, 2010.
93 Fombonne, 2005.
94 http://deevybee.blogspot.com/2011/08/open-letter-to-baroness-susan.html.
95 Twenge & Campbell, 2009.
96 Twenge, Campbell, & Freeman, 2012.
97 Narcissism is vanity or self-conceit. In mythology, the self-admiring Narcissus was changed into the flower of the same name (more commonly known as the daffodil).
98 Wetzel, Brown, Hill, Chung, Robins, & Roberts, 2017.
99 Twenge, Joiner, Rogers, & Martin, 2018a.
100 More recently, Twenge and her colleagues have tried to parry this criticism in a new article in which their 'evidence' still remains a correlation, but efforts have been made to rule out all the other possible influences. See: Twenge, Martin, & Campbell, 2018b.
101 Song, Zmyslinski-Seelig, Kim, Drent, Victor, Omori, & Allen, 2014.
102 The term became widely known through the work of Stanley Cohen, 2011.
103 https://nl.wikipedia.org/wiki/Morele_paniek.
104 Birdsall & Siewert, 2013.
105 This theme was also dealt with in De Bruyckere & Smits, 2015.
106 Ra, Cho, Stone, De La Cerda, Goldenson, Moroney, Tung, Lee, & Leventhal, 2018.

107 Ferguson, 2017.
108 Source: https://erasmusmc.nl/corp_home/corp_news-center/2015/2015-04/bijziendheid.voorkomen.met.buiten.spelen/</URI>
See, amongst others: Tideman, Polling, Van der Schans, Verhoeven, & Klaver, 2016.
109 Ghose, 2013.
110 Brown, Shifrin, & Hill, 2015.
111 Chassiakos, Radesky, Christakis, Moreno, & Cross, 2016.
112 Livingstone, 2016.
113 See http://edition.cnn.com/2016/10/21/health/screen-time-media-rules-children-aap/index.html.
114 Hallahan, Kauffman, & Pullen, 2009.
115 Sligte, Bulterman-Bos, & Huizinga, 2009.
116 Peterson & Seligman, 2004.
117 Park et al., 2004.
118 Ofman, 2001.
119 Korthagen & Vasalos, 2005.
120 Colvin, 2008.
121 Ericsson & Pool, 2016b.
122 O'Keefe, Dweck, & Walton, 2018.
123 Gardner, 2016.
124 Legg & Hutter, 2007.
125 Ritchie, 2015.
126 Gregory & Zangwill, 1987.
127 Nicolas, Andrieu, Croizet, Sanitioso, & Burman, 2013.
128 Ritchie, 2015
129 See, amongst others:
- Benyamin, Pourcain, Davis, Davies, Hansell, Brion, & Haworth, 2014.
- Burt, 1966.
- Davies, Tenesa, Payton, Yang, Harris, Liewald, Ke ... & Deary, 2011.
- Posthuma, De Geus, Baaré, Pol, Kahn, & Boomsma, 2002.

130 www.tweelingenregister.org/.
131 Plomin & Deary, 2015.
132 See, amongst others:
- Pietschnig & Voracek, 2015.
- Trahan, Stuebing, Fletcher, & Hiscock, 2014.

133 See, amongst others:
- Johnson, 2005.
- Kaufman, Zhou, Reynolds, Kaufman, Green, & Weiss, 2014.
- Woodley, Te Nijenhuis, Must, & Must, 2014.
- Flynn, 2012.
- Pietschnig & Gittler, 2015.
- Dutton & Lynn, 2015.
- Teasdale & Owen, 2005.
- Dutton & Lynn, 2013.
- Wang & Lynn, 2018.

134 Nisbett, Aronson, Blair, Dickens, Flynn, Halpern, & Turkheimer, 2012.
135 Ritchie & Tucker-Drob, 2018.
136 De Bruyckere, Kirschner, & Hulshof, 2015a

137 Chitty, 2007.
138 Galton, 1883.
139 Bashford & Levine, 2010.
140 Jensen, 1969.
141 Herrnstein & Murray, 1994.
142 Cattell, 1949.
143 Anastasi & Urbina, 1997.
144 See, amongst others:
- Hartigan & Wigdor, 1989.
- Neisser, Boodoo, Bouchard, Boykin, Brody, Ceci, & Urbina, 1996.
- Wigdor, 1982.

145 See:
- Freedle & Kostin, 1997.
- Sackett, Schmitt, Ellingson, & Kabin, 2001.

146 Lilienfeld, Lynn, Ruscio, & Beyerstein, 2010.
147 See, amongst others:
- Gottfredson & Deary, 2004.
- Wrulich, Brunner, Stadler, Schalke, Keller, & Martin, 2014.
- Lynn, Harvey, & Nyborg, 2009.
- Deary, Batty, & Gale, 2008.
- Robertson, Smeets, Lubinski, & Benbow, 2010.
- Colom & Flores-Mendoza, 2007.

148 Neisser, Boodoo, Bouchard, Boykin, Brody, Ceci, & Urbina, 1996. Because schools and their success are determined by cultural standards, it would be strange if a culturally specific test did not correlate well with success in a culture-related institution with culture-related objectives.
149 Deary, Strand, Smith, & Fernandes, 2007.
150 Johnson, Carothers, & Deary, 2008.
151 Ritchie, 2015.

Myths about Educational Policy

In our first book we discussed a series of educational myths relating to educational policy. However, in recent years we've investigated so many new myths in this same field that we now feel obliged to devote a section of this current book to the same contentious but highly important subject.

The various themes covered deal with the assessment, evaluation, and rewarding of extremely good teachers. While we certainly don't deny the need for good teachers, there's clearly something unusual going on with regard to the current approach of policy-makers towards these superwomen and -men.

One of the things that most struck us during our preparatory work for this chapter is how often a particular position or opinion is embraced without very much really being known about the possible effects. This applies, for example, to the debate about year/mixed-grade classes or multi-age classes, which we'll look at later. Another similar theme – but one that we won't discuss, simply because we found almost no reliable research material about its likely impact – is co-teaching that sees a renewed popularity in some regions.

The Importance of Excellent Teachers

It's indisputable that excellent teachers can make a real difference. Consider, for example, the research conducted by Hanushek, which measured not only the impact of the quality of teachers on learning, but also on later economic consequences for the student.[1] Other research has similarly confirmed the importance of strong and effective teachers; for example, in relation to the post-education earning power of students (see Figure 4.1 below).[2]

Effective Teachers Raise Students' Earnings

(Figure 1)

The economic value of an effective teacher grows with larger classes, and the economic costs of having an ineffective teacher are substantial.

Annual Impact of Teacher Quality on the Lifetime Incomes of a Class of Students*

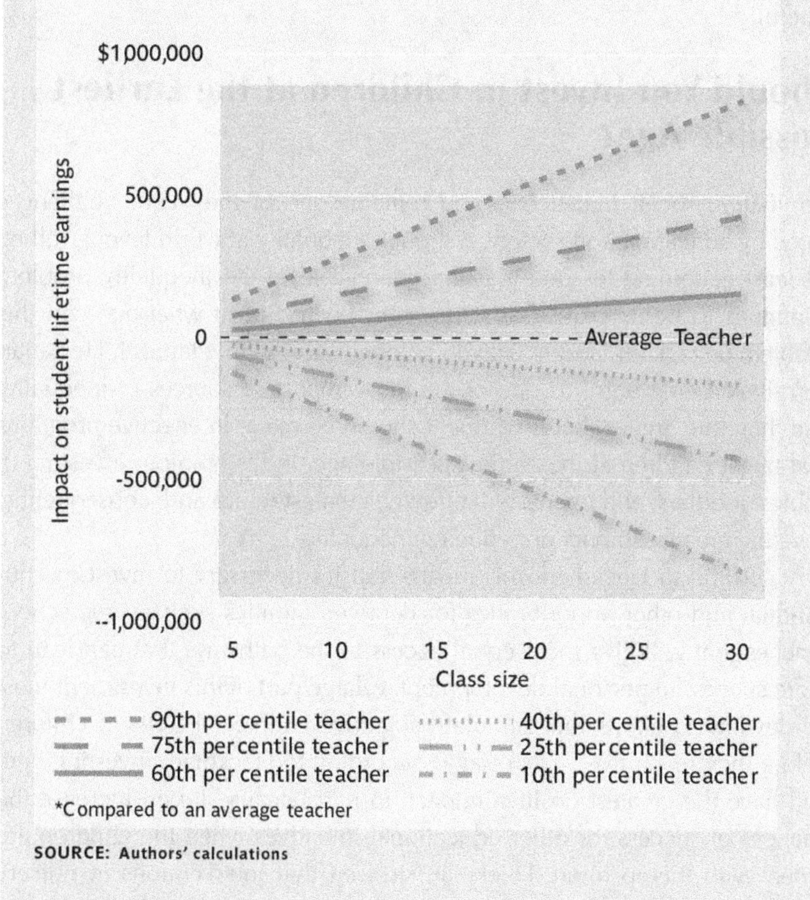

Figure 4.1

Source: Chetty, Friedmann, & Rockoff, 2011.

Although in reality an expensive option, this is being increasingly adopted on a wide scale and is seen as a solution for various problems. However, it was not without good reason that one of the first summary studies in this field (2001) was entitled 'Where are the data?',[3] and it seems to us that very little has changed during the past two decades. We certainly found case studies, and plenty of them, but real effectiveness research is still very hard to find.

The most important lesson that we learned after reading all the available material on the different themes covered in the following pages is this: be careful!

Should You Invest in Children at the Earliest Possible Age?

Eliminating social injustice is and remains one of the major challenges faced by education and society. Although inequality at world level is falling (at least according to some), at the national level the inequality problem continues to be as crucial as it has ever been. But at what age can this problem be tackled most effectively? Nobel Prize winner James J. Heckman describes 'being born' as one of the most important sources of inequality and therefore argues that investment should be made in effective programs that target children at the earliest possible age. In his opinion, investing in babies, toddlers, and infants will offer the greatest return and, consequently, have the greatest impact on reducing inequality.

According to Heckman, this means that it's necessary to invest in educational and other opportunities for deprived families such as free school lunches that will give them equal access to the pathways that can lead to more successful personal development. A large part of this investment must be devoted to efforts that stimulate cognitive and social skills in children before they reach five years of age. According to Heckman, investing here will have the greatest positive impact, in part because it will increase the chances of success for other educational initiatives when the children are older. With this in mind, Heckman stressed that interventions in nursery schools from the age of three years onwards already run the risk of being too late due to their decreasing effectiveness.[4]

This basic idea that early investments in young people have the greatest possible influence has since been elaborated into what is now known as the Heckman curve (see Figure 4.2).

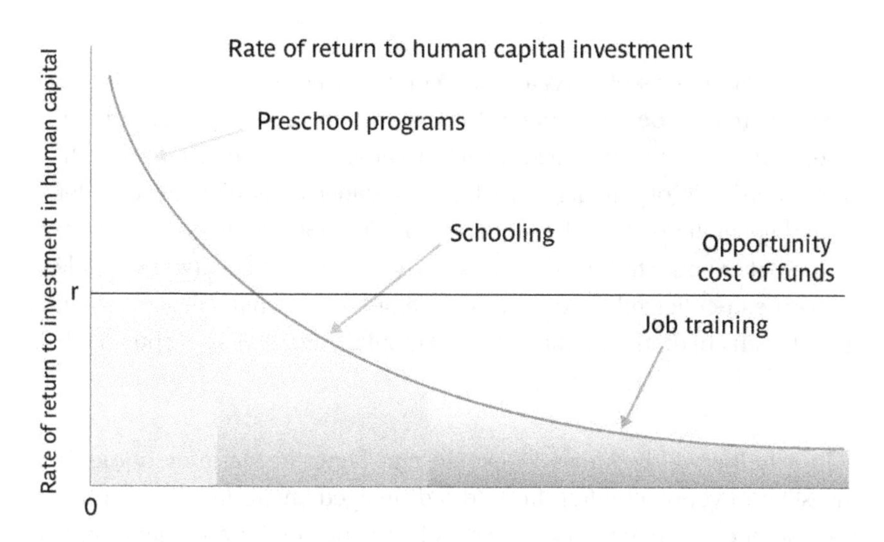

Figure 4.2 Human Capital Investment.
Source: Based on Carneiro & Heckman, 2003.

Having examined social inequality in depth, Cunha and Heckman reached the conclusion that the gulf between children from difference socio-economic backgrounds has already been firmly established before the child first attends school.[5] The skill level of a child younger than five is highly correlated with certain family related factors such as the parents' educational level.[6] What's more, the gap between children from different environments is not only noticeable, but is also a lasting one.[7] The family circumstances in which children grow up, therefore, have an important impact on the development of the skills of those children both in terms of nature (via genetic factors) and nurture (via environmental factors). What's more, within this context nature and nurture can have a considerable effect on each other, which can be strengthened positively or negatively, depending on the situation.

30 Million Words

The 30 Million Words initiative[8] launched by Professor Dana Suskind (University of Chicago), based on research by Betty Hart and Todd Risley, has demonstrated that some children – particularly those from deprived backgrounds and/or neighborhoods – have heard 30 million fewer and less varied words than children from better areas by the time they're four years old.[9] As a result, children who hear more and different words are better prepared to deal with the challenges of primary education. This latter group, which was followed in the research until the third year of primary school, have a wider vocabulary, read better and generally perform better at school. The bottom line seems to be: the better your start in life, the better your future. Recently, this study has been criticized,[10] but its basic premise of a significant skill deficit between children from different backgrounds still seems indisputable.[11]

In a further study, James Heckman and Dimitriy Masterov argued that investing in young children from 'disadvantaged environments' can have a positive effect in many areas, such as less contact with criminality in later life and fewer drop-outs from secondary education. In other words, early investment can help to counteract some of the hereditary drawbacks that many of these children face.[12]

Heckman has been repeatedly challenged for the narrowness of the evidence which he uses to make these claims. Heckman and Masterov only studied a number of relatively small projects from the 1960s and 1970s (i.e., the High/Scope Perry Pre-school Project, the Carolina Abecedarian Project, the Chicago Child-Parent Centers), so that it's unclear to what extent valid generalizations can be made and, in particular, whether their conclusions can be scaled up as a basis for wider educational policy.[13]

Right or Wrong? The Arguments

Heckman gives fifteen arguments for investing in the early formation of the minds of very young children which can be grouped into three broad groups, as specified by researchers like Doyle, Knudsen and even Heckman himself[14]:

- arguments based on avoiding high-risk factors in children from families with a low socio-economic status (SES);
- arguments based on developmental and neuroscientific research; and
- technological and economic arguments.

With regard to high-risk factors, Heckman and Masterov describe how children from a low SES background generally have poorer health, not only in terms of poor levels of illness prevention but also in terms of the severity of any illnesses contracted. In their eyes, this can be attributed to both genetic and environmental factors. What's more, this can continue to have an impact in adulthood. Similarly, children from low SES families also score lower than average on tests of verbal and cognitive performance and higher than average for emotional and behavioral problems. In particular, the influence of the mother on the upbringing of the child appears to play a crucial role in the child's development, as does the presence or absence of books and other learning materials in the home. Though the sources used by Doyle and his colleagues to substantiate these claims date from the 1990s, more recent studies have reached the same general conclusions. Fernald and colleagues have found that the difference in SES has a clear effect on vocabulary, with children from lower SES families already falling six months behind the average at age two.[15] A 2011 overview study by Walker and colleagues published in *The Lancet*, confirmed the existence of a number of risks faced more frequently by children from lower SES families including slower physical growth, greater likelihood of exposure to lead with its resulting cognitive and physical problems (usually due to old lead plumbing or peeling lead-painted walls), greater likelihood of exposure to violence, etc. Shonkoff and colleagues described how what they called 'toxic stress' at an early age can have an enormous influence on later learning development and the functioning of the individual.[16]

If we examine the second group of developmental and neuroscientific arguments, Heckman and his various co-authors make clear that the results are primarily indicative, rather than conclusive. Although researchers no longer speak of critical periods, preferring instead to refer to sensitive periods, and although Heckman tends to use both terms interchangeably, this is an area where he again probably has a point. The theory of the critical period has now been accepted by many researchers as no more than a myth.[17] To date, it has not been possible to identify and substantiate the existence of any critical period for human learning, in the sense that if you don't learn something during that particular critical period, you will never be able to learn it. In contrast, there is plenty of evidence to support the idea of sensitive periods for learning, periods when learning is easier. But this is not to say that it's no longer possible to learn effectively at a later age. At birth, children are able to distinguish all the many different sounds around them. However, this capability already begins to deteriorate between their sixth and twelfth month of life.[18] This explains, for example, why Japanese people, as they get older, find it harder to differentiate between the 'l' and the 'r' sounds. In other words, in terms of learning it's not a matter of 'later is impossible', but rather 'later is more difficult'. While it remains true that for learning many things the old adage 'the earlier, the better' still applies, but the idea that it's too late once a certain period in your life has passed is too pessimistic. Much has been written over the plasticity of the human brain, and it's certainly beneficial for our learning capabilities at any age.[19] In this context, recent research has once again opened the door to the prospect of inducing sensitive periods of learning later in life by the use of medication. This could mean that the cost for interventions to stimulate, for example, later second or third language learning might fall significantly if this learning becomes easier for older learners.[20]

Other studies, such as a study by Shonkoff and colleagues, also confirm the positive effects of early interventions but there are other reasons to start early. Hanson and colleagues described how stress during the early years of life can lead to negative behavior later. Kim and colleagues have shown how stress caused by poverty can affect brain development. Skoe and colleagues[21] put forward a neurological model to explain how lack of stimulation at an early age can have a lasting impact on learning in later life, within the framework of which they showed that the difference in vocabulary richness identified by Fernald and colleagues can also have implications in terms of development.[22]

When considering all these findings, it's important to note that the researchers – Hanson and colleagues are particularly clear on this point – do not regard their outcomes as deterministic or all-decisive. It's more a matter of the previously mentioned difference between critical and sensitive learning periods. The increased likelihood of a negative impact due to less positive environmental factors during one's early years, take for example brain development, doesn't mean that these children are doomed to ignorance and that they are incapable of making up any lost ground in later years. It's probably more difficult and therefore, in terms of Heckman's reasoning, 'more expensive', but it's not impossible.

The technological and economic arguments in this debate focus on Heckman's claim that each learning phase of life requires the right support. This is what he calls 'a multi-stage technology', which, as a result of further research, we know yields more benefits for children from families with a low SES than for children from families with a higher SES.[23] Heckman's technological arguments also imply a need to monitor early investment in young children.

Heckman supports his belief in the importance of multi-stage technology and, above all, the importance of early investment by referring (amongst other things) to the previously mentioned successful programs of the 1960s and 1970s in the US where these investments positively affected young children. Since then, there have been many other examples across the globe of similar projects where positive effects were generated, in some cases even by offering parents support *before* childbirth. In Jamaica, for example, researchers noted positive effects of providing psycho-social support to the parents of pre-school children. This intervention consisted of two one-hour visits over a period of two weeks. During these visits, the parents were given advice about parenting and the mothers were encouraged to play with their children in a way that would stimulate the child's cognitive and personal development. Twenty years after this randomized intervention took place, the researchers went back to the participants. They discovered that the average income of the participants in the study was 42% higher than that of the control group. The focus on supporting the bond between parents and child (especially in families with a low SES) has also been shown to be beneficial in the United Kingdom.[24]

On the basis of a cohort study in the United States, Claessens and colleagues concluded that even greater benefits could be gained from nursery school if the level of the linguistic and mathematical education was challenging.[25] In contrast, an evaluation of various initiatives relating to pre-school and early school education in the Netherlands conducted by researchers at the Radboud University revealed that these initiatives later yielded no real gain for cognitive skills such as language and arithmetic.[26]

Rather than looking at the results of individual studies or countries, it's sometimes more interesting to examine the review studies in which these various national findings are scientifically compared. For example, in 2010 Nores and Barnett investigated 56 scientific studies involving a total of 30 interventions aimed at young children in twenty-three countries (all outside the United States). Their aim was to establish what gains had been achieved, if any, with respect to cognitive development, behavior, health, and schooling.[27] They concluded that in each of these domains lasting benefits could be demonstrated, although the effect of these benefits – which is greater in countries with a strong economy – decreases over time. In similar fashion, Camilli and his colleagues[28] examined 123 different studies to assess the influence of early intervention programs in the United States, with an emphasis on pre-school interventions involving children before they go to nursery school. They too concluded that there were clear positive effects of early intervention, particularly with regard to cognitive development, but also, once again, with a diminishing return as the years pass. Both studies underlined the importance of continued support. A further (non-peer reviewed) report by the RAND Corporation studied comparable interventions in Europe and came to the conclusion that such programs could be a useful instrument for reducing inequality, although it was conceded that the results suggested that significant differences between individual programs and countries would remain.[29]

Perhaps self-evidently, all the studies recorded that the programs need to be of high quality to achieve the best results. But what exactly does this mean? Examination of the review studies suggests the following key characteristics:

- The importance of direct instruction. Here the researchers observed differences over time, but this is in keeping with the findings of other studies into the importance of direct instruction for children with a learning deficit.[30]
- The importance of more individual instruction.
- Camilli and colleagues found (to their amazement) that programs offering extra services, such as family support, achieved poorer results. One explanation might be that these extra services 'use up' time that might otherwise be devoted specifically to learning.
- Nores and Barnett concluded that programs focussing on direct care or on education or both have the greatest effect, with the educational component being particularly important.
- A specific focus on a specific age group can also have an added value.

As far as this last characteristic is concerned, Nores and Barnett (along with some of the other review studies) noted that there is significant room for improvement in the quality of the research methodology, above all with regard to the need for clear and unambiguous indicators or points of comparison.

Some Educational Reservations

The perceived importance of direct instruction and the strong emphasis on the educational component in the review studies may be off-putting for many people. Likewise, arguments favoring lowering the starting age for nursery school or setting of the bar in language and arithmetic higher might have a similar effect.[31]

Wilna Meijer has identified what she sees as a double tendency in thinking about schooling; namely, that education is currently confronted with the dual processes of 'deschooling' or 'unschooling' and what could be described as a 'scholarization' making it more school-like. With 'deschooling', Meijer not only refers to the many extra tasks that teachers are now expected to perform, but also – like Biesta[32] (among others) – to the shift away from formal 'schooling' towards more individual 'learning'. This latter phenomenon applies primarily to children at a later age, while during the early toddler and nursery school period young children are becoming increasingly more school-like.[33]

Bearing all these findings and recommendations in mind, it's possible (with little ill will) to imagine that children from families with a low SES are almost being 'punished' for their situation by sending them at a very early age to school or to a more school-like environment. Direct instruction, as mentioned earlier, is indeed more effective than, say, discovery-based learning, and certainly for children from families with a low SES, but the general well-being associated with this approach is significantly less. The emphasis is often placed on cognitive development, specifically on language and arithmetic. And while we've just demonstrated that this results in increased effectiveness, the other side of the coin might be, for example, that the time available for play and more informal elements comes under increasing pressure.[34]

Arguments in favor of the importance of playing and of allowing 'children to be children' may sound 'romantic', but these aspects have been shown to have a clear added value. Other informal activities, such as the combination of play with music can benefit spatial awareness and listening skills.[35]

Focusing on Parents?

Whereas the different interventions considered so far generally revolve around programs that can support alleviating or making good the deficiencies of the young child's environment, recent work by Mullainathan and Shafir argues that the elimination of the cares and worries created by poverty can also be an important way to further stimulate the development of children and can perhaps help to compensate for (or at least offset) the consequences of the pedagogic reservations discussed above.[36] In this context, for example, Newman and colleagues found a positive connection between the availability of affordable housing and the cognitive development of young infants.[37] The 'mental bandwidth' of parents that might otherwise be consumed by worrying about how to pay the rent or the mortgage is now free to be spent on supporting their offspring. Children quickly notice when their parents are under stress and – as mentioned earlier – the presence of stress during the earliest years of life can have a lasting impact on the development of the brain (amongst other things).[38]

In 2011, Sendhil Mullainathan and Saugato Datta wrote an essay on good parenting that emphasized this point.[39] According to them, there was only one certainty about parenting: if you are inattentive, unengaged and inconsistent, you will not be a good parent. Sadly, this kind of negative behavior is more frequently found in families with low incomes. Why this is so is a matter for much (and often heated) discussion. Many of the proposed solutions in the professional literature (and beyond) focus on skills learning that can help correct this negative behavior. Mullainathan and Datta suggest that the focus might be better placed elsewhere[40]:

> Good parenting requires psychic resources. Complex decisions must be made. Sacrifices must be made in the moment. This is hard for anyone, whatever their income: we all have limited reserves of self-control, and attention and other psychic resources. [...]
>
> Low-income parents, however, also face a tax on their psychic resources. Many things that are trifling and routine to the well-off give sleepless nights to those less fortunate. To take a simple example, everyone may face the same bank overdraft fees – but steering clear of them is pretty easy for the well-off, while for the poor it requires constant attention, steely reserve and enormous amounts of self-control. For the well-off, monthly bills are automatically deducted and there is still some slack left over. For those with less income, finding ways to ensure that rent, utilities and phone bills are paid for out of small, irregular paychecks is an act of complicated financial jugglery.

The researchers argue that every program that seeks to assist low income families in their educational task is doomed to failure as long as the everyday stress associated with that low income is not eliminated or at least reduced: 'So, what does it take to be a good parent? Freedom of mind. And that is a luxury low-income parents often cannot afford.' As a result, investing in situations in which the bond between the child and the parents is optimally strengthened and the negative influences are limited to a minimum can lead directly to lower levels of early school dropout.[41]

But Is It Really a Curve?

During the intervening years since his first publication, Heckman has added an important dimension to his curve. He has now come to the conclusion that the good early development of which he is such an exponent needs to be maintained and followed up by effective education stretching into adulthood. Taken together, this package of educational measures will create a better situation for people, which can only be of benefit to the economy and to society as a whole in the years ahead. This can be summarized in what is now known as the Heckman Equation: Invest + Develop + Sustain = Gain.

Conclusion: Nuanced

The Heckman curve suggests that investing in children as early as possible, preferably before they reach the age of three, offers the highest possible return on investment for educational resources. Heckman himself, however, now promotes the Heckman Equation, which, in addition to investment and development, has now added continued educational support to his recipe for success.

Is It a Good Idea to Put Children of Different Ages Together in the Same Class?

It's becoming an increasingly popular phenomenon: multi-age classes. The idea is not new and the reasons for putting children of different ages together in the same class are many and varied.

The Jena Plan and Multi-Grade Classes

Jena-plan education is based on the principle of mixed-grade classes. Peter Petersen, the father of this form of education, combined three different grades into a single class. He regarded this system as being comparable with the classic guild system of medieval times. In the first year, you are the youngest and least experienced member of the class (the apprentice). In the second year, you become familiar with everything and make progress in what you need to learn (the journeyman). Finally, in the third year you are the oldest and most experienced (the master), so that you perhaps have most right to speak in the discussions that form an essential part of the plan's learning process. Unfortunately, you then transfer to the next mixed-grade class, so that you become the youngest again ...[42]

Sometimes, multi-age classes are a matter of necessity; for example, when schools have a shortage of teachers, students and/or resources.[43] This is something that is becoming increasingly common nowadays in response to, among other things, demographic change and economic fluctuations. But whatever the reasons for introducing such classes, there are a number of things to be said in their favor:

- The classes reflect the increasing diversity of society.
- Lessons are no longer geared to the 'average' student, who happens by chance to be born in the same period as her or his classmates.
- It's easier to divide students into homogeneous or heterogeneous sub-groups.
- Students can receive lessons from the same teacher over a longer period, which makes it possible to build up a better relationship of trust.
- And so on ....[44]

The Relative Age Effect

Why are so many good soccer players born in the first half of the year?[45] Why are more children with ADHD born in the second half of the year?[46] Why are younger children in the same class more often referred for mental health issues?[47] This is known as the relative age effect (or, sometimes, the birth month effect). Children born early in the year can sometimes be almost a year older than some of their classmates who were born at the end of the year. If we take the football example, it's obvious that at a young age a physical difference of 12 months is important: the older children are generally bigger, stronger and faster. In theory, it should be less important for academic matters: a child born in November or December is not by definition 'less clever' than a child born in January or February. Even so, the effect is reflected in school results more often than you might think, which can be seen as a possible argument in favor of mixed-grade classes that focus less on student age. That being said, all is not lost for those with an autumn or winter birthday: research has also shown that children born later in the year score better when they get to university.[48]

But how effective are mixed-grade classes? This question has been investigated for a number of decades, but the results of the various meta-analyses are far from clear. The conclusions range from no effect in the research conducted by Veenman[49] to a slight negative effect.[50] It will therefore come as no surprise that the effect size for the combined meta-analyses calculated by John Hattie is just .04, which is significantly less than the effect size for average education (which ranges between .15 and .40).[51] On the basis of the same sources mentioned above, Hattie concludes that there is little reason to assume that mixed-grade classes would be more effective, most probably because the majority of teachers fail to adequately adjust their teaching approach to reflect the new situation. However, the previously cited work by Veenman does suggest that mixed-grade classes might at least have limited benefit in terms of general well-being and learning motivation.

Older research into mixed-grade classes seem primarily concerned with reassuring people that such classes will not hinder learning. This is very different from the arguments with which we started this section, which suggested that multi-age classes might actually improve learning. However, these arguments are based on sources that are even older, so that we are forced to conclude that the current state of research is far from optimal. Why? The reasons for setting up mixed-grade classes can be varied, which introduce a degree of distortion. The way in which the classes are set up can also vary. Moreover, it has become apparent over the years that this is a difficult theme to investigate with randomized controlled trials, while for many of the studies that have been completed there was no clear control group to validate the results.

Has the situation improved in recent decades? Might it not be the case that in a changing society mixed-grade classes are now more appropriate?

Maybe – although honesty compels us to say that the uncertainty evident in the older meta-analyses is still present today. In a research report published by the University of Leuven in 2016 reference was made to various recent studies, but the overall picture remains vague. Jaime Thomas[52] found no effects on performance when comparing single grade and mixed-grade classes for the third year of pre-school to the second year of primary school. Similarly, Wilkinson and Hamilton[53] found no effects at the primary school level. In contrast, Lindström and Lindahl[54] found a significant negative effect at the upper primary level. Mariano and Kirby[55] likewise identified a negative effect in multi-year classes in the second grade of primary education. Differential effects have not yet been sufficiently investigated, although Leuven and Rønning[56] found that multi-age classes can sometimes be positive for the youngest children in the group, whereas this way of grouping tends to be negative for their oldest classmates. Guo and colleagues[57] also identified positive effects for the vocabulary of preschoolers, with the effect again being greatest for the youngest children in the class and almost negligible for the older ones.[58]

Following the appearance of the Leuven report in 2016, additional research has been published but the trends remain largely unaltered, with further supporting evidence for a more negative than positive effect for older children.[59]

The discussion about the value or otherwise of mixed-grade classes is unlikely to die down. Various possible advantages and disadvantages have been named by the proponents of the different sides of the argument, but the essence of the situation remains that to date the only positive learning effect has been identified amongst the youngest students in a class, but often at the expense of a negative impact on the older ones. Mixed-grade classes are, as mentioned, sometimes unavoidable as an 'emergency' solution for a particular set of circumstances. It's therefore comforting to know that the research, in general, suggests that this can do little real harm. But actively encouraging mixed-grade classes as a preferred solution for various educational challenges is, at best, questionable. In the absence of systematically researched evidence, the advantages found are often anecdotal and theoretical.

Conclusion: Nuanced

Dick Clark's research on the use of media in education in 1983 made apparent that it was not the medium that made a difference, but the method.[60] Much the same is true of mixed-grade classes: it's not the system that is important; but rather the way the teacher implements the system. (S)he is the primary reason for any differences in the effects of mixed-grade classes in relation to single grade classes. It should be noted, however, that here we are talking explicitly about student performance and not about student socialization and other matters, which were the pedagogic aspects that the pioneers of mixed-grade classes, like Peter Petersen, had more in mind.

Does More (Lesson) Time Mean More Learning?

A former British Minister of Education, Michael Gove, is just one of those who argue in favor of extending the length of the school day in an effort to raise the standard of education.[61] It sounds logical: give children more hours of lessons and they'll learn more. The OECD also seems to be saying much the same thing in one of its PISA in Focus reports.[62] As is so often the case, however, reality is much more complex.

Difficult to Research

We've already noted in the section of our previous book dealing with the influence of class size on learning that PISA only provides insights into certain correlations, without establishing evidence for causal relationships. As a result, and on the basis of a comparison between different countries and their total number of lesson hours – not only in PISA but also in the TIMSS (Trends in Mathematics and Science Study) and PIRLS (Progress in International Reading Literacy Study) studies, which investigated how well a particular country or region performs – all we can say is that there is a connection between more hours and more learning. We cannot, however, say with certainty that more hours lead to more learning. The OECD claims to have identified such a connection in its report, but that connection is far from clear and unambiguous. It's certainly true that in many good performing regions the average number of lesson hours is higher, but this does not necessarily always go hand in hand with better student performance. More lessons with bad teachers or poor educational practices can actually lead to the opposite result.

For his analysis for the Dutch Central Bureau of Statistics, Mark Groen also used PISA data, but he examined it from the perspective of economic educational efficiency. An educational system of a country becomes more efficient when the costs of education, corrected for (amongst other things) differences in purchasing power, are lower and its score in international tests (in this case PISA) are higher. Groen's analysis showed that efficient educational countries actually tend to have fewer hours of lessons.[63] Of course, this kind of reasoning can be dangerous, because it does not look at how well a particular country or region performs in absolute figures, but simply compares that performance with the financial investment needed to achieve it. A country that spends next to nothing on education and achieves moderate performance may be labeled 'more efficient' than a country that proportionally spends much more and records significantly higher scores in the PISA comparison.

That being said, the efficiency reasoning is not wholly without validity, since it makes clear that what happens *during* the lessons is also important – perhaps even more important than the total number of hours of teaching. And we know from various other studies (see, for example, the earlier section on the 10,000 hour rule) that practice and repetition outside of formal lessons are also crucial for improving overall performance.

What Happens If Countries Introduce More Hours of Lessons?

An interesting but perhaps more difficult way to investigate this question is to increase the number of lesson hours and see if it has a positive effect. This is what occurred in Mexico. Unfortunately for those who hold that more hours are better, the results were disappointing:

- There was hardly any learning gain.
- The divide between 'poor' and 'rich' students was widened.[64]

Germany experienced something similar. When the country scored poorly in the first PISA results published in 2000, the government responded with various measures designed to correct the situation, including a lengthening of the school day. In this context, it needs to be noted that before this change students in Germany often had relatively short hours, not more than four hours on some days. Be that as it may, increasing the number of school hours was seen as an important factor in Germany's increasing good scores in subsequent international comparisons.[65] However, researchers who investigated precisely this element came to the conclusion that, on average, the learning gain was small and that, as in Mexico, the gap between students from rich and poor backgrounds grew significantly.[66]

How can this be explained? If all students are given more lessons, and in the case of Germany also new content, those from better environments in terms of SES will benefit more, because they have greater prior knowledge. Many studies have shown that children from such backgrounds have an advantage over their classmates from deprived backgrounds for a variety of reasons, including the higher educational level of their parents, a greater diversity of educational stimuli in the home, parents who talk more with them, and parents who are more inclined to help them with their homework.[67] It was these factors, for example, that led Dietrichson and colleagues to note that the introduction of almost any (linear) measure in education[68] will increase the 'rich-poor' divide, a divide that can only be reduced by giving more time specifically to the students who need it.[69] John Carroll established in 1963, that students differ in the amount of time they need to learn something.[70]

More Time For Lessons Also Means Less Time For Other Things

If children and adolescents spend a lot of time in school, they have less time for other activities. This is an educational dilemma worth mentioning, because there is evidence that 'doing something else' is also important for effective learning. For example, there is a clear link between taking regular breaks and better learning,[71] while the effectiveness of spaced practice and repetition with increasingly longer breaks has also been demonstrated.[72] Similarly, if children use their free time for physical activity, this also has a learning benefit.[73] This is equally true for getting enough sleep (too little sleep results in poorer learning).[74] Even having a good breakfast impacts learning potential![75]

Conclusion: Nuanced

:-|

More lesson time can lead to more learning if, as was the case in Germany, the initial number of lesson hours is relatively low. But more time does not automatically lead to more learning. If all students are given more lessons, there is a danger that the gap between rich and poor students will increase. For this reason, it's better to target any extra available time on the children who need it most. Equally, we must remember that hours spent away from school also have a positive impact on learning, so that significantly reducing the number of such hours is not necessarily a good thing.

Do Teachers Make a Difference?

When compiling the list of myths we wanted to discuss in this book, in part we were guided by the matters most frequently raised in recent years on our blogs and in our lectures. One of the most popular claims is that 'teachers make all the difference' and it can sometimes be painful when we need to confront people with the honest question: 'Is that really the case?' Hence the reason for this section.

A Consequence of Effectiveness Research?

In a speech in 2015, Frans Janssens explained why the statement 'The teacher is the most important factor in a student's school career' is a myth. He argued that this popular idea developed as a consequence of growing attention to effectiveness research in education.[76] And he is right: this kind of research does highlight the impact of teachers and their actions on learning performance.[77] Of course, it's equally true that good teachers do play an important role, a point regularly emphasized by popular writers and researchers in evidence-based education such as John Hattie and Robert Marzano. But are teachers the most decisive factor in learning success?

If you look at the following well-known graphic (see Figure 4.3) included by Hattie in his book *Teachers Make a Difference. What is the Research Evidence?* you can see that there is someone else who is even more crucial.[78]

This may well be true, if you look, for example, at the results of twin research into the extent to which heredity can explain differences in school results, which concluded that it accounted for 58% of the difference in core subjects (such as language and mathematics), although this varied from subject to subject.[79] It's important to note, however, that this is something that is notoriously difficult to accurately assess. Heredity often determines the upper and lower limits of a person's potential, but it is that person's

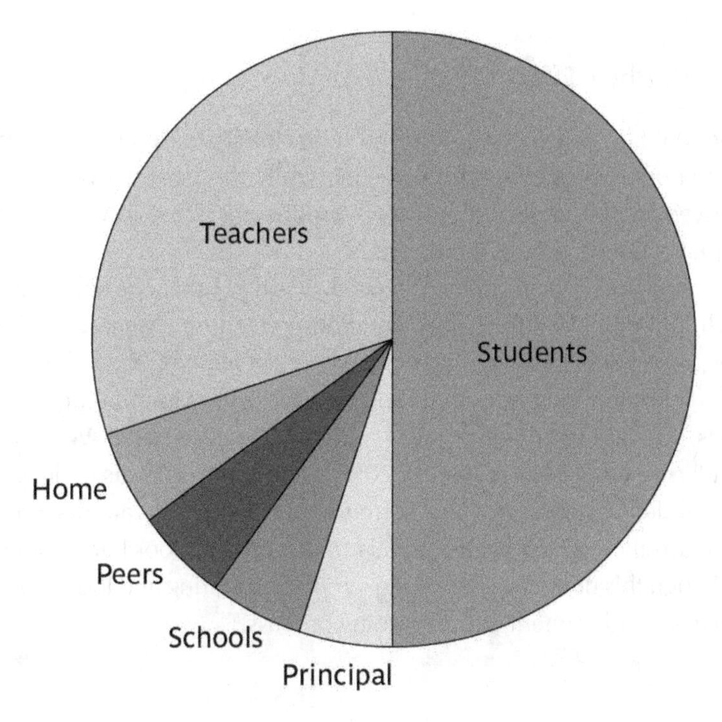

Figure 4.3 Relative contribution to learning.
Source: Hattie, 2003.

environment which then determines how and what level the person will develop between those limits.[80]

If we look at the share allocated to teachers in this process, it tends to average out at around 30% (a ballpark figure also mentioned in various sources).[81] However, there are reasons to assume that this percentage, if anything, overestimates teacher influence. To begin with, there are many relevant factors that they are simply unable to influence, such as the genetic make-up of their students and their home situations.

What they can influence – and do influence to an important degree – is the percentages themselves, with Hattie as a case in point. How they organize and give their lessons can have a significant effect. Some teachers can work wonders in closing the gap between students from rich and poor environments, reversing the Matthew effect that is frequently found in education.[82] Moreover, the teachers, together with their headmasters/principals and school boards, also have a huge influence on the learning climate. So yes, teachers do play an important role, but...

The Matthew Effect

The Matthew effect is a term used in sociology to describe the phenomenon of how the rich get richer, while the poor get poorer. It's derived from a verse in the Bible – Matthew 25:29 – in which Jesus explains the parable of the talents.[83]

In education, the term is often used, amongst others by Keith Stanovich,[84] to describe the phenomenon observed during research of how people develop their reading skills when first learning to read. People who learn to read easily from an early age will read more and more texts, so that they practice more and become even better. With poor readers, the opposite is true. In 2017, Dietrichson and his colleagues concluded that many of the current practices in education serve to increase the gap between students from rich and poor backgrounds, although this does not apply, for example, to tutoring and the resulting necessary adjustment of the learning process.[85]

More Complex than You Think

Focusing on percentages of this kind can soon lead to difficulties, because everything affects everything else. It's easiest to demonstrate this by using a concrete example.

The graph in Figure 4.4 illustrates the difference in the effect of inexperienced teachers and experienced teachers on learning performance in mathematics.[86]

The problem is that the effect of an inexperienced teacher can vary, not only from teacher to teacher, but also from class to class and from student to student. In particular, the effect can be different on children from families with a lower SES: they can experience more negative effects from less good or less experienced teachers. Yet even if you argue that the quality of the teacher is more important than the SES of the student for learning, as is the case with Ken Rowe,[87] this argument is no longer relevant if you know – as research has confirmed – that in most countries it's precisely these least experienced teachers who are most likely to end up teaching those poorer students.[88]

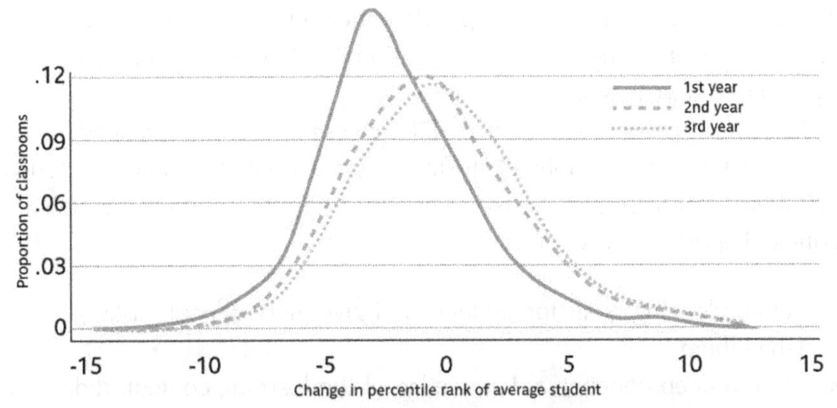

Note: Classroom-level impacts on average student performance, controlling for baseline scores, student demographics, and program participation. LAUSD elementary teachers, < 4 years' experience.

Figure 4.4

Source: Gordon, Kane, & ... Staiger, 2006

In other words, this example of the influence of teaching experience on mathematics learning brings together the following elements:

- The experience of the teachers.
- The SES of the student's home background, which for children from poorer families increases the likelihood of being taught by inexperienced teachers.
- The school policy or, in wider terms, the educational policy that makes it possible for these less experienced teachers to be allocated to poorer children.

And this is before we even start thinking about the impact of genetic factors, which, irrespective of socio-economic factors, unquestionably have a major impact on learning performance in mathematics, so that there can be large learning differences amongst children from both poor *and* rich backgrounds. To say which of these factors has the greatest effect is difficult, because they interact with each other in so many different ways. For example, if you look at the question about who influences a student's learning, you quickly run up against further questions about which aspects of the learning process can be influenced and which cannot. This tends to turn the focus onto teachers and can lead to unrealistic pressure, because it confronts them with so many problematical elements about which they can do nothing (home situation, educational policy, etc.), yet they are still expected to find a solution.[89]

But there is more. There are also differences between experienced teachers and expert teachers. John Hattie investigated this matter[90] and concluded that there are no fewer than sixteen points of difference, three of which are critical. Expert teachers:

- Set challenging goals for students and give them difficult tasks to challenge them.
- Have a deep conceptual knowledge of the learning content, didactics, and how people learn. As a consequence, their knowledge is better organised and they're better able to transfer and explain the connections between new content and students' pre knowledge. They're also better at connecting learning content with other topics in the curriculum.
- Are better at monitoring problems that students have and give them more relevant and useful feedback.

These are the three characteristics that separate the teaching wheat from the chaff.

Conclusion: Nuanced

Do teachers really make the difference? The evidence suggests that even if high quality teachers do not necessarily make 'the' difference, they can certainly make an important difference. Consequently, this section is not an excuse for teachers to:

- lose hope;
- no longer do their best; or
- think that they do not have a positive impact.

It's important for policy-makers who like to say that 'teachers make the difference' to be aware that they themselves also have an impact on the situation, which in turn can either increase or reduce the impact of the teachers.

Can Students Correctly Assess the Quality of Their Teachers?

Constantly assessing one another has become an integral part of our modern way of life, from TripAdvisor® to tinder®. And for some people this is also the best way to improve the quality of our education: employ only good teachers and get rid of the bad ones. In fact, research has already been carried out into the positive effect that good teachers can have on the learning of their students in comparison with bad and/or mediocre teachers.[91] This is known as 'teacher added value'. Of course, it's also possible to ask the 'customers' themselves – the students – what they think about the men and women who teach them. But would that really be such a good idea?

Shall We Ask the Students?

While teachers have been evaluating students for a long, long time, it's only more recently that we've seen the emergence of the trend for allowing the students to assess their teachers. What's more, both in the selection and in the assessment of teachers, this kind of subjective judgment is playing an increasingly important role. Rightly or wrongly?

In 2016, Uttl, White and Gonzalez conducted a meta-study of the available research on this very theme, with the aim of establishing how accurately students were able to assess the quality of their teachers. To do this, they compared the student assessments with the actual effectiveness of the teachers involved.[92] Are teachers who help students to learn better judged as being better by those same students? Uttl and his colleagues concluded that there is hardly any correlation between student assessments and what they learn: just .03, which in statistical terms is effectively zero. The researchers commented:

> The entire notion that we could measure professors' teaching effectiveness by simple ways such as asking students to answer a few questions about their perceptions of their course experiences, instructors' knowledge, and the like seems unrealistic ... students do not learn more from professors with higher SETs (Student Evaluation of Teaching).

Of course, this does not mean that students will necessarily learn less from higher rated teachers or vice versa for more poorly rated teachers, but it does mean that there is no causal relationship. After all, this – as the researchers themselves point out – is not wholly illogical: it's easy to imagine students enjoying an entertaining lesson in which the learning content is minimal or non-existent. This is an important point. In a 2017 study Uttl and Smibert argued that it's both unfair and dishonest to use this kind of unreliable system of measurement as a basis to determine (in part, at least) the careers of teachers.[93] It's an argument that continues to be relevant, since new research published since the meta-analysis has shown that the problem still exists.[94]

But is this anything new? Twenty years ago, Krautman and Sander[95] investigated the relationship between student grades and teacher assessments and concluded that the assessments closely reflected the grades that the students expected to get. As a result, Krautman spoke of teachers 'buying' more favorable assessments by being generous in the awarding of good grades, resulting in 'grade inflation' – students being awarded increasingly more points for the same level of performance. A 2016 review by Kornell and Hausman seemed to confirm this.[96] They found that the students of high scoring teachers scored better at the end of a series of lessons with that teacher, but that an examination of improved learning ability, measured in terms of performance in a subsequent series of lessons in a follow-up subject, showed that it was often teachers with a relatively low score from their students who achieved better learning results.

To find a possible explanation for this, we need to go even further back into research history. In 1972, Rodin and Rodin published an article in the respected journal *Science* about the relationship between subjective and objective measurements for determining what makes a good teacher.[97] In their study, the three teachers who received the lowest (anonymous) subjective scores also received the highest objective scores (based on empirical measurement of how much their students learned). The researchers suggested that the reason for this is possibly that students dislike teachers who make them work (too?) hard to achieve results; in other words, harder than the students wanted to work. The authors concluded: 'If how much students learn is considered to be a major component of good teaching, it must be concluded that good teaching is not validly measured by student evaluations.'

Perceived 'overworking' is just one factor that can influence student assessments. Uttl and Smibert found that teachers who teach subjects involving more mathematical calculations are often assessed more harshly. The previously mentioned meta-analysis by Uttl and colleagues also established that assessments are sometimes influenced by the gender of the teacher.[98] A series of tests showed that female teachers are often evaluated differently (i.e. score lower) than their male colleagues. This contention was confirmed by more recent research.[99] In a study in an online environment (where it was not possible to visually identify the teacher's gender), teachers who were identified as 'male' received better assessments than those identified as 'female' – even if the teacher was a woman in both cases!

Of course, nowadays there are plenty of online sites, such as RateMyProfessor.com, where thousands of students can evaluate their teachers and professors. Andrew Rosen has analyzed the huge mountain of data available from this site and again reached the conclusion that female educators often receive significantly poorer assessments than the men, although this can vary from discipline to discipline. Reflecting the Uttl and Smibert findings, Rosen also discovered that the teachers of science subjects (mathematics, physics, etc) are more severely assessed than teachers of other subjects.

Conclusion: Myth

If we look at the actual learning return, student evaluations say little about the quality of their teachers.

Is It a Good Idea to Pay More to the Better Teachers?

It sounds so logical: Pay good teachers more, so that all teachers will be encouraged to improve their teaching. At the same time, there are those who regard this suggestion as too 'neo-liberal', while others say that it's no more than a 'zombie' idea: an idea that has been repeatedly refuted by the evidence but simply refuses to die. So is merit pay a good idea or not? There are two main problems.

What Is a Good Teacher and, More Importantly, How Do You Recognize Her/Him?

In theory, it's simple: sack the bad teachers and pay the remaining good ones more. But in practice, it's not as easy as it sounds to separate the good from the bad.[100] We've just seen how hard it is for students to assess their teachers effectively. And it's not much easier for the rest of us.

Dylan Wiliam has summarized the complexities of the situation:

- The level of teacher performance varies. Good teachers have bad days and bad teachers have good days. So bearing this in mind, how do you decide when to assess and how often to assess?
- Context is crucial. Teachers will seem to be much better at their job if they are giving lessons to a class of motivated students or students from better socio-economic backgrounds. However, according to Wiliam, it's almost impossible to tell the difference between a group of motivated students receiving bad lessons and a group of unmotivated students receiving good lessons.
- Teacher performance in class does not necessarily equate with learning. If lessons are hard, requiring effort from students to complete them, they are more likely to remember the lesson content longer. It's therefore perfectly possible that a seemingly smooth and efficient lesson will have a lower long-term learning effect, while a lesson that gives rise to a degree of confusion, which can only be clarified after considerable effort, will have a higher long-term learning effect.[101]

How Often Do You Need to Observe a Teacher to Get a Reliable Picture of Her/His Ability?

In 2012, Hill and colleagues calculated how often teachers need to be observed to get a valid and reliable impression of their level of performance. Although the researchers advised caution when dealing with their recommendations, they nevertheless suggested a minimum of six observed lessons, each viewed by five qualified observers.[102] But that was the easy part. The hard part was the subsequent necessity to develop and validate an evaluation protocol. So how exactly do you decide what makes a good teacher?

Of course, it's always possible to use standard tests to measure how much learning added-value a teacher generates. This involves testing students both before and after a given period of learning. These VAM (Value-Added Measures) tests are very popular in the United States, but are contentious and of doubtful reliability. More important (in a negative sense), they reduce teaching to the level of mere qualifications, whereas education needs to be about so much more (for example, socialization and personal development).[103]

And if the weight attached to these tests increases – if, for example, they help to determine the level of your salary – the possibility of fraud becomes more likely.[104]

But Does It Work?

Merit pay is also a subject of much discussion outside the educational field. Research suggests that it has hardly any effect on the performance of managers in the public sector, other than to increase the level of staff dissatisfaction. Or to put it another way: it sounds like a great idea but it seldom, if ever, seems to work.[105] Ryan and Deci's self-determination theory seeks to offer an alternative to this kind of motivation scheme, which actually takes us back to the era of the behaviorist 'carrot and stick' approach.[106] Dan Pink built further on this idea in his book *Drive*, where he essentially suggested that rewards can only work when tasks are fairly uniform and require little creativity. As soon as tasks demand something more of the people completing them, this type of simplistic reward system can even have a negative effect.[107]

In recent years, the merit pay theme has also been researched extensively in education. A 2007 review concluded that the problems which every sector encounters with regard to merit pay would be no different in the field of education, notwithstanding the fact that there were a limited number of studies suggesting a possible positive effect.[108] But how big is that effect likely to be? A meta-analysis from 2017 quotes a figure of just .05.[109] Hattie recorded a comparable effect in 2015[110] and repeated it in his updated list, also published in 2017.[111] Moreover, the different sources indicate that even this limited effect is dependent on the way in which the merit pay is organized. In particular, the perception of the system as being 'fair' is crucial.[112] Even then, there is still a number of negative aspects that need to be considered. The system can put added pressure on collaboration between different members of staff[113] and can also potentially make it more difficult to keep some teachers on board. For example, a teacher who helps another teacher to give better lessons may later find her- or himself disadvantaged, if the merit pay 'cake' needs to be divided amongst more good teachers. At the end of the day, however, the fundamental problem still remains: How on earth do you decide what makes a good teacher?

Merit Pay Based on Level of Attendance?

Dylan Wiliam offers an example of merit pay that might work, although it's more in keeping with the ideas of Ryan and Deci and Dan Pink. The wages of teachers in a randomized controlled trial at Seva Mandir, a non-governmental organization in India, was linked to their level of attendance. It was decided to focus on attendance because in rural parts of the country as many as a third of all teachers regularly fail to turn up for work. To confirm their teachers' presence, the students were issued cameras that allowed them to photograph the teachers in the morning and again in the evening. The teachers in the control group received a fixed wage of 1,000 rupees per month. The wages of the teachers in the intervention group were based purely on attendance. If the teacher was only present for ten days or less, (s)he received a salary for that month of just 500 rupees. For every day of attendance over and above ten days, (s)he received an additional 50 rupees per day. The results of the trial demonstrated that this method of remuneration had a hugely positive impact on overall attendance, with the added bonus that student learning also improved, because the number of lesson hours significantly increased. This is hardly surprising. If there is no teacher, there is no instruction; if there is no instruction, there is no learning – or at least it becomes very difficult. This was also evident in other research projects where the amount of study time was not monitored. The more someone studies, the greater the likelihood that this someone will learn more. This means that the effect of an intervention can actually be attributed to the fact of 'more studying', and not to the intervention itself. Wiliam argues – correctly in our opinion – that this approach does not run contrary to the insights of, for example, Dan Pink, because it relates to a simple matter of behavior: making the effort to attend. The question is to what extent this approach can be applied in other places where there is not such a problem with the absence of teachers.[114]

Conclusion: Myth

:-\

Although some people think the idea sounds logical, and although from time to time merit pay systems appear that seem to be successful, the average effect is very limited. It hardly seems worth the effort when confronted with the potential disadvantages and the inevitable stumbling block of how you decide who is a good teacher and who isn't.

Notes

1 Hanushek, 2011.
2 Also see Chetty, Friedman, & Rockoff, 2011.
3 Murawski & Lee Swanson, 2001.
4 Heckman, 2006.
Doyle, Harmon, Heckman, & Tremblay, 2009.
5 Cunha & Heckman, 2007.
6 Carneiro & Heckman, 2003.
7 Heckman, 2007.
8 https://cri.uchicago.edu/portfolio/thirty-million-words/www.lena.org/wp-content/uploads/2016/07/LENA-Conference-2013-Dana-Suskind.pdf.
9 Hart & Risley, 1995.
10 Sperry, Sperry, & Miller, 2018.
11 See, amongst others, the analysis by Daniel Willingham: www.danielwillingham.com/daniel-willingham-science-and-education-blog/the-debunking-of-hart-risley-and-how-we-use-science
12 Heckman & Masterov, 2007.
13 Heckman, 2013.
14 Heckman, 2008.
Knudsen, Heckman, Cameron, & Shonkoff, 2006.
Doyle,Harmon, Heckman, & Tremblay, 2009.
15 Fernald, Marchman, & Weisleder, 2013.
16 Walker, Wachs, Grantham-McGregor, Black, Nelson, Huffman, & Richter, 2011.
Shonkoff, Garner, Siegel, Dobbins, Earls, McGuinn, & Wood, 2012.
17 Something we've discussed in our previous book Urban Myths about Learning and Education
18 See, amongst others:
- Byrnes, 2001.
- Goswami, 2006.
19 See, amongst others:
- Byrnes, 2001.
- Pinker, 2003.
20 Gervain, Vines, Chen, Seo, Hensch, Werker, & Young, 2013.
21 Skoe, Krizman, & Kraus, 2013.

22 Heckman, Farah, & Meaney, 2010.
Hanson, Nacewicz, Sutterer, Cayo, Schaefer, Rudolph, & Davidson, 2015.
Kim, Evans, Angstadt, Ho, Sripada, Swain, Liberzon, & Phan, 2013.
23 Geoffroy, Côté, Borge, Larouche, Séguin, & Rutter, 2007.
24 Gertler, Heckman, Pinto, Zanolini, Vermeersch, Walker, & Grantham-McGregor, 2013.
Allen, 2011.
25 Claessens,Engel, & Curran, 2014.
26 Bruggers, Driessen, & Gesthuizen, 2014.
27 Nores & Barnett, 2010.
28 Camilli,Vargas, Ryan, & Barnett, 2010.
29 Guerin, 2014.
30 Hattie & Yates, 2013.
31 Veen, 2013.
32 For an overview: De Bruyckere, Struyf, & Kavadias, 2015b.
33 Meijer, 2013.
34 Miller & Almon, 2009
35 Jarvis, Newman, & Swiniarski, 2014.
Putkinen, Saarikivi, & Tervaniemi, 2013.
Oostermeijer, Boonen, & Jolles, 2014.
36 Mullainathan & Shafir, 2013.
37 Newman & Holupka, 2014.
38 Noble, Houston, Kan, & Sowell, 2012.
39 Mullainathan & Datta, 2011.
40 Mullainathan & Datta, 2011, p. 9.
41 Moullin, Waldfogel, & Washbrook, 2014.
42 Winters & Velthausz, 2014.
43 See, amongst others:
- Joubert, 2010.
- Joyce, 2014.

44 See:
- Masrifatin, 2016.
- Lindström & Lindahl, 2011. Klasse (2017). *Jaarklassen, weg ermee* (www.klasse.be/93172/jaarklassen-weg-ermee/).

45 See, amongst others:
- Dudink, 1994.
- Helsen, Van Winckel, & Williams, 2005.
- Musch & Grondin, 2001.

46 Sayal, Chudal, Hinkka-Yli-Salomäki, Joelsson, & Sourander, 2017.
47 Berg & Berg, 2014.
48 See, amongst others:
- Billari & Pellizzari, 2008.
- Roberts & Stott, 2015.

49 See:
- Veenman, 1995.
- Veenman, 1996.

50 Mason & Burns, 1996.
51 Hattie, 2009.
52 Thomas, 2012.

53 Wilkinson & Hamilton, 2003.
54 Lindström & Lindahl, 2011.
55 Mariano & Kirby, 2009.
56 Leuven & Rønning, 2011.
57 Guo, Tompkins, Justice, & Petscher, 2014.
58 Vandecandelaere, Van Den Branden, Juchtmans, Vandenbroeck, & De Fraine, 2016.
59 Ansari & Pianta, 2018.
60 Clark, 1983.
61 www.theguardian.com/politics/2013/apr/18/michael-gove-longer-school-day-holidays.
62 OECD, 2016.
63 Groen, 2015.
64 Agüero & Beleche, 2013.
65 Schleicher, 2017.
66 Huebener, Kuger, & Marcus, 2017.
67 American Psychological Association, *Education and Socio-economic Status* (www.apa.org/pi/ses/resources/publications/education.aspx). '10 theories on the relationship between socio-economic status & academic achievement' (www.teachthought.com/learning/10-theories-on-the-relationship-between-socioeconomic-status-and-academic-achievement/).
68 Linear measures are measures that are applied to everyone. For example, more lesson hours were imposed on students who didn't really need them.
69 Dietrichson, Bøg, Filges, & Klint Jørgensen, 2017.
70 Carroll, 1963.
71 See, amongst others:
   - Ashley & Pearson, 2012.
72 Benjamin & Tullis, 2010.
73 Hillman, Pontifex, Castelli, Khan, Raine, Scudder, Drolette, Moore, Chien-Ting, & Kamijo, 2014.
74 See, amongst others:
   - Chee & Choo, 2004.
   - Drummond & Brown, 2001.
   - Harrison & Horne, 2000.
   - Koslowsky & Babkoff, 1992.
   - Titova, Hogenkamp, Jacobsson, Feldman, Schiöth, & Benedict, 2015.
   - Thomas, Sing, Belenky, Holcomb, Mayberg, Dannals, Wagner, Thorne, Popp, Rowland, Welsh, Balwinski & Redmond, 2000.
75 Frisvold, 2015.
76 Janssens, 2015.
77 See, amongst others:
   - Brophy & Good, 1986.
   - Muijs, Kyriakides, van der Werf, Creemers, Timperley, & Earl, 2014.
78 Hattie, 2003.
79 See, amongst others:
   - Krapohl et al., 2014.
   - Shakeshaft, Trzaskowski, McMillan, Rimfeld, Krapohl, Haworth, & Plomin, 2013.

80 See the FAQs on: http://ssgac.org/documents/FAQsRietveldetal2013Science.pdf, which is part of this study: Rietveld, Medland, Derringer, Yang, Esko, Martin, & Albrecht, 2013.
81 See (in addition to the previously mentioned overview by Hattie, 2003):
- Rivkin, Hanushek, & Kain, 2005.
- Sirin, 2005.

82 Dietrichson, Bøg, Filges, & Klint Jørgensen, 2017.
83 Matthew effect (https://en.wikipedia.org/wiki/Matthew_effect).
84 Stanovich, 2009.
85 Dietrichson, Bøg, Filges, & KlintJørgensen, 2017.
86 Gordon, Kane, & Staiger, 2006.
87 Rowe, 2003.
88 OECD, 2015.
89 Janssens, 2015
90 Hattie, 2003.
91 Chetty, Friedman, & Rockoff, 2014.
92 Uttl, White, & Gonzalez, 2017.
93 Uttl & Smibert, 2017.
94 See, amongst others:
- Lee, Connolly, Dancy, Henderson, & Christensen, 2018.
- Turner, Hatton, & Theresa, 2018.

95 Krautmann & Sander, 1999.
96 Kornell & Hausman, 2016.
97 Rodin & Rodin, 1972.
98 Boring, 2017.
99 MacNell, Driscoll, & Hunt, 2015.
100 Ingvarson & Rowe, 2008.
101 Wiliam, 2018.
102 Hill, Charalambous, & Kraft, 2012.
103 Biesta & Pols, 2012.
104 Levitt & Dubner, 2005.
105 See:
- Marsden & Richardson, 1994.
- Pearce, Stevenson, & Perry, 1985.
- For a summary of the fifty years of research that suggests this: Dow Scott, Somersan, & Repsold, 2015.
- Campbell, Campbell, & Chia, 1998.

106 Ryan & Deci, 2000.
107 Pink, 2011.
108 Podgursky & Springer, 2007.
109 Pham, Nguyen, & Springer, 2017.
110 Hattie, 2015.
111 See: www.evidencebasedteaching.org.au/hatties-2017-updated-list/.
112 Meng & Wu, 2015.
113 Brewer, Myers, & Zhang, 2015.
114 See:
- Duflo, Hanna, & Ryan, 2012.
- Wiliam, 2018.

5 Evidence-Based Education as an Educational Myth

It was during the summer of 2018 that a man came up to us after one of our presentations and asked if we knew that Australian [*sic*] professor Hattie. Hattie is a New Zealander, we told him, but yes, of course we knew of him. The man continued by explaining that, in his opinion, Hattie was the person responsible for him having to retire a year earlier than scheduled. What was the case? One fine day, the directors of his school announced that, in keeping with the ideas of John Hattie, henceforth homework would for all intents and purposes be forbidden because it didn't work and class sizes would be increased since class size had no effect on learning. Less work and bigger classes meant fewer teachers, and so the man was 'let go' a year early ...

In a conversation we had previously had with Hattie he also said how he had noticed that in some countries his work had been used in a similar way, namely as an excuse to cut back on resources in teacher training, since that was also supposed to have little effect on student learning. But this had never been his intention.[1]

These are just a few of the examples of how Hattie's research and, by extension, evidence-based education is sometimes being used – or rather abused.

Under the motto 'Be most critical of those things that you most fervently believe', it seems appropriate to us to end this book by also looking critically at evidence-based education as a possible myth. This quickly leads us to two key questions. (1) Are there problems with educational research? (2) How is educational research used?

Are There Problems with Educational Research?

This might sound like a strange question to ask at the end of a book based as far as possible on educational research. But it's true that educational research is faced with a number of problems. First, educational research – like any research – has its limitations. Here is a list of some of the most important ones, without any pretense of being complete:

- Research is carried out within a particular context, but there is no certainty that the results will be replicated in a different context.
- The teacher is perhaps the most context-dependent variable in educational research. Often, it's the researcher or a trained assistant who takes on the role of the teacher in the research setting. This person has no connection, no past and no future with the student. As a result, students react differently during research interventions than they would normally do with their own teacher. Also, the personality characteristics of the teacher and her/his perceived authenticity and attitude towards the students also influences how the intervention develops in practice.
- Linked to this is the concept of intervention fidelity. This is a form of validity that requires that the way the teacher implements the intervention is the same the way the researcher(s) intended. Often, what the teacher actually does in the class is different from what the research team had in mind and had already tested in a research context.
- There are also limitations with regard to measurement instruments. For example, in the section earlier in the book on homework we referred to a study which suggested that until recently the time that pupils were thought to spend on homework was incorrectly estimated by a wide margin.[2]
- Much educational research looks at correlational rather than causal relationships. Think, for example, of PISA where it's far from clear what the 'cause' is and what the 'effect' is. Similarly, in our previous book we discussed how research into the influence of class size offered little real clarity, since it's only based on a limited number of longitudinal studies working with randomly selected groups.
- Randomized Controlled Trials (RCT) are capable of establishing whether a causal relationship exists, but this approach is relatively rare in

educational research. What's more, even these RCT studies have their limitations, as Dylan Wiliam has commented. RCTs attempt to research specific elements, but in education the different elements often interact with each other in a complex manner. You might wish to study the effects of homework, but homework is also impacted by factors such as age, socio-economic background, type of feedback given, etc. Trying to encompass the entirety of this complexity within a single research framework is extremely difficult. In addition, Wiliam contends that in education it's also difficult to deal with both groups – the intervention group and the control group – in a sufficiently similar manner (except, of course, for the variable you wish to investigate). A further complication is that within the different groups, different teachers can do things in very different ways, which can also influence the research outcomes.[3]

- RCTs can show what things could work, but often fail to explain how they work, and certainly not in your own classroom.[4]
- Much educational research is 'underpowered'; in other words, the sample groups are too small to draw hard conclusions.[5] We saw this in the section on growth mindset, where much of the supposed effect disappeared when a larger sample group was used in a replication.
- In recent years, there has been much criticism of the statistics used by Hattie in his meta-meta-analysis, in particular his somewhat unconventional (some might even say inappropriate) use of the measure for effect sizes (Cohen's *d*).[6] There was also the complaint that he did not really look at the quality of the meta-analyses he was examining, which was also a fault made by some of the original meta-analyses themselves.[7] This was something that Hattie readily admitted during our conversation with him. In this way, for example, he explained the original high score for learning styles by the inclusion of a meta-analysis which – unbeknownst to him – was strongly suspected of scientific fraud.

To these specific educational research problems can also be added the challenges faced by all scientific research. For example, we can speak of a publication bias when the published research is not representative of all the research that has been conducted.[8] There is a greater likelihood that positive results that confirm something will make it into print, whereas negative or inconclusive results will either not be offered for publication or will be rejected. At the same time, there is also the related problem of publication pressure. This leads some researchers to search for spectacular results that are more likely to attract the attention of the leading scientific journals, even though nil-results can sometimes be just as important if not more so, although much less 'glamorous' from a publication perspective. Publication bias can certainly have a distorting effect on meta-analyses that only examine published sources, and this is before we even begin to consider the impact of the increasing number of instances of research fraud that have come to light in recent years. These are challenges that the entire scientific world is struggling to address.

In the various sections on (educational) psychology, we referred repeatedly to the recent replication crisis affecting this domain. In part, this crisis can be explained by the factors we discussed earlier in the book, but in reality the problems associated with replication are nothing new. What's more, the replication crisis is actually something positive in our opinion: it shows that science is not standing still. It's a good thing that researchers are checking and rechecking to see whether or not certain studies – even classic, groundbreaking studies – can be confirmed. If they can, that's fine. But if they can't, then why not? Can earlier insights be refined or amended? Or, in some cases, can they even be dismissed? In this way, research, if properly carried out, can have a self-purifying effect. Another result of this crisis is that researchers are now opting more and more to preregister their research. By doing this, they tell in advance what and how they'll carry out the research, making it impossible to hide if the results didn't go as expected. At the same time, this negates the publication bias as the publication of the results are guaranteed – if you did exactly what you said you would in the preregistration – regardless of the results! We'll finally get to see what doesn't work.

Unfortunately, replication is not yet something that has become properly embedded in the world of education. In 2014, just 1% of the studies published in top journals were replication studies.[9] True, there are many more studies on comparable themes – otherwise meta-analyses would not be possible – but pure replications find it much harder to make their way into print.

Are There Problems with the Translation of Educational Research?

In the anecdote with which we started this chapter, the problem was not so much Hattie's research itself, but rather the way that the insights resulting from that research were interpreted and translated into daily practice. The conclusions went much further than the research itself envisaged or warranted. Looking at results in this way, simply to see what might have a 'significant' effect, without taking proper account of the complexity of education, is asking for trouble. In his book *The Ingredients for Great Teaching,* Pedro De Bruyckere explained the level of complexity that underlies just a single and seemingly simple figure cited by Hattie.[10] The figure in question relates to the effect size of web-based learning.

The graph in Figure 5.1 weighs 318 effect sizes for web-based learning against each other. Hattie gave web-based learning an effect size of .18,[11] which is far below the generally accepted minimum score of .40 for an approach to be regarded as having added value. But to use this score as a basis for a blanket statement such as 'online learning does not work' is much too simplistic and can easily be refuted by reference to the graph. The scores each reflect a specific purpose, context and approach.

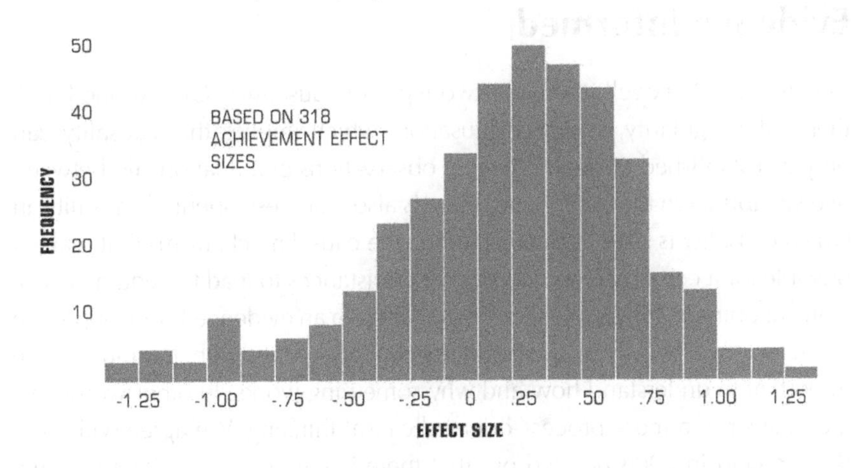

Figure 5.1
Source: *Bernard and colleagues, 2004.*

This example comes from the standard work on technology in education by Ruth Colvin Clark and Richard Mayer,[12] where they needed a couple of hundred pages to explain why online learning really does work (maybe). In this book, we also needed a number of pages to explain the circumstances in which homework can have either a positive or a negative effect.

Any close examination of educational research from the perspective of the user will soon reveal a considerable degree of confusion between cause and effect. In John Hattie's 2017 review of effect sizes, 'teacher estimates of pupil achievement' stood right at the top of his list, with an impressive effect size of 1.62. But before you commit yourself as a school to following up on this figure, you first need to know it primarily relates to how well teachers estimate their students' performance. In the same list, 'teacher expectations' only has a much more modest effect size of .43.[13]

This demonstrates that perhaps it is unwise simply to focus on the approaches or interventions with a high effect size. It's possible that an approach with a modest effect size can more easily be added to your educational repertoire than one with a large effect size that demands a great deal of time and effort to achieve the promised results. This is why the Teaching and Learning Toolkit issued by the Education Endowment Foundation balances the effect size of an approach against both the quality of the relevant research and the amount of effort and money needed to implement the approach, so that schools can make more balanced and better informed choices.[14]

Evidence Informed

According to Maxwell, there are two types of causality.[15] On the one hand, there's the regularity model of causation, which implies that causality can only be established through repeated observations of a relationship between two variables. On the other hand, there is also a process-oriented causality, in which causality is seen as understanding the causal mechanisms that make it possible for a certain combination of circumstances to lead to certain effects.

In our opinion, things are likely to go wrong in an evidence-based approach if you focus too heavily on the regularity concept of causation. It is much more important to understand how and why something works. In other words, we are in favor of a more process-oriented causal thinking. We agree with Roel Bosker, who in 2008 pointed out that there is little benefit in knowing that something works better 'on average', if you don't know how you're going to make it work in your own class.[16]

Evidence-based practice is an interdisciplinary approach that has its roots in medical science. Originally, the approach was described as being like a 'three-legged stool', because it integrates three basic principles:

1. The best available research evidence bearing on whether and why a treatment works.
2. Clinical expertise (clinical judgment and experience) to rapidly identify each patient's unique health state and diagnosis, their individual risks and benefits of potential interventions.
3. Client preferences and values.[17]

Globally speaking, if a decision is made on the intake and working of a medicine, then it means that it was tested and approved for a certain specifically defined population (e.g., an adult with a certain body mass index (BMI) and with specific symptoms and pathologies) and the instruction to take a pill in the morning on an empty stomach but followed by food intake allows for a wide range of specific circumstances (at home, in the car, on the beach, when and wherever, as long as it's on an empty stomach in the morning).

Our definition of evidence informed education is the use of empirically obtained scientific evidence about how children can best learn, as a basis for making informed decisions about how education in practical terms can best be organized. Consequently, 'evidence informed' still means 'based on empirically obtained scientific research' – and this is the 'leg' on which we focus in this book – but within the learning sciences it's much more difficult to define and control the 'circumstances' on which the other two 'legs' depend. In education, we are all too often faced with vague and unpredictable circumstances, which can significantly influence the effect of learning interventions.

In other words, what works at 9 am in one class may not work at 3 pm in another class. If that trouble-maker Peter is absent today, things may turn out differently than if he was present. For this reason, we must be constantly aware, as the designers of learning interventions, that if we use the available scientific evidence there is every possibility that what works in one context may not necessarily work in a different context (lesson, subject, age, school type, time of day, etc.).

All these potential problems persuade us that it's better to argue for an evidence-informed approach, rather than an evidence-based approach for education. And if we can avoid the things we know really don't work, that would be a great start!

Conclusion? Nuanced!

Notes

1 For a full report on this conversation, see: https://theeconomyofmeaning.com/2015/11/11/a-talk-with-john-hattie-about-inclusive-education-teacher-training-and-learning-styles/.
2 Rawson, Stahovich, & Mayer, 2017.
3 Wiliam, 2014.
4 Gravemeijer & Kirschner, 2007.
5 Ioannidis, 2005.
6 See, amongst others:
   - Bergeron & Rivard, 2017.
7 https://robertslavinsblog.wordpress.com/2018/06/21/john-hattie-is-wrong/
8 Rothstein, Sutton, & Borenstein, 2006.
9 Makel & Plucker, 2014.
10 De Bruyckere, 2017.
11 Hattie, 2009.
12 Clark & Mayer, 2016.
13 www.evidencebasedteaching.org.au/hatties-2017-updated-list/.
14 See: https://educationendowmentfoundation.org.uk/evidence-summaries/teaching-learning-toolkit.
15 Maxwell, 2004.
16 Bosker, 2008.
17 https://nl.wikipedia.org/wiki/Evidence-based_practice.

References

Abeysekera, L., & Dawson, P. (2015). Motivation and cognitive load in the flipped classroom: Definition, rationale and a call for research. *Higher Education Research & Development, 34*(1), 1–14.

Abrami, P. C., Bernard, R. M., Borokhovski, E., Waddington, D. I., Wade, C. A., & Persson, T. (2015). Strategies for teaching students to think critically: A meta-analysis. *Review of Educational Research, 85*, 275–314.

Aghuzumtsyan, R., & Poghosyan, S. (2014). The impact of chess lessons on formation and development of the students (retrieved from www.iccs.chessacademy.am/uploads/images/h_impact_of_chess_lessons_on_formation_and_development_of_the_students-article.pdf).

Agüero, J. M., & Beleche, T. (2013). Test-Mex: Estimating the effects of school year length on student performance in Mexico. *Journal of Development Economics, 103*, 353–361.

Allen, G. (2011). *Early intervention: Smart investment, massive savings, the second independent report to Her Majesty's Government*. London: The Stationery Office.

Altenmüller, E. (2006). Neuronale Auswirkungen musikalischen Lernens im Kindes- und Jugendalter und Transfereffekte auf Intelligenzleistungen [Neuronal effects of musical learning in childhood and adolescence and transfer effects on intelligence performance]. In Bundesministerium für Bildung und Forschung (Ed.) *Macht Mozart schlau? Die Förderung kognitiver Kompetenzen durch Musik [Does Mozart make one smart? Facilitation of cognitive abilities through music]* (pp. 59–70). Bonn: Bundesministerium für Bildung und Forschung.

Amemiya, J., & Wang, M.-T. (2018). Why effort praise can backfire in adolescence. *Child Development Perspectives, 12*(3), 199–203.

American Association of Colleges and Universities. (2007). *College learning for the new global century*. Washington, DC: AACU.

Anastasi, A., & Urbina, S. (1997, 7th ed.). *Psychological testing*. Upper Saddle River, NJ: Prentice Hall.

Ansari, A., & Pianta, R. C. (2018). Effects of an early childhood educator coaching intervention on preschoolers: The role of classroom age composition. *Early Childhood Research Quarterly, 44,* 101–113.

Ashley, S., & Pearson, J. (2012). When more equals less: Overtraining inhibits perceptual learning owing to lack of wakeful consolidation. *Proceedings of the Royal Society B, 279*(1745), 4143–4147.

Bacolod, M., Mehay, S., & Pema, E. (2018). Who succeeds in distance learning? Evidence from quantile panel data estimation. *Southern Economic Journal, 84,* 1129–1145.

Baer, D. (2014, June 2). Malcolm Gladwell explains what everyone gets wrong about his famous '10,000 hour rule'. *Business Insider* (retrieved from www.businessinsider.com/malcolm-gladwell-explains-the-10000-hour-rule-2014-6?international=true&r=US&IR=T May, 3, 2018).

Bahník, Š., & Vranka, M. A. (2017). Growth mindset is not associated with scholastic aptitude in a large sample of university applicants. *Personality and Individual Differences, 117,* 139–143.

Bailey, R., Madigan, D. J., Cope, E., & Nicholls, A. R. (2018). The prevalence of pseudoscientific ideas and neuromyths among sports coaches. *Frontiers in Psychology, 9,* 641.

Bandler, R., & Grinder, J. (1979). *Frogs into princes Neurolinguistic programming.* Moab, UT: Real People Press.

Bashford, A., & Levine, P. (Eds.). (2010). *The Oxford handbook of the history of eugenics.* New York, NY: OUP USA.

Bassett, D. S., Yang, M., Wymbs, N. F., & Grafton, S. T. (2015). Learning-induced autonomy of sensorimotor systems. *Nature Neuroscience, 18,* 744–751.

BBC World Service (2017). Have 65% of future jobs not yet been invented? *More or less* (retrieved from www.bbc.co.uk/programmes/p053ln9f).

Beard, M. (2006, July 10). Does Latin 'train the brain'? *The Times Literary Supplement* (retrieved from www.the-tls.co.uk/does-latin-train-the-brain/).

Beck, C. E., & Beck, E. A. (1984). Test of the eye-movement hypothesis of Neurolinguistic Programming: A rebuttal of conclusions. *Perceptual and Motor Skills, 58*(1), 175–176.

Bell, S. T. (2007). Deep-level composition variables as predictors of team performance: A meta-analysis. *Journal of Applied Psychology, 92,* 595–615.

Benjamin, A. S., & Tullis, J. (2010). What makes distributed practice effective? *Cognitive Psychology, 61,* 228–247.

Benyamin, B., Pourcain, B., Davis, O. S., Davies, G., Hansell, N. K., Brion, M. J., & Haworth, C. M. A. (2014). Childhood intelligence is heritable, highly polygenic and associated with FNBP1L. *Molecular Psychiatry, 19*(2), 253.

Berg, S., & Berg, E. (2014). The youngest children in each school cohort are overrepresented in referrals to mental health services. *The Journal of Clinical Psychiatry, 75,* 530–534.

Bergeron, P. J., & Rivard, L. (2017). How to engage in pseudoscience with real data: A criticism of John Hattie's arguments in Visible Learning from the perspective of a statistician. *McGill Journal of Education/Revue des sciences de l'éducation de McGill, 52*(1), 237–246.

Bernard, R. M., Abrami, P. C., Lou, Y., Borokhovski, E., Wade, A., Wozney, L., Wallet, P. A., ... Huang, B. (2004). How does distance education compare with classroom instruction? A meta-analysis of the empirical literature. *Review of Educational Research, 74*, 379–439. doi:10.3102/00346543074003379.

Bess, T. L., & Harvey, R. J. (2002). Bimodal score distributions and the Myers-Briggs Type Indicator: Fact or artifact? *Journal of Personality Assessment, 78*, 176–186.

Bettinger, E. P., Fox, L., Loeb, S., & Taylor, E. S. (2017). Virtual classrooms: How online college courses affect student success. *American Economic Review, 107*, 2855–2875.

Beunk, G. (2014). Hoofd, hart en handen. In Murre, P., de Muynck, B., & Vermeulen, H. (Eds.) *Vitale idealen, voorbeeldige praktijken II* (pp. 90–105). Amsterdam: Buijten & Schipperheijn.

Biesta, G., & Pols, W. (2012). *Goed onderwijs en de cultuur van het meten*. Amsterdam: BoomLemma.

Biggs, J. B., & Collis, K. F. (2014). *Evaluating the quality of learning: The SOLO taxonomy (Structure of the Observed Learning Outcome)*. San Diego, CA: Academic Press.

Billari, F. C., & Pellizzari, M. (2008). *The younger, the better? Relative age effects at university*. IZA discussion papers, No. 3795.

Binet, A. (1975). *Modern ideas about children*. (S. Heisler, Trans.). Menlo Park, CA: Suzanne Heisler, Publisher.

Birdsall, C., & Siewert, S. (2013). Of sound mind: Mental distress and sound in twentieth-century media culture. *Tijdschrift voor Mediageschiedenis, 16*(1), 27–45.

Bishop, J. L., & Verleger, M. A. (2013, June). The flipped classroom: A survey of the research. *ASEE National Conference Proceedings, Atlanta (GA), 30*(9), 1–18.

Blackwell, B., Bloomfield, S., & Buncher, C. R. (1972). Demonstration to medical students of placebo responses and non-drug factors. *The Lancet, 299*(7763), 1279–1282.

Blakeslee, S. (1998, October 13). Placebos prove so powerful even experts are surprised: New studies explore the brain's triumph over reality. *The New York Times* (retrieved from www.nytimes.com/1998/10/13/science/placebos-prove-so-powerful-even-experts-are-surprised-new-studies-explore-brain.Html).

Blinder, A. S. (2006). Offshoring: The next industrial revolution? *Foreign Affairs, 85*(2), 113–128.

Bloom, B. S. (1956). *Taxonomy of educational objectives: The classification of educational goals. Handbook 1: Cognitive domain*. New York, NY: David McKay Co.

Blum, B. (2018). The lifespan of a lie. *Medium* (retrieved from https://medium.com/s/trustissues/the-lifespan-of-a-lie-d869212b1f62).

Boone, M. (2007). *Historici en hun métier: een inleiding tot de historische kritiek*. Gent: Academia Press.

Boring, A. (2017). Gender biases in student evaluations of teaching. *Journal of Public Economics, 145*, 27–41.

Bos, N., Groeneveld, C., Van Bruggen, J., & Brand Gruwel, S. (2016). The use of recorded lectures in education and the impact on lecture attendance and exam performance. *British Journal of Educational Technology, 47*, 906–917.

Bosker, R. J. (2008). Naar meer evidence based onderwijs [Towards more evidence based education]. *Pedagogische Studiën, 85*, 49–51.

Bracke, E., & Bradshaw, C. (2017). The impact of learning Latin on school pupils: A review of existing data. *The Language Learning Journal*, 1–11.

Brewer, T. J., Myers, P. S., & Zhang, M. (2015). Islands unto themselves: How merit pay schemes may undermine positive teacher collaboration. *Critical Questions in Education*, 6(2), 45–54.

Brophy, J., & Good, T. (1986). Teacher behavior and student achievement. In M. Wittrock (Ed.) *Handbook of research on teaching* (pp. 328–375). New York, NY: Macmillan.

Brown, A., Shifrin, D. L., & Hill, D. L. (2015). Beyond 'turn it off': How to advise families on media use. *AAP News, 36*(10), 54–54.

Bruggers, I., Driessen, G., & Gesthuizen, M. (2014). Voor-en vroegschoolse voorzieningen, effectief of niet? De samenhang tussen deelname aan voor- en vroegschoolse voorzieningen en de taal- en rekenprestaties van leerlingen op de korte en langere termijn. *Mens en Maatschappij, 89*(2), 117–150.

Burgoyne, A. P., Sala, G., Gobet, F., Macnamara, B. N., Campitelli, G., & Hambrick, D. Z. (2016). The relationship between cognitive ability and chess skill: A comprehensive meta-analysis. *Intelligence, 59*, 72–83.

Burgstahler, S. (2007). *Universal design of instruction: Definition, principles, and examples*. Washington, DC: University of Washington (retrieved from www.washington.edu/doit/Brochures/Academics/instruction.Html).

Burt, C. (1966). The genetic determination of differences in intelligence: A study of monozygotic twins reared together and apart. *British Journal of Psychology, 57*(1–2), 137–153.

Byrnes, J. P. (2001). *Minds, brains, and learning: Understanding the psychological and educational relevance of neuroscientific research*. New York, NY: Guilford Press.

Camilli, G., Vargas, S., Ryan, S., & Barnett, W. S. (2010). Meta-analysis of the effects of early education interventions on cognitive and social development. *The Teachers College Record, 112*, 579–620.

Campbell, D. J., Campbell, K. M., & Chia, H. B. (1998). Merit pay, performance appraisal, and individual motivation: An analysis and alternative. *Human Resource Management: Published in Cooperation with the School of Business Administration, the University of Michigan and in Alliance with the Society of Human Resources Management, 37*(2), 131–146.

Capp, M. J. (2017). The effectiveness of universal design for learning: A meta-analysis of literature between 2013 and 2016. *International Journal of Inclusive Education, 21*, 791–807.

Capraro, R. M., & Capraro, M. M. (2002). Myers-Briggs type indicator score reliability across studies: A meta-analytic reliability generalization study. *Educational and Psychological Measurement, 62*, 590–602.

Carey, J., Churches, R., Hutchinson, G., Jones, J., & Tosey, P. (2010). *Neuro-linguistic programming and learning: Teacher case studies on the impact of NLP in education*. CFBT Education Trust (retrieved from https://files.eric.ed.Gov/fulltext/ED508368.pdf).

Carlisle, J. F. (1993). The influence of study of a second language on improvement in spelling: A longitudinal study. *Reading and Writing, 5*, 339–353.

Carneiro, P., & Heckman, J. J. (2003). *Human capital policy*. Cambridge, MA: National Bureau of Economic Research.

Carroll, J. (2007). *Ready, set, done: How to innovate when faster is the new fast*. Mississauga: Oblio Press.

Carroll, J. B. (1963). A model of school learning. *Teachers College Record, 64*, 723–733.

Carskadon, T. G., & Cook, D. D. (1982). Validity of MBTI descriptions as perceived by recipients unfamiliar with type. *Research in Psychological Type, 5*, 89–94.

Castles, A., Rastle, K., & Nation, K. (2018). Ending the reading wars: Reading acquisition from novice to expert. *Psychological Science in the Public Interest, 19*(1), 5–51.

Cattell, R. (1949). *Culture free intelligence test, scale 1, handbook*. Champaign, IL: Institute of Personality and Ability Testing.

Chall, J. S. (1967). *Learning to read: The great debate*. New York, NY: McGraw Hill.

Chao, M. M., Visaria, S., Mukhopadhyay, A., & Dehejia, R. (2017). Do rewards reinforce the growth mindset? Joint effects of the growth mindset and incentive schemes in a field intervention. *Journal of Experimental Psychology: General, 146*, 1402–1419.

Chassiakos, Y. L. R., Radesky, J., Christakis, D., Moreno, M. A., & Cross, C. (2016). Children and adolescents and digital media. *Pediatrics, 138*(5), e20162593.

Chee, M. W. L., & Choo, W. C. (2004). Functional imaging of working memory after 24 hr of total sleep deprivation. *The Journal of Neuroscience, 24*, 4560–4567.

Cherry, L. L., & Macdonald, N. H. (1983). The UNIXTM Writers' Workbench software. *Byte, 8*, 241–248.

Chetty, R., Friedman, J. N., & Rockoff, J. E. (2011). *The long-term impacts of teachers: Teacher value-added and student outcomes in adulthood* (No. w17699). Cambridge, MA: National Bureau of Economic Research.

Chetty, R., Friedman, J. N., & Rockoff, J. E. (2014). Measuring the impacts of teachers II: Teacher value-added and student outcomes in adulthood: Dataset. *American Economic Review, 104*, 2633–2679.

Chevalier, A., Dolton, P., & Luhrmann, M. (2014). *'Making it count': Evidence from a field study on assessment rules, study incentives and student performance*. Institute for the Study of Labor Working Paper 8582 (retrieved from https://core.ac.uk/download/pdf/39422426.pdf).

Chitty, C. (2007). *Eugenics, race and intelligence in education*. London, UK: Bloomsbury Publishing.

Claessens, A., Engel, M., & Curran, F. C. (2014). Academic content, student learning, and the persistence of preschool effects. *American Educational Research Journal, 51*, 403–434.

Clark, J. M., & Paivio, A. (1991). Dual coding theory and education. *Educational Psychology Review, 3*, 149–210.

Clark, R. C., & Mayer, R. E. (2016). *E-learning and the science of instruction: Proven guidelines for consumers and designers of multimedia learning*. Hoboken, NJ: John Wiley & Sons.

Clark, R. E. (1983). Reconsidering research on learning from media. *Review of Educational Research, 53*, 445–459.

Clements, D. (1985). Research on Logo in education: Is the turtle slow but steady, or not even in the race? *Computers in the Schools, 2*(2–3), 55–71.

Clements, D. H., & Gullo, D. F. (1984). Effects of computer programming on young children's cognition. *Journal of Educational Psychology, 76*, 1051–1058.

Cohen, S. (2011). *Folk devils and moral panics*. Abingdon: Routledge.

Collard, P. (2008). *Key note address to conference CITE*. Chorley: Creativity in Initial Teacher Education.

Colom, R., & Flores-Mendoza, C. E. (2007). Intelligence predicts scholastic achievement irrespective of SES factors: Evidence from Brazil. *Intelligence, 35*, 243–251.

Colvin, G. (2008). *Talent is overrated. What really separates world-class performers from everybody else*. London: Penguin Books.

Cooper, H. (1989). Synthesis of research on homework. *Educational Leadership, 47*(3), 85–91.

Cooper, H., Robinson, J., & Patall, E. (2006). Does homework improve academic achievement? A synthesis of research 1987-2003. *Review of Educational Research, 76*, 1–62.

Cornhill, H., & Case-Smith, J. (1996). Factors that relate good and poor handwriting. *The American Journal of Occupational Therapy, 50*, 732–739.

Credé, M., Tynan, M. C., & Harms, P. D. (2017). Much ado about grit: A meta-analytic synthesis of the grit literature. *Journal of Personality and Social Psychology, 113*, 492–511.

Crum, A. J., & Langer, E. J. (2007). Mind-set matters: Exercise and the placebo effect. *Psychological Science, 18*(2), 165–571.

Cuddy, L. L., Balkwill, L. L., Peretz, I., & Holden, R. R. (2005). Musical difficulties are rare: A study of 'tone deafness' among university students. *Annals of the New York Academy of Sciences, 1060*, 311–324.

Cunha, F., & Heckman, J. (2007). *The technology of skill formation*. (No. w12840). Cambridge, MA: National Bureau of Economic Research.

Dahl, M. (2016). Don't believe the hype about grit, pleads the scientist behind the concept. *Science of Us* (retrieved from: www.thecut.com/2016/05/dont-believe-the-hype-about-grit-pleads-the-scientist-behind-the-concept.Html).

Daly, L., & Beloglovsky, M. (2014). *Loose parts: Inspiring play in young children*. St Paul, MN: Redleaf Press.

Darley, J. M., & Latané, B. (1968). Bystander intervention in emergencies: Diffusion of responsibility. *Journal of Personality and Social Psychology, 8*, 377–383.

Dave, R. H. (1970). *Psychomotor levels in developing and writing behavioral objectives* (pp. 20–21). R. J. Armstrong (Ed.). Tucson, AZ: Educational Innovators Press.

Davidson, C. N. (2011). *Now you see it: How the brain science of attention will transform the way we live, work and learn*. Solon, OH: Findaway World LLC.

Davies, G., Tenesa, A., Payton, A., Yang, J., Harris, S. E., Liewald, D., Ke, X., ... & Deary, I. J. (2011). Genome-wide association studies establish that human intelligence is highly heritable and polygenic. *Molecular Psychiatry, 16*, 996–1005.

Davies, P. L., Schelly, C. L., & Spooner, C. L. (2013). Measuring the effectiveness of Universal Design for Learning intervention in postsecondary education. *Journal of Postsecondary Education and Disability, 26*, 195–220.

Davis, O. S., Band, G., Pirinen, M., Haworth, C. M., Meaburn, E. L., Kovas, Y., & Curtis, C. J. (2014). The correlation between reading and mathematics ability at age twelve has a substantial genetic component. *Nature Communications, 5*, 4204.

Dawson, M. E., Schell, A. M., & Filion, D. L. (2007). The electrodermal system. *Handbook of Psychophysiology, 2*, 200–223.

de Block, A. (1975). *Taxonomie van leerdoelen*. Antwerp, Belgium: Standaard Wetenschappelijke Uitgeverij.

De Bruyckere, P. (2017). *Klaskit*. Leuven, Belgium: LannooCampus/Anderz.

De Bruyckere, P. (2018). *The ingredients for great teaching*. London: Sage Publishing.

De Bruyckere, P. (in prep.). *Learning styles still live in thinking about educational technology*.

De Bruyckere, P., Kirschner, P. A., & Hulshof, C. D. (2015a). *Urban myths about learning and education*. San Diego, CA: Academic Press.

De Bruyckere, P., & Smits, B. (2015). *Ik was 10 in 2015*. Leuven, Belgium: Lannoo-Campus.

De Bruyckere, P., Struyf, E., & Kavadias, D. (2015b). Rousseau and Arendt in the iPad class, the old roots of present day discussions on technology in schools. *Pedagogische Studien, 92*, 202–209.

De Groot, A. D. (1946). *Het denken van den schaker*. Amsterdam: Noord-Hollandsche Uitgevers Maatschappij.

De Rooy, P. (2018). *Een geschiedenis van het onderwijs in Nederland* [A history of education in the Netherlands]. Amsterdam: Wereldbibliotheek.

De Stefano, F. (2007). Vaccines and autism: Evidence does not support a causal association. *Clinical Pharmacology & Therapeutics, 82*, 756–759.

Deary, I. J., Batty, G. D., & Gale, C. R. (2008). Childhood intelligence predicts voter turnout, voting preferences, and political involvement in adulthood: The 1970 British Cohort Study. *Intelligence, 36*, 548–555.

Deary, I. J., Strand, S., Smith, P., & Fernandes, C. (2007). Intelligence and educational achievement. *Intelligence, 35*, 13–21.

DeBacker, T. K., Heddy, B. C., Kershen, J. L., Crowson, H. M., Looney, K., & Goldman, J. A. (2018). Effects of a one-shot growth mindset intervention on beliefs about intelligence and achievement goals. *Educational Psychology, 38*, 711–733.

Dede, C. (2010). Comparing frameworks for 21st century skills. *21st Century Skills: Rethinking How Students Learn, 20*, 51–76.

Deer, B. (2011). How the case against the MMR vaccine was fixed. *British Medical Journal, 342*, c5347.

Dietrichson, J., Bøg, M., Filges, T., & KlintJørgensen, A. M. (2017). Academic interventions for elementary and middle school students with low socioeconomic status: A systematic review and meta-analysis. *Review of Educational Research, 87*, 243–282.

Digman, J. M. (1990). Personality structure: Emergence of the five-factor model. *Annual Review of Psychology, 41*, 417–440.

Doli ski, D., Grzyb, T., Folwarczny, M., Grzybała, P., Krzyszycha, K., Martynowska, K., & Trojanowski, J. (2017). Would you deliver an electric shock in 2015? Obedience in the experimental paradigm developed by Stanley Milgram in the 50 years following the original studies. *Social Psychological and Personality Science, 8*, 927–933.

Dow Scott, K., Somersan, R., & Repsold, B. (2015). Is there merit in merit pay? A survey of reward professionals. *World at Work Journal, 24*(1), 6–17.

Doyle, O., Harmon, C. P., Heckman, J. J., & Tremblay, R. E. (2009). Investing in early human development: Timing and economic efficiency. *Economics & Human Biology, 7*(1), 1–6.

Druckman, D., & Swets, J. A. (Eds.). (1988). *Enhancing human performance: Issues, theories, and techniques*. Washington, DC: National Academy Press.

Drummond, S. P. A., & Brown, G. G. (2001). The effects of total sleep deprivation on cerebral responses to cognitive performance. *Neuropsychopharmacology, 25*, 68–73.

Dubner, J. S. (2016, May 4). How to get more grit in your life. *The Freakonomics Podcast* (retrieved from http://freakonomics.com/podcast/grit/).

Duckworth, A. (2016, March 26). Don't grade schools on grit. *The New York Times*.

Duckworth, A. L., Peterson, C., & Matthews, M. D., & Kelly, D. R. (2007). Grit: Perseverance and passion for long-term goals. *Journal of Personality and Social Psychology, 92*, 1087–1101.

Dudink, A. (1994). Birth date and sporting success. *Nature, 368*(6472), 592.

Duflo, E., Hanna, R., & Ryan, S. P. (2012). Incentives work: Getting teachers to come to school. *American Economic Review, 102*, 1241–1278.

Duggan, G. B., & Payne, S. J. (2009, September). Text skimming: The process and effectiveness of foraging through text under time pressure. *Journal of Experimental Psychology: Applied, 15*, 228–242.

Dunning, D. (2008). *Introduction to type and learning*. Palo Alto, CA: CPP.

Dutton, E., & Lynn, R. (2013). A negative Flynn effect in Finland, 1997-2009. *Intelligence, 41*, 817–820.

Dutton, E., & Lynn, R. (2015). A negative Flynn Effect in France, 1999 to 2008-9. *Intelligence, 51*, 67–70.

Düvel, N., Wolf, A., & Kopiez, R. (2017). Neuromyths in music education: Prevalence and predictors of misconceptions among teachers and students. *Frontiers in Psychology, 8*, 629.

Dweck, C. S. (1975). The role of expectations and attributions in the alleviation of learned helplessness. *Journal of Personality and Social Psychology, 31*, 674–685.

Dweck, C. S. (1999). *Self-theories: Their role in motivation, personality, and development*. Philadelphia, PA: Psychology Press.

Dweck, C. S. (2006). *Mindset: The new psychology of success*. New York, NY: Random House.

Dweck, C. S. (2012). Mindsets and human nature: Promoting change in the Middle East, the schoolyard, the racial divide, and willpower. *American Psychologist, 67*, 614–622.

Dweck, C. S. (2015). Carol Dweck Revisits the 'Growth Mindset'. *Education Week, 35*(5), 20–24.

Dweck, C. S. (2017). From needs to goals and representations: Foundations for a unified theory of motivation, personality, and development. *Psychological Review, 124*, 689–719.

Dweck, C. S., & Leggett, E. L. (1988). A social-cognitive approach to motivation and personality. *Psychological Review, 95*, 256–273.

Dweck, C. S., & Reppucci, N. D. (1973). Learned helplessness and reinforcement responsibility in children. *Journal of Personality and Social Psychology, 25*(1), 109–116.

Edwards, M. R., & Clinton, M. E. (2018). A study exploring the impact of lecture capture availability and lecture capture usage on student attendance and attainment. *Higher Education*, 1–19.

Elich, M., Thompson, R. W., & Miller, L. (1985). Mental imagery as revealed by eye movements and spoken predicates: A test of neurolinguistic programming. *Journal of Counseling Psychology, 32*, 622–625.

Epstein, J. L., & Van Voorhis, F. L. (2001). More than minutes: Teachers' roles in designing homework. *Educational Psychologist, 36*, 181–193.

Ericsson, A., & Pool, R. (2016a). *Peak: Secrets from the new science of expertise*. Boston, MA: Houghton Mifflin Harcourt.

Ericsson, A., & Pool, R. (2016b, October 4). Malcolm Gladwell got us wrong: Our research was key to the 10,000 hour rule, but here's what got oversimplified. *Salon* (retrieved from www.salon.com/2016/04/10/malcolm_gladwell_got_us_wrong_our_research_was_key_to_the_10000_hour_rule_but_heres_what_got_oversimplified/).

Fan, H., Xu, J., Cai, Z., He, J., & Fan, X. (2017). Homework and students' achievement in math and science: A 30-year meta-analysis, 1986-2015. *Educational Research Review, 20*, 35–54.

Farthouat, J., Atas, A., Wens, V., De Tiege, X., & Peigneux, P. (2018). Lack of frequency-tagged magnetic responses suggests statistical regularities remain undetected during NREM sleep. *Scientific Reports, 8*(1), 11719.

Ferguson, C. J. (2017). Everything in moderation: Moderate use of screens unassociated with child behavior problems. *Psychiatric Quarterly, 88*, 797–805.

Fernald, A., Marchman, V. A., & Weisleder, A. (2013). SES differences in language processing skill and vocabulary are evident at 18 months. *Developmental Science, 16*, 234–248.

Fernandes, L., Maley, M., & Cruickshank, C. (2008). The impact of online lecture recordings on learning outcomes in pharmacology. *Journal of the International Association of Medical Science Educators, 18*, 62–70.

Fernández-Alonso, R., Suárez-Álvarez, J., & Muñiz, J. (2015). Adolescents' homework performance in mathematics and science: Personal factors and teaching practices. *Journal of Educational Psychology, 107*, 1075.

Finnish National Agency for Education (2015, February 9). *Writing by hand will still be taught in Finnish schools* (retrieved from www.oph.fi/english/current_issues/101/0/writing_by_hand_will_still_be_taught_in_finnish_schools).

Flesch, R. (1955). *Why Johnny can't read – and what you can do about it*. New York, NY: Harper & Brothers.

Flynn, J. R. (2012). *Are we getting smarter? Rising IQ in the twenty-first century*. New York, NY: Cambridge University Press.

Fombonne, E. (2005). The changing epidemiology of autism. *Journal of Applied Research in Intellectual Disabilities, 18*, 281–294.

Forehand, M. (2010). Bloom's taxonomy. *Emerging Perspectives on Learning, Teaching, and Technology, 41*, 47.

Forrin, N. D., & MacLeod, C. M. (2018). This time it's personal: The memory benefit of hearing oneself. *Memory, 26*, 574–579.

Frase, L. T., Keenan, S. A., & Dever, J. J. (1980). Human performance in computer-aided writing and documentation. In P. A. Kolers, M. E. Wrolstad & H. Bouma (Eds.) *Processing of visible language 2* (pp. 405–416). New York, NY: Plenum.

Freedle, R., & Kostin, I. (1997). Predicting black and white differential item functioning in verbal analogy performance. *Intelligence, 24*, 417–444.

Frey, C. B., & Osborne, M. A. (2017). The future of employment: How susceptible are jobs to computerization? *Technological Forecasting and Social Change, 114*, 254–280.

Frisvold, D. E. (2015). Nutrition and cognitive achievement: An evaluation of the School Breakfast Program. *Journal of Public Economics, 124*, 91–104 (www.sciencedirect.com/science/article/pii/S0047272714002497).

Galton, F. (1883). *Inquiries into human faculty and its development*. London: Macmillan.

Gardner, H. (2016). Multiple Intelligences: Prelude, Theory, and Aftermath. In R. J. Sternberg, S. T. Fiske & D. J. Foss (Eds.) *Scientists making a difference*. (pp. 167–170). Cambridge, MA: Cambridge University Press.

Geary, D. C. (2007). Educating the evolved mind: Reflections and refinements. In J. S. Carlson & J. R. Levin (Eds.) *Educating the Evolved Mind* (pp. 177–203, Vol. 2, Psychological perspectives on contenporary educational issues). Greenwich, CT: Information Age.

Geoffroy, M. C., Côté, S. M., Borge, A. I., Larouche, F., Séguin, J. R., & Rutter, M. (2007). Association between nonmaternal care in the first year of life and children's receptive language skills prior to school entry: The moderating role of socioeconomic status. *Journal of Child Psychology and Psychiatry, 48*, 490–497.

Gertler, P., Heckman, J., Pinto, R., Zanolini, A., Vermeersch, C., Walker, S., & Grantham-McGregor, S. (2013). *Labor market returns to early childhood stimulation: A 20-year follow-up to an experimental intervention in Jamaica* (No. w19185). Cambridge, MA: National Bureau of Economic Research.

Gervain, J., Vines, B. W., Chen, L. M., Seo, R. J., Hensch, T. K., Werker, J. F., & Young, A. H. (2013). Valproate reopens critical-period learning of absolute pitch. *Frontiers in Systems Neuroscience, 102*, 7.

Ghose, T. (2013). Pediatricians: No more than 2 hours screen time daily for kids: The American Academy of Pediatrics' new guidelines also advise against TVs or Internet access in children's bedrooms. *Scientific American* (retrieved from www.scientificamerican.com/article/pediatricians-no-more-than-2-hour-screen-time-kids/).

Gillette, C., Rudolph, M., Kimble, C., Rockich-Winston, N., Smith, L., & Broedel-Zaugg, K. (2018). A systematic review and meta-analysis of student pharmacist outcomes comparing flipped classroom and lecture. *American Journal of Pharmaceutical Education*, e-View. doi:10.5688/ajpe6898.

Gladwell, M. (2008). *Outliers: The story of success*. New York, NY: Hachette.

Gobet, F., & Campitelli, G. (2006). Educational benefits of chess instruction: A critical review. In *Chess and education: Selected essays from the Koltanowski conference* (pp. 124–143). Chess Program at the University of Texas at Dallas (TX).

Godlee, F., Smith, J., & Marcovitch, H. (2011). Wakefield's article linking MMR vaccine and autism was fraudulent: Clear evidence of falsification of data should now close the door on this damaging vaccine scare. *BMJ: British Medical Journal, 342*(7788), 64–66.

Gold, B. P., Frank, M. J., Bogert, B., & Brattico, E. (2013). Pleasurable music affects reinforcement learning according to the listener. *Frontiers in Psychology, 4*, Article 541.

Goodman, K. S. (1967). Reading: A psycholinguistic guessing game. *Journal of the Reading Specialist, 6*, 126–135.

Gordon, R. J., Kane, T. J., & Staiger, D. (2006). *Identifying effective teachers using performance on the job*. Washington, DC: Brookings Institution.

Goswami, U. (2006). Neuroscience and education: From research to practice? *Nature Reviews Neuroscience, 7*, 406–413.

Gottfredson, L. S., & Deary, I. J. (2004). Intelligence predicts health and longevity, but why? *Current Directions in Psychological Science, 13*(1), 1–4.

Graham, S., Liu, X., Bartlett, B., Ng, C., Harris, K. R., Aitken, A., & Talukdar, J. (2017). Reading for writing: A meta-analysis of the impact of reading interventions on writing. *Review of Educational Research*, 0034654317746927.

Grant, A. (2013, September 18). Goodbye to MBTI: The fad that won't die. *Psychology Today* (retrieved from www.psychologytoday.com/intl/blog/give-and-take/201309/goodbye-mbti-the-fad-won-t-die).

Gravemeijer, K. P. E., & Kirschner, P. A. (2007). Naar meer evidence-based onderwijs? *Pedagogische Studiën, 84*, 463–472.

Greenfield, S. (2015). *Mind change: How digital technologies are leaving their mark on our brains*. London: Random House.

Gregory, R. L., & Zangwill, O. L. (1987). *The Oxford companion to the mind*. Oxford: Oxford University Press.

Grinder, J., & Bandler, R. (1976). *The structure of magic II*. Palo Alto, CA: Science and Behavior Books.

Groen, M. (2015). Kan het onderwijs in Netherlands efficiënter? *CBS Scientific Paper* (retrieved from www.cbs.nl/-/media/imported/documents/2015/05/kan-het-onderwijs-in-Netherlands-efficienter-2012-wp.pdf).

Gross-Loh, C. (2016, December 16). Don't let praise become a consolation prize. *The Atlantic* (retrieved from www.theatlantic.com/education/archive/2016/12/how-praise-became-a-consolation-prize/510845/).

Guerin, B. (2014). *Breaking the cycle of disadvantage: Early childhood interventions and progression to higher education in Europe*. Cambridge, UK: Rand (retrieved from www.rand.org/pubs/research_reports/RR553.Html).

Guo, Y., Tompkins, V., Justice, L., & Petscher, Y. (2014). Classroom age composition and vocabulary development among at-risk preschoolers. *Early Education and Development, 25*, 1016–1034.

Haag, L., & Stern, E. (2003). In search of the benefits of learning Latin. *Journal of Educational Psychology, 95*, 174–178.

Halat, E., & Karakus, F. (2014). Integration of WebQuest in a social studies course and motivation of pre-service teachers. *The Georgia Social Studies Journal, 4*(1), 20–31.

Hallahan, D. P., Kauffman, J. M., & Pullen, P. C. (2009). *Exceptional learners: An introduction to special education*. Boston, MA: Pearson Education.

Hambrick, D. Z., Altmann, E. M., Oswald, F. L., Meinz, E. J., Gobet, F., & Campitelli, G. (2014). Accounting for expert performance: The devil is in the details. *Intelligence, 45*, 112–114.

Haney, C., Banks, C., & Zimbardo, P. (1972). *Interpersonal dynamics in a simulated prison* (No. ONR-TR-Z-09). Stanford, CA: University Department of Psychology.

Hanson, J. L., Nacewicz, B. M., Sutterer, M. J., Cayo, A. A., Schaefer, S. M., Rudolph, K. D., & Davidson, R. J. (2015). Behavioral problems after early life stress: Contributions of the hippocampus and amygdala. *Biological Psychiatry, 77*, 314–323.

Hanushek, E. A. (2011). How much is a good teacher worth? *Education Next, 11*(3), 40–45.

Harris, T. (2002). NLP: If it works, use it … or is there censorship around? *Humanising Language Teaching, 4*(5) (retrieved from http://old.Hltmag.co.uk/sep02/mart3.Htm).

Harrison, Y., & Horne, J. A. (2000). Sleep loss and temporal memory. *Journal of Experimental Psychology: Applied, 53*, 271–279.

Harrow, A. (1972). *A taxonomy of psychomotor domain: A guide for developing behavioral objectives*. New York, NY: David McKay.

Hart, B., & Risley, T. R. (1995). *Meaningful differences in the everyday experience of young American children*. Baltimore, MD: Paul H. Brookes Publishing Company.

Hartigan, J., & Wigdor, A. (1989). Fairness in employment testing. *Science, 245*(4913), 14.

Hattie, J. (2003, October). *Teachers make a difference: What is the research evidence?* Paper presented at the Australian Council for Educational Research Annual Conference on Building Teacher Quality, Melbourne (retrieved from www.acer.edu.au/documents/rc2003_hattie_teachersmakeadifference.pdf).

Hattie, J. (2009). *Visible learning: A synthesis of over 800 meta-analyses relating to achievement*. Abingdon: Routledge.

Hattie, J. (2015). The applicability of Visible Learning to higher education. *Scholarship of Teaching and Learning in Psychology, 1*(1), 79.

Hattie, J., Biggs, J., & Purdie, N. (1996). Effects of learning skills interventions on student learning: A meta-analysis. *Review of Educational Research, 66*, 99–136.

Hattie, J., & Yates, G. C. (2013). *Visible Learning and the science of how we learn.* Abingdon: Routledge.

Heckman, D. A., Farah, M. J., & Meaney, M. J. (2010). Socioeconomic status and the brain: Mechanistic insights from human and animal research. *Nature Reviews Neuroscience, 11*, 651–659.

Heckman, J. J. (2006). Skill formation and the economics of investing in disadvantaged children. *Science, 312*(5782), 1900–1902.

Heckman, J. J. (2007). The economics, technology, and neuroscience of human capability formation. *Proceedings of the National Academy of Sciences, 104*(33), 13250–13255.

Heckman, J. (2008). The case for investing in disadvantaged young children. In First Focus (Ed.) *Big ideas for children: Investing in our nation's future* (pp.49–58). Washington, DC: In Focus.

Heckman, J. J. (2013, September 14). Lifelines for poor children. *The New York Times*.

Heckman, J. J., & Masterov, D. V. (2007). The productivity argument for investing in young children. *Applied Economic Perspectives and Policy, 29*, 446–493.

Helsen, W. F., Van Winckel, J., & Williams, A. M. (2005). The relative age effect in youth soccer across Europe. *Journal of Sports Sciences, 23*, 629–636.

Hempenstall, K. (1997). The whole language phonics controversy: An historical perspective. *Educational Psychology, 17*, 399–418.

Hempenstall, K. (2016). *Read about it: Scientific evidence for effective teaching of reading*. Sydney, Australia: Centre for Independent Studies.

Henry, M. J., & McAuley, J. D. (2010). On the prevalence of congenital amusia. *Music Perception: An Interdisciplinary Journal, 27*, 413–418.

Herman, A. M. (1999). *Futurework: Trends and challenges for work in the 21st century*. US Department of Labor (retrieved from www.Dol.gov/oasam/programs/history/herman/reports/futurework/report.Htm).

Herrnstein, R. J., & Murray, C. A. (1994). *The bell curve: Intelligence and class structure in American life*. New York, NY: The Free Press.

Hew, K. F., & Lo, C. K. (2018). Flipped classroom improves student learning in health professions education: A meta-analysis. *BMC Medical Education, 18*(1), 38.

Hill, H. C., Charalambous, C. Y., & Kraft, M. A. (2012). When rater reliability is not enough: Teacher observation systems and a case for the generalizability study. *Educational Researcher, 41*(2), 56–64.

Hillman, C. H., Pontifex, M. B., Castelli, D. M., Khan, N. A., Raine, L. B., Scudder, M. R., Drolette, R., Moore, R. D., Chien-Ting, W., & Kamijo, K. (2014). Effects of the FITKids randomized controlled trial on executive control and brain function. *Pediatrics, 134*(4), e1063–e1071.

Horton, R. (2004). A statement by the editors of The Lancet. *The Lancet, 363*(9411), 820–821.

Huang, R. H., & Shih, Y. N. (2011). Effects of background music on concentration of workers. *Work, 38*, 383–387.

Huebener, M., Kuger, S., & Marcus, J. (2017). Increased instruction hours and the widening gap in student performance. *Labour Economics, 47*, 15–34.

Hughes, R. W. (2014). Auditory distraction: A duplex mechanism account. *PsyCh Journal, 3*(1), 30–41.

Hunter, J. E., & Hunter, R. F. (1984). Validity and utility of alternative predictors of job performance. *Psychological Bulletin, 96*, 72–98.

Ingvarson, L., & Rowe, K. (2008). Conceptualising and evaluating teacher quality: Substantive and methodological issues. *Australian Journal of Education, 52*(1), 5–35.

Ioannidis, J. P. (2005). Why most published research findings are false. *PLoS Medicine, 2*(8), e124.

Jacob, R., & Parkinson, J. (2015). The potential for school-based interventions that target executive function to improve academic achievement: A review. *Review of Educational Research, 85*, 512–552.

Jaggars, S. S., & Xu, D. (2016). How do online course design features influence student performance? *Computers & Education, 95*, 270–284.

James, K. H., & Engelhardt, L. (2012). The effects of handwriting experience on functional brain development in pre-literate children. *Trends in Neuroscience and Education, 1*(1), 32–42.

Jäncke, L. (2008a). *Macht Musik schlau? Neue Erkenntnisse aus den Neurowissenschaften und der kognitiven Psychologie [Does music make one smart? New findings from neuroscience and cognitive psychology]*. Bern, Switzerland: Huber.

Jäncke, L. (2008b). Music, memory and emotion. *Journal of Biology, 7*(6), 7–21.

Janssens, F. J. G. (2015). *Broodje aap, noot, mies: Vier mythes over onderwijs*. Cura ao, Netherlandsse Antillen: Inter-Continental University of the Caribbean.

Jarvis, P., Newman, S., & Swiniarski, L. (2014). On 'becoming social': The importance of collaborative free play in childhood. *International Journal of Play, 3*(1), 53–68.

Jaschke, A. C., Honing, H., & Scherder, E. J. (2018). Longitudinal analysis of music education on executive functions in primary school children. *Frontiers in Neuroscience, 12*, 103.

Jensen, A. (1969). How much can we boost IQ and scholastic achievement. *Harvard Educational Review, 39*(1), 1–123.

Johnson, S. (2005). *Everything bad is good for you: How today's popular culture is actually making us smarter*. Grand Rapids, MI: Riverhead Publishing.

Johnson, W., Carothers, A., & Deary, I. J. (2008). Sex differences in variability in general intelligence: A new look at the old question. *Perspectives on Psychological Science, 3*, 518–531.

Josephs, D. C. (1958). The emerging American scene. *The School Review, 66*(1), 19–31.

Joubert, J. (2010). Multi-grade teaching in South Africa. *Commonwealth Education Online* (retrieved from www.cedol.org/wp-content/uploads/2012/02/58-62-2010.pdf).

Joyce, T. J., Crockett, S., Jaeger, D. A., Altindag, O., & O'Connell, S. D. (2014). *Does classroom time matter? A randomized field experiment of hybrid and traditional lecture formats in economics* (No. w20006). Cambridge, MA: National Bureau of Economic Research.

Joyce, T. M. (2014). Quality basic education for all: Challenges in multi-grade teaching in rural schools. *Mediterranean Journal of Social Sciences, 5*, 531.

Just, M., Masson, M., & Carpenter, P. (1980). The differences between speed reading and skimming. *Bulletin of the Psychonomic Society, 16*, 171.

Just, M. A., & Carpenter, P. A. (1987). *The psychology of reading and language comprehension*. Boston, MA: Allyn & Bacon.

Kaiser, M. L., Albaret, J. M., & Doudin, P. A. (2009). Relationship between visual-motor integration, eye-hand coordination, and quality of handwriting. *Journal of Occupational Therapy, Schools & Early Intervention, 2*, 87–95.

Kaufman, A. S., Zhou, X., Reynolds, M. R., Kaufman, N. L., Green, G. P., & Weiss, L. G. (2014). The possible societal impact of the decrease in US blood lead levels on adult IQ. *Environmental Research, 132*, 413–420.

Kennedy, M. J., Thomas, C. N., Meyer, J. P., Alves, K. D., & Lloyd, J. W. (2014). Using evidence-based multimedia to improve vocabulary performance of adolescents with LD: A UDL approach. *Learning Disability Quarterly, 37*(2), 71–86.

Kereluik, K., Mishra, P., Fahnoe, C., & Terry, L. (2013). What knowledge is of most worth: Teacher knowledge for 21st century learning. *Journal of Digital Learning in Teacher Education, 29*(4), 127–140.

Kersey, A. J., & James, K. H. (2013). Brain activation patterns resulting from learning letter forms through active self-production and passive observation in young children. *Frontiers in Psychology, 4*, 567.

Kidd, D. (2009). Formative assessment models and their impact on initial teacher training. *Learning and Teaching in Action, 8*(1), 21–28.

Kim, P., Evans, G. W., Angstadt, M., Ho, S. S., Sripada, C. S., Swain, J. E., Liberzon, I., & Phan, K. L. (2013). Effects of childhood poverty and chronic stress on emotion regulatory brain function in adulthood. *Proceedings of the National Academy of Sciences, 110*(46), 18442–18447.

Kimball, B. A. (1986). *Orators & philosophers: A history of the idea of liberal education*. New York, NY: Teachers College Press.

Kirschner, P. A. (2017). *Het Voorbereiden van leerlingen op (nog) niet bestaande banen*. Heerlen, Netherlands: Open Universiteit (retrieved from www.innovatiefinwerk.nl/sites/innovatiefinwerk.nl/files/field/bijlage/rapport_paul_kirschner_nsvp_-_herzien_dec._2017_2.pdf).

Klasse (2017). *Jaarklassen, weg ermee* (www.klasse.be/93172/jaarklassen-weg-ermee/).

Klein, D. (2007). A quarter century of US 'math wars' and political partisanship. *BSHM Bulletin, 22*(1), 22–33.

Knudsen, E. I., Heckman, J. J., Cameron, J. L., & Shonkoff, J. P. (2006). Economic, neurobiological, and behavioral perspectives on building America's future workforce. *Proceedings of the National Academy of Sciences, 103*(27), 10155–10162.

Kohn, A. (2006). *The homework myth: Why our kids get too much of a bad thing*. Boston, MA: Da Capo Lifelong Books.

Kohn, A. (2015, August 16). The perils of 'Growth Mindset' education: Why we're trying to fix our kids when we should be fixing the system (retrieved 16 March 2018, from www.salon.com/2015/08/16/the_education_fad_thats_hurting_our_kids_what_you_need_to_know_about_growth_mindset_theory_and_the_harmful_lessons_it_imparts/).

Kornell, N., & Hausman, H. (2016). Do the best teachers get the best ratings? *Frontiers in Psychology, 7*, 570.

Korthagen, F., & Vasalos, A. (2005). Levels in reflection: Core reflection as a means to enhance professional growth. *Teachers and Teaching, 11*(1), 47–71.

Koslowsky, M., & Babkoff, H. (1992). Meta-analysis of the relationship between total sleep deprivation and performance. *Chronobiology International, 9*, 132–136.

Krapohl, E., Rimfeld, K., Shakeshaft, N. G., Trzaskowski, M., McMillan, A., Pingault, J-P., Asbury, K., Harlaar, N., Kovas, Y., Dale, P., & Plomin, R. (2014). The high heritability of educational achievement reflects many genetically influenced traits, not just intelligence. *Proceedings of the National Academy of Sciences, 111*(42), 15273–15278.

Krathwohl, D. R. (2002). A revision of Bloom's taxonomy: An overview. *Theory into Practice, 41*, 212–218.

Krathwohl, D. R., Bloom, B. S., & Masia, B. B. (1964). *Taxonomy of educational objectives, Book II. Affective domain*. New York, NY: David McKay Company.

Krautmann, A. C., & Sander, W. (1999). Grades and student evaluations of teachers. *Economics of Education Review, 18*(1), 59–63.

Kuipers, B. S., Higgs, M. J., Tolkacheva, N. V., & de Witte, M. C. (2009). The influence of Myers-Briggs type indicator profiles on team development processes: An empirical study in the manufacturing industry. *Small Group Research, 40*, 436–464.

Lancaster, S. J. (2013). The flipped lecture. *New Directions in the Teaching of Physical Sciences, 9*, 28–32.

Lankton, S. (1980). *Practical magic* (p. 7). Cupertino, CA: Meta.

Laurie, V. (2011, November 5). Creative educating for the future. *The Australian* (retrieved from www.theaustralian.com.au/arts/creative-educating-for-the-future/newsstory/138b992d67805d43f596a9a2311040a8?sv=84b3f6943dbc30bde7021275ce27750a&nk=ced65cf16652f0da0d9db900b837778c-1525813312).

Le, H., Oh, I. S., Robbins, S. B., Ilies, R., Holland, E., & Westrick, P. (2011). Too much of a good thing: Curvilinear relationships between personality traits and job performance. *Journal of Applied Psychology, 96*, 113–133.

Lee, K., & Ashton, M. C. (2014). The dark triad, the big five, and the HEXACO model. *Personality and Individual Differences, 67*, 2–5.

Lee, L. J., Connolly, M. E., Dancy, M. H., Henderson, C. R., & Christensen, W. M. (2018). A comparison of student evaluations of instruction vs. students' conceptual learning gains. *American Journal of Physics, 86*, 531–535.

Legg, S., & Hutter, M. (2007). A collection of definitions of intelligence. *Frontiers in Artificial Intelligence and Applications, 157*(17), 9.

Lehmann, J. A., & Seufert, T. (2017). The influence of background music on learning in the light of different theoretical perspectives and the role of working memory capacity. *Frontiers in Psychology, 8*, 1902.

Leuven, E., & Rønning, M. (2011). *Classroom grade composition and student achievement*. Bonn, Germany: IZA Discussion Paper.

Levitt, S. D., & Dubner, S. J. (2005). *Freakonomics*. New York, NY: William Morrow/Harper Collins.

Lilienfeld, S. O. (2010). *50 great myths of popular psychology: Shattering widespread misconceptions about human behavior*. Chichester, UK: Wiley-Blackwell.

Lilienfeld, S. O., Lynn, S. J., Ruscio, J., & Beyerstein, B. L. (2010). *50 Great myths of popular psychology*. Malden, MA: Wiley-Blackwell.

Lindström, E. A., & Lindahl, E. (2011). The effect of mixed-age classes in Sweden. *Scandinavian Journal of Educational Research, 55*, 121–144.

Littlefield, J., Delclos, V. R., Lever, S., Clayton, K. N., Bransford, J. D., & Franks, J. J. (1988). Learning LOGO: Method of teaching, transfer of general skills, and attitudes toward school and computers. In R. E. Mayer (Ed.) *Teaching and learning computer programming: Multiple research perspectives* (pp. 111–135). Hillsdale, NJ: Lawrence Erlbaum Associates, Inc.

Livingstone, S. (2016). New 'screen time' rules from the American Academy of Pediatrics. *Parenting for a Digital Future* (retrieved from http://blogs.Lse.ac.uk/mediapolicyproject/2016/10/24/new-screen-time-rules-from-the-american-academy-of-pediatrics/).

Longcamp, M., Boucard, C., Gilhodes, J. C., & Velay, J. L. (2006). Remembering the orientation of newly learned characters depends on the associated writing knowledge: A comparison between handwriting and typing. *Human Movement Science, 25*, 646–656.

Lye, S. Y., & Koh, J. H. L. (2014). Review on teaching and learning of computational thinking through programming: What is next for K-12? *Computers in Human Behavior, 41*, 51–61.

Lynn, R., Harvey, J., & Nyborg, H. (2009). Average intelligence predicts atheism rates across 137 nations. *Intelligence, 37*(1), 11–15.

Macnamara, B. N., Hambrick, D. Z., & Oswald, F. L. (2014). Deliberate practice and performance in music, games, sports, education, and professions: A meta-analysis. *Psychological Science, 25*, 1608–1618.

Macnamara, B. N., Moreau, D., & Hambrick, D. Z. (2016). The relationship between deliberate practice and performance in sports: A meta-analysis. *Perspectives on Psychological Science, 11*, 333–350.

MacNell, L., Driscoll, A., & Hunt, A. N. (2015). What's in a name: Exposing gender bias in student ratings of teaching. *Innovative Higher Education, 40*, 291–303.

Makel, M. C., & Plucker, J. A. (2014). Facts are more important than novelty: Replication in the education sciences. *Educational Researcher, 43*, 304–316.

Maltese, A. V., Tai, R. H., & Fan, X. (2012). When is homework worth the time? Evaluating the association between homework and achievement in high school science and math. *The High School Journal, 96*(1), 52–72.

Mangen, A., Anda, L. G., Oxborough, G. H., & Brønnick, K. (2015). Handwriting versus keyboard writing: Effect on word recall. *Journal of Writing Research, 7*, 227–247.

Mariano, L. T., & Kirby, S. N. (2009). *Achievement of students in multigrade classrooms: Evidence from the Los Angeles Unified School District*. Cambridge: RAND.

Marsden, D., & Richardson, R. (1994). Performing for pay? The effects of 'merit pay' on motivation in a public service. *British Journal of Industrial Relations, 32*, 243–261.

Marzano, R. J., & Heflebower, T. (2012). *Klaar voor de 21e eeuw. Vaardigheden voor een veranderende wereld*. Vlissingen, Netherlands: Bazalt.

Masciantonio, R. (1977). Tangible benefits of the study of Latin: A review of research. *Foreign Language Annals, 10*, 375–382.

Mason, D. A., & Burns, R. B. (1996). 'Simply no worse and simply no better' may simply be wrong: A critique of Veenman's conclusion about multigrade classes. *Review of Educational Research*, 66, 307–322.

Masrifatin, Y. (2016). Non-graded education: Recognition of individual differences. *Educatio: Jurnal Pendidikan STAIM Nganjuk, 1*(2), 136–155.

Masters, K. (2014). Nipping an education myth in the bud: Poh's brain activity during lectures. *Medical Teacher, 36*, 732–735.

Matari , M. J. (2007). *The robotics primer*. Cambridge, MA: MIT Press.

Mauger, P. (1966). The flexible school. *Forum, 8*, 2.

Mavrou, K., Charalampous, E., & Michaelides, M. (2013). Graphic symbols for all: Using symbols in developing the ability of questioning in young children. *Journal of Assistive Technologies, 7*(1), 22–33.

Maxwell, J. A. (2004). Causal explanation, qualitative research, and scientific inquiry in education. *Educational Researcher, 33*(3), 3–11.

Mayer, R. E. (1975). Different problem-solving competencies established in learning computer programming with and without meaningful models. *Journal of Educational Psychology, 67*(6), 725–734.

Mayer, R. E. (2009). *Multimedia learning*. New York, NY: Cambridge University Press.

Mayer, R. E., & Moreno, R. (2003). Nine ways to reduce cognitive load in multimedia learning. *Educational Psychologist, 38*, 43–52.

Mayne, R. (2017). A critical look at NLP in ELT. *English Australia Journal, 33*(1), 43.

Mazur, E. (2011, August). The scientific approach to teaching: Research as a basis for course design. In: *Proceedings of the Seventh International Workshop on Computing Education Research* (pp. 1–2). ACM.

Meijer, W. A. J. (2013). *Onderwijs, weer weten waarom*. Amsterdam: Uitgeverij SWP.

Meikle, J., & Boseley, S. (2010). MMR row doctor Andrew Wakefield struck off register. *The Guardian* (retrieved from www.theguardian.com/society/2010/may/24/mmr-doctor-andrew-wakefield-struck-off).

Meng, F., & Wu, J. (2015). Merit pay fairness, leader-member exchange, and job engagement: Evidence from Mainland China. *Review of Public Personnel Administration, 35*(1), 47–69.

Metiri Group & NCREL. (2003). *EnGauge 21st century skills: Literacy in the digital age*. Chicago, IL: NCREL.

Middlebrooks, C. D., Kerr, T., & Castel, A. D. (2017). Selectively distracted: Divided attention and memory for important information. *Psychological Science, 28*, 1103–1115.

Miellet, S., O'Donnell, P. J., & Sereno, S. C. (2009). Parafoveal magnification: Visual acuity does not modulate the perceptual span in reading. *Psychological Science, 20*, 721–728.

Milgram, S. (1963). Behavioral study of obedience. *Journal of Abnormal and Social Psychology, 67*, 371–378.

Milgram, S. (1974). *Obedience to authority*. New York, NY: Harper & Row.

Miller, E., & Almon, J. (2009). *Crisis in the kindergarten: Why children need to play in school*. College Park, MD: Alliance for Childhood.

Miller, G. E. (1990). The assessment of clinical skills/competence/performance. *Academic Medicine, 65*, 63–67.

Millrood, R. (2004). The role of NLP in teachers' classroom discourse. *ELT Journal, 58*(1), 28–37.

Mirzakhanyana, R., Gevorgyana, S., Sargsyana, V., & Daveyana, H. (2017). Analysis of the efficiency of teaching chess in schools. *Sociology, 7*(1), 36–42.

Mischel, W. (2014). *The marshmallow test: Understanding self-control and how to master it*. New York, NY: Random House.

Mishra, P., & The Deep-Play Research Group. (2012). Rethinking technology & creativity in the 21st century: Crayons are the future. *Tech Trends, 56*(5), 13–16.

Morshead, R. W. (1965). Taxonomy of educational objectives handbook II: Affective domain. *Studies in Philosophy and Education, 4*(1), 164–170.

Moullin, S., Waldfogel, J., & Washbrook, E. (2014, March 21). *Baby Bonds Parenting, attachment and a secure base for children* (retrieved July 12, 2014, from www.suttontrust.com/our-work/research/item/baby-bonds/).

Mueller, C. M., & Dweck, C. S. (1998). Praise for intelligence can undermine children's motivation and performance. *Journal of Personality and Social Psychology, 75*(1), 33–52.

Mueller, P. A., & Oppenheimer, D. M. (2014). The pen is mightier than the keyboard: Advantages of longhand over laptop note taking. *Psychological Science, 25*, 1159–1168.

Muijs, D., Kyriakides L., van der Werf, G., Creemers, B., Timperley, H., & Earl, L. (2014). State of the art – Teacher effectiveness and professional learning. *School Effectiveness and School Improvement: An International Journal of Research, Policy and Practice, 25*, 231–256.

Mullainathan, S., & Datta, S. (2011). *Stress impacts good parenting*. In: W. K. Kellogg Foundation. Annual Report 2011 (retrieved from www.ideas42.org/publication/view/stress-impacts-good-parenting-the-behavioral-economists-perspective/).

Mullainathan, S., & Shafir, E. (2013). *Scarcity: Why having too little means so much*. London: Macmillan.

Murawski, W. W., & Lee Swanson, H. (2001). A meta-analysis of co-teaching research: Where are the data? *Remedial and Special Education, 22*, 258–267.

Musch, J., & Grondin, S. (2001). Unequal competition as an impediment to personal development: A review of the relative age effect in sport. *Developmental Review, 21*(2), 147–167.

Myers, I. B., McCaulley, M. H., Quenk, N. L., & Hammer, A. L. (1998). *Manual: A guide to the development and use of the Myers- Briggs Type Indicator*. Palo Alto, CA: Consulting Psychologists Press.

National Institute of Child Health and Human Development (2000). *Report of the National Reading Panel: Teaching children to read: An evidence-based assessment of the scientific literature on reading and its implications for reading instruction* (NIH Publication No. 00-4754). Washington, DC: Government Printing Office.

National Research Council (2003). *The polygraph and lie detection*. Committee to Review the Scientific Evidence on the Polygraph. Division of Behavioral and Social Sciences and Education. Washington, DC: The National Academies Press.

Neisser, U., Boodoo, G., Bouchard Jr, T. J., Boykin, A. W., Brody, N., Ceci, P., & Urbina, S. (1996). Intelligence: Knowns and unknowns. *American Psychologist, 51*(2), 77–101.

Neve, P., Livingstone, D., Hunter, G., & Alsop, G. (2013). *2nd Annual Conference on the Aiming for Excellence in STEM Learning and Teaching* (retrieved from www.paulneve.com/hea-stem2013_final.pdf).

Newman, S. J., & Holupka, C. S. (2014). Housing affordability and child well-being. *Housing Policy Debate*, 1–36, (ahead-of-print).

Nicolas, S., Andrieu, B., Croizet, J. C., Sanitioso, R. B., & Burman, J. T. (2013). Sick? Or slow? On the origins of intelligence as a psychological object. *Intelligence, 41*, 699–711.

Nisbett, R. E., Aronson, J., Blair, C., Dickens, W., Flynn, J., Halpern, D. F., & Turkheimer, E. (2012). Intelligence: New findings and theoretical developments. *American Psychologist, 67*(2), 130.

Noble, K. G., Houston, S. M., Kan, E., & Sowell, E. R. (2012). Neural correlates of socioeconomic status in the developing human brain. *Developmental Science, 15*, 516–527.

Norcross, J. C., Koocher, G. P., & Garofalo, A. (2006). Discredited psychological treatments and tests: A Delphi poll. *Professional Psychology: Research and Practice, 37*, 515–522.

Nores, M., & Barnett, W. S. (2010). Benefits of early childhood interventions across the world: (Under) Investing in the very young. *Economics of Education Review, 29*, 271–282.

Núñez, J. C., Suárez, N., Rosário, P., Vallejo, G., Cerezo, R., & Valle, A. (2014). Teachers' feedback on homework, homework-related behaviors and academic achievement. *The Journal of Educational Research, 1*, 1–13.

O'Brien, E. J., Albrecht, J. E., Hakala, C. M., & Rizzella, M. L. (1995). Activation and suppression of antecedents during reinstatement. *Journal of Experimental Psychology: Learning, Memory, and Cognition, 21*, 626–634.

O'Keefe, P. A., Dweck, C. S., & Walton, G. M. (2018). Implicit theories of interest: Finding your passion or developing it. *Psychological Science*. doi:10.1177/0956797618780643

OECD. (2015). Supporting new teachers. In *Teaching in focus* (Vol. 11). Paris, France: OECD Publishing (https://doi.org/10.1787/5js1p1r88lg5-en).

OECD. (2016). How is learning time organized in primary and secondary education? In *Education indicators in focus* (No. 38). Paris, France: OECD Publishing.

Ofman, D. (2001). *Core qualities: A gateway to human resources*. Schiedam, Netherlands: Scriptum.

Oostermeijer, M., Boonen, A. J., & Jolles, J. (2014). The relation between children's constructive play activities, spatial ability, and mathematical word problem-solving performance: A mediation analysis in sixth-grade students. *Frontiers in Psychology, 5*, 782.

Orosz, G., Péter-Szarka, S., Bőthe, B., Tóth-Király, I., & Berger, R. (2017). How not to do a mindset intervention: Learning from a mindset intervention among students with good grades. *Frontiers in Psychology, 8*, 1–11.

Paivio, A. (1986). *Mental representations: A dual coding approach*. Oxford: Oxford University Press.

Pan, S. C., & Rickard, T. C. (2018). Transfer of test-enhanced learning: Meta-analytic review and synthesis. *Psychological Bulletin, 144*, 710–756.

Papert, S. (1980). *Mindstorms: Children, computers, and powerful ideas*. New York, NY: Basic Books.

Papert, S. (1996). An exploration in the space of mathematics educations. *International Journal of Computers for Mathematical Learning, 1*(1), 95–123.

Park, N., Peterson, C., & Seligman, M. E. (2004). Strengths of character and well-being. *Journal of Social and Clinical Psychology, 23*(5), 603–619.

Partnership for 21st Century Skills. (2006). *A state leader's action guide to 21st century skills: A new vision for education*. Tucson, AZ: Partnership for 21st Century Skills.

Peal, R. (2014). *Progressively worse: The burden of bad ideas in British schools*. London: Civitas, Institute for the Study of Civil Society.

Pearce, J. L., Stevenson, W. B., & Perry, J. L. (1985). Managerial compensation based on organizational performance: A time series analysis of the effects of merit pay. *Academy of Management Journal, 28*, 261–278.

Pennebaker, J. W., Gosling, S. D., & Ferrell, J. D. (2013). Daily online testing in large classes: Boosting college performance while reducing achievement gaps. *PLoS One, 8*(11).

Perham, N., & Currie, H. (2014). Does listening to preferred music improve reading comprehension performance? *Applied Cognitive Psychology, 2*, 279–284.

Perkins, D. N., & Salomon, G. (1992, 2nd ed.). Transfer of Learning. In *Contribution to the international Encyclopedia of education*. Oxford: Pergamon Press.

Peterson, C., & Seligman, M. E. (2004). *Character strengths and virtues: A handbook and classification* (Vol. 1). Oxford: Oxford University Press.

Pham, L. D., Nguyen, T. D., & Springer, M. G. (2017, April 3). *Teacher merit pay and student test scores: A meta-analysis*. Nashville, TN: Vanderbilt University.

Pietschnig, J., & Gittler, G. (2015). A reversal of the Flynn effect for spatial perception in German-speaking countries: Evidence from a cross-temporal IRT-based meta-analysis (1977-2014). *Intelligence, 53*, 145–153.

Pietschnig, J., & Voracek, M. (2015). One century of global IQ gains: A formal meta-analysis of the Flynn effect (1909–2013). *Perspectives on Psychological Science, 10*, 282–306.

Pink, D. H. (2011). *Drive: The surprising truth about what motivates us*. London: Penguin.

Pinker, S. (2003). *The blank slate: The modern denial of human nature*. London: Penguin.

Pishghadam, R., & Shayesteh, S. (2014). Neuro-linguistic programming (NLP) for language teachers: Revalidation of an NLP scale. *Theory and Practice in Language Studies, 4*, 2096–2104.

Pittenger, D. J. (1993). The utility of the Myers-Briggs Type Indicator. *Review of Educational Research, 63*, 467–488.

Pittenger, D. J. (2005). Cautionary comments regarding the Myers-Briggs Type Indicator. *Consulting Psychology Journal: Practice and Research, 57*, 210–221.

Plomin, R., & Deary, I. J. (2015). Genetics and intelligence differences: Five special findings. *Molecular Psychiatry, 20*(1), 98–108.

Podgursky, M. J., & Springer, M. G. (2007). Teacher performance pay: A review. *Journal of Policy Analysis and Management: The Journal of the Association for Public Policy Analysis and Management, 26*, 909–950.

Poh, M. Z., Swenson, N. C., & Picard, R. W. (2010). A wearable sensor for unobtrusive, long-term assessment of electrodermal activity. *IEEE Transactions on Biomedical Engineering, 57*, 1243–1252.

Popova, A., Kirschner, P. A., & Joiner, R. (2013). Effects of primer podcasts on stimulating learning from lectures: How do students engage? *British Journal of Educational Technology, 45*, 330–339.

Popova, A., Kirschner, P. A., & Joiner, R. (2014). Enhancing learning from lectures with epistemic primer podcasts activity – A pilot study. *International Journal of Learning Technology, 9*, 323–337.

Poropat, A. E. (2014). Other-rated personality and academic performance: Evidence and implications. *Learning and Individual Differences, 34*, 24–32.

Posthuma, D., De Geus, E. J., Baaré, W. F., Pol, H. E. H., Kahn, R. S., & Boomsma, D. I. (2002). The association between brain volume and intelligence is of genetic origin. *Nature Neuroscience, 5*(2), 83.

Putkinen, V., Saarikivi, K., & Tervaniemi, M. (2013). Do informal musical activities shape auditory skill development in preschool-age children? *Frontiers in Psychology, 4*, 572.

Ra, C. K., Cho, J., Stone, M. D., De La Cerda, J., Goldenson, N. I., Moroney, E., Tung, I., Lee, S. S., & Leventhal, A. M. (2018). Association of digital media use with subsequent symptoms of attention-deficit/hyperactivity disorder among adolescents. *Journal of the American Medical Association, 320*, 255–263.

Rawson, K., Stahovich, T. F., & Mayer, R. E. (2017). Homework and achievement: Using smartpen technology to find the connection. *Journal of Educational Psychology, 109*, 208–219.

Rayner, K., Schotter, E. R., Masson, M. E., Potter, M. C., & Treiman, R. (2016). So much to read, so little time: How do we read, and can speed reading help? *Psychological Science in the Public Interest, 17*(1), 4–34.

Reavis, R. D., Miller, S. E., Grimes, J. A., & Fomukong, A.-N. N. M. (2018). Effort as person-focused praise: 'Hard worker' has negative effects for adults after a failure. *The Journal of Genetic Psychology, 179*(3), 117–122.

Reigeluth, C. M. (Ed.). (1983). *Instructional-design theories and models: An overview of their current status*. Hillsdale, NJ: Erlbaum Associates.

Revell, J., & Norman, S. (1999). *Handing over: NLP-based activities for language learning*. London: Saffire Press.

Richter, C. P. (1957). On the phenomenon of sudden death in animals and man. *Psychosomatic Medicine, 19*, 191–198.

Rietveld, C. A., Medland, S. E., Derringer, J., Yang, J., Esko, T., Martin, N. W., & Albrecht, E. (2013). GWAS of 126,559 individuals identifies genetic variants associated with educational attainment. *Science, 340*(6139), 1467–1471.

Rimfeld, K., Kovas, Y., Dale, P. S., & Plomin, R. (2016). True grit and genetics: Predicting academic achievement from personality. *Journal of Personality and Social Psychology, 111*, 780–789.

Ris, E. W. (2015). Grit: A short history of a useful concept. *Journal of Educational Controversy, 10*(1), 3–18.

Ritchie, S. (2015). *Intelligence: All that matters*. London: Hodder & Stoughton.

Ritchie, S. J., & Tucker-Drob, E. M. (2018). How much does education improve intelligence? A meta-analysis. *Psychological Science, 29*, 1358–1369.

Rivkin, S. G., Hanushek, E. A., & Kain, J. F. (2005). Teachers, schools, and academic achievement. *Econometrica, 73*, 417–458.

Roberts, S. J., & Stott, T. (2015). A new factor in UK students' university attainment: The relative age effect reversal? *Quality Assurance in Education, 23*, 295–305.

Robertson, K. F., Smeets, S., Lubinski, D., & Benbow, C. P. (2010). Beyond the threshold hypothesis: Even among the gifted and top math/science graduate students, cognitive abilities, vocational interests, and lifestyle preferences matter for career choice, performance, and persistence. *Current Directions in Psychological Science, 19*, 346–351.

Rodin, M., & Rodin, B. (1972). Student evaluations of teachers. *Science, 177*(4055), 1164–1166.

Romiszowski, A. J. (2016). *Designing instructional systems: Decision making in course planning and curriculum design*. Abingdon: Routledge.

Rosário, P., Núñez, J. C., Vallejo, G., Cunha, J., Nunes, T., Mourão, R., & Pinto, R. (2015). Does homework design matter? The role of homework's purpose in student mathematics achievement. *Contemporary Educational Psychology, 43*, 10–24.

Rose, D. H., & Meyer, A. (2002). *Teaching every student in the digital age: Universal design for learning*. Alexandria, VA: Association for Supervision and Curriculum Development.

Rosenberg, M. (2013). *Spotlight on learning styles*. Peaslake, Surrey: Delta Publishing.

Rothstein, H. R., Sutton, A. J., & Borenstein, M. (Eds.). (2006). *Publication bias in meta-analysis: Prevention, assessment and adjustments*. New York, NY: Wiley.

Rowe, K. J. (2003, October 19-21). The importance of teacher quality as a key determinant of students' experiences and outcomes of schooling. *Paper presented at the 2003 ACER Research Conference (Background paper for Keynote Address)*, Carlton Crest Hotel, Melbourne (available in pdf format at www.acer.edu.au/research/programs/learningprocess.Html).

Royer, J. M. (1979). Theories of the transfer of learning. *Educational Psychologist, 14*(1), 53–69.

Ryan, R. M., & Deci, E. L. (2000). Intrinsic and extrinsic motivations: Classic definitions and new directions. *Contemporary Educational Psychology, 25*, 54–67.

Rybanska, V., McKay, R., Jong, J., & Whitehouse, H. (2018). Rituals improve children's ability to delay gratification. *Child Development, 89*, 349–359.

Sackett, P. R., Schmitt, N., Ellingson, J. E., & Kabin, M. B. (2001). High-stakes testing in employment, credentialing, and higher education: Prospects in a post-affirmative-action world. *American Psychologist, 56*, 302–318.

Sala, G., Foley, J. P., & Gobet, F. (2017). The effects of chess instruction on pupils' cognitive and academic skills: State of the art and theoretical challenges. *Frontiers in Psychology, 8*, 238.

Sala, G., & Gobet, F. (2017). Does far transfer exist? Negative evidence from chess, music, and working memory training. *Current Directions in Psychological Science, 26*, 515–520.

Salgado, J. F., Anderson, N., & Tauriz, G. (2015). The validity of ipsative and quasi ipsative forced choice personality inventories for different occupational groups: A comprehensive meta analysis. *Journal of Occupational and Organizational Psychology, 88*, 797–834.

Saxe, L. (1991). Science and the CQT polygraph. *Integrative Physiological and Behavioral Science, 26*, 223–231.

Sayal, K., Chudal, R., Hinkka-Yli-Salomäki, S., Joelsson, P., & Sourander, A. (2017). Relative age within the school year and diagnosis of attention-deficit hyperactivity disorder: A nationwide population-based study. *The Lancet Psychiatry, 4*, 868–875.

Schellenberg, E. G. (2004). Music lessons enhance IQ. *Psychological Science, 15*, 511–514.

Schleicher, A. (2017). Seeing education through the prism of PISA. *European Journal of Education, 52*, 124–130.

Schmitt, S. A., McClelland, M. M., Tominey, S. L., & Acock, A. C. (2015). Strengthening school readiness for Head Start children: Evaluation of a self-regulation intervention. *Early Childhood Research Quarterly, 30*, 20–31.

Schultz, L. (2005). Bloom's taxonomy. *Old Dominion University* (retrieved from www.psianw.org/newsletter-articles/blooms-taxonomy-levels-of-understanding).

Shakeshaft, N. G., Trzaskowski, M., McMillan, A., Rimfeld, K., Krapohl, E., Haworth, C. M., & Plomin, R. (2013). Strong genetic influence on a UK nationwide test of educational achievement at the end of compulsory education at age 16. *PLoS One, 8*(12), e80341.

Shonkoff, J. P., Garner, A. S., Siegel, B. S., Dobbins, M. I., Earls, M. F., McGuinn, L., & Wood, D. L. (2012). The lifelong effects of early childhood adversity and toxic stress. *Pediatrics, 129*(1), e232–e246.

Silva, E. (2009). Measuring skills for 21st-century learning. *Phi Delta Kappan, 90*, 630–634.

Simpson, E. J. (1972). *The classification of educational objectives in the psychomotor domain*. Washington, DC: Gryphon House.

Singley, M. K., & Anderson, J. R. (1989). *The transfer of cognitive skill (No. 9)*. Cambridge, MA: Harvard University Press.

Sirin, S. R. (2005). Socioeconomic status and academic achievement: A meta-analytic review of research. *Review of Educational Research, 75*, 417–453.

Sisk, V. F., Burgoyne, A. P., Sun, J., Butler, J. L., & Macnamara, B. N. (2018). To what extent and under which circumstances are growth mind-sets important to academic achievement? Two meta-analyses. *Psychological Science, 29*, 549–571.

Skoe, E., Krizman, J., & Kraus, N. (2013). The impoverished brain: Disparities in maternal education affect the neural response to sound. *Journal of Neuroscience, 33*, 17221–17231.

Sligte, H., Bulterman-Bos, J., & Huizinga, M. (2009). Maatwerk voor latente talenten? Uitblinken op alle niveaus. *SCO-rapport, (820)*. p. 22.

SLO. (2014). *Digitale geletterdheid en 21steeeuwse vaardigheden in het funderend onderwijs: Een conceptueel kader*. Enschede, Netherlands: SLO.

Smith, C. R. (1983). *Writer's Workbench: Applications in the classroom*. Paper presented at the annual meeting of the Conference on College Composition and Communication, Detroit (MI).

Smoker, T. J., Murphy, C. E., & Rockwell, A. K. (2009). Comparing memory for handwriting versus typing. *Proceedings of the Human Factors and Ergonomics Society Annual Meeting, October 2009, 53*, 1744–1747.

Song, H., Zmyslinski-Seelig, A., Kim, J., Drent, A., Victor, A., Omori, K., & Allen, M. (2014). Does Facebook make you lonely? A meta analysis. *Computers in Human Behavior, 36*, 446–452.

Sperry, D. E., Sperry, L. L., & Miller, P. J. (2018). Reexamining the verbal environments of children from different socioeconomic backgrounds. *Child Development*. doi:10.1111/cdev.13072

Stanovich, K. E. (2009). Matthew effects in reading: Some consequences of individual differences in the acquisition of literacy. *Journal of Education, 189*(1–2), 23–55.

Stehr-Green, P., Tull, P., Stellfeld, M., Mortenson, P. B., & Simpson, D. (2003). Autism and thimerosal-containing vaccines: Lack of consistent evidence for an association. *American Journal of Preventive Medicine, 25*(2), 101–106.

Strack, F., Martin, L. L., & Stepper, S. (1988). Inhibiting and facilitating conditions of the human smile: A nonobtrusive test of the facial feedback hypothesis. *Journal of Personality and Social Psychology, 54*, 768–777.

Strieker, L. J., & Ross, J. (1962). A description and evaluation of the Myers-Briggs-Type Indicator. In *Research Bulletin #RB-62-6*. Princeton, NJ: Educational Testing Service.

Swain, F. (2011). Susan Greenfield: Living online is changing our brains. *New Scientist, 3*. https://www.newscientist.com/article/mg21128236-400-susan-greenfield-living-online-is-changing-our-brains/

Sweller, J. (2005). The redundancy principle in multimedia learning. In R. E. Mayer (Ed.) *The Cambridge handbook of multimedia learning* (pp. 159–167). New York, NY: Cambridge University Press.

Sweller, J., Clark, R., & Kirschner, P. (2010). Teaching general problem-solving skills is not a substitute for, or a viable addition to, teaching mathematics. *Notices of the American Mathematical Society, 57*, 1303–1304.

Szpunar, K. K., Khan, N. Y., & Schacter, D. L. (2013). Interpolated memory tests reduce mind wandering and improve learning of online lectures. *Proceedings of the National Academy of Sciences, 110*, 6313–6317.

Talwar, R., & Hancock, T. (2010). The shape of jobs to come. Possible new careers emerging from advances in science and technology (2010 – 2030), *Fast Future Research* (retrieved from http://fastfuture.com/wpcontent/uploads/2010/01/FastFuture_Shapeofjobstocome_FullReport1.pdf).

Tampio, N. (2016, June 2). Teaching 'grit' is bad for children, and bad for democracy. *Aeon.co*. (https://aeon.co/ideas/teaching-grit-is-bad-for-children-and-bad-for-democracy).

Taylor, L. E., Swerdfeger, A. L., & Eslick, G. D. (2014). Vaccines are not associated with autism: An evidence-based meta-analysis of case-control and cohort studies. *Vaccine, 32*, 3623–3629.

Teasdale, T. W., & Owen, D. R. (2005). A long-term rise and recent decline in intelligence test performance: The Flynn Effect in reverse. *Personality and Individual Differences, 39*, 837–843.

Tedre, M., & Denning, P. J. (2016, November). *The long quest for computational thinking*. In: Proceedings of the 16th Koli Calling International Conference on Computing Education Research (pp. 120–129). ACM.

ter Bogt, T. F. M., Keijsers, L., & Meeus, W. H. J. (2013). Early adolescent music preferences and minor delinquency. *Pediatrics, 131*(2), e380–e389.

Thomas, J. L. (2012). Combination classes and educational achievement. *Economics of Education Review, 31*, 1058–1066.

Thomas, M., Sing, H., Belenky, G., Holcomb, H., Mayberg, H., Dannals, R., Wagner H., Thorne D., Popp K., Rowland L., Welsh A., Balwinski S., & Redmond D. (2000). Neural basis of alertness and cognitive performance impairments during sleepiness. Effects of 24 h of sleep deprivation on waking human regional brain activity. *Journal of Sleep Research, 9,* 335–352.

Thomason, T. C., Arbuckle, T., & Cady, D. (1980). Test of the eye-movement hypothesis of Neurolinguistic Programming. *Perceptual and Motor Skills, 51,* 230.

Thorndike, E. L. (1923). The influence of first year Latin upon the ability to read English. *School Sociology, 17,* 165–168.

Tideman, J. W. L., Polling, J. R., Van der Schans, A., Verhoeven, V., & Klaver, C. (2016). Bijziendheid, een groeiend probleem. *Netherlands Tijdschrift Voor Geneeskunde, 160*(48).

Titova, O. E., Hogenkamp, P. S., Jacobsson, J. A., Feldman, I., Schiöth, H. B., & Benedict, C. (2015). Associations of self-reported sleep disturbance and duration with academic failure in community-dwelling Swedish adolescents: Sleep and academic performance at school. *Sleep Medicine, 16*(1), 87–93.

Tosey, P., & Mathison, J. (2009). *Neuro-linguistic programming: A critical appreciation for managers and developers*. Basingstk B: Macmillan.

Trahan, L. H., Stuebing, K. K., Fletcher, J. M., & Hiscock, M. (2014). The Flynn effect: A meta-analysis. *Psychological Bulletin, 140,* 1332.

Traphagan, T., Kucsera, J. V., & Kishi, K. (2010). Impact of class lecture webcasting on attendance and learning. *Educational Technology Research and Development, 58*(1), 19–37.

Trautwein, U., Köller, O., Schmitz, B., & Baumert, J. (2002). Do homework assignments enhance achievement? A multilevel analysis in 7th grade mathematics. *Contemporary Educational Psychology, 27,* 26–50.

Tricot, A., & Sweller, J. (2014). Domain-specific knowledge and why teaching generic skills does not work. *Educational Psychology Review, 26,* 265–283.

Tu, J. J., & Johnson, J. R. (1990). Can computer programming improve problem-solving ability? *ACM SIGCSE Bulletin, 22*(2), 30–33.

Tucker-Drob, E. M., Briley, D. A., Engelhardt, L. E., Mann, F. D., & Harden, K. P. (2016). Genetically-mediated associations between measures of childhood character and academic achievement. *Journal of Personality and Social Psychology, 111,* 790–815.

Turner, K. M., Hatton, D., & Theresa, M. (2018). Student evaluations of teachers and courses: Time to wake up and shake up. *Nursing Education Perspectives, 39*(3), 130–131.

Twenge, J. M., & Campbell, W. K. (2009). *The narcissism epidemic: Living in the age of entitlement*. New York, NY: Simon & Schuster.

Twenge, J. M., Campbell, W. K., & Freeman, E. C. (2012). Generational differences in young adults' life goals, concern for others, and civic orientation, 1966–2009. *Journal of Personality and Social Psychology, 102,* 1045–1062.

Twenge, J. M., Joiner, T. E., Rogers, M. L., & Martin, G. N. (2018a). Increases in depressive symptoms, suicide-related outcomes, and suicide rates among US adolescents after 2010 and links to increased new media screen time. *Clinical Psychological Science*, *6*(1), 3–17.

Twenge, J. M., Martin, G. N., & Campbell, W. K. (2018b). Decreases in psychological well-being among American adolescents after 2012 and links to screen time during the rise of smartphone technology. *Emotion*, *18*(6), 765–780.

UN CRPD Committee. (2016). General Comment No. 4. *UN Doc CRPD/C/GC/4*. (retrieved October 10, 2018 from https://tbinternet.ohchr.org/_layouts/treatybodyexternal/Download.aspx?symbolno=CRPD/C/GC/4&Lang=en).

Uttl, B., & Smibert, D. (2017). Student evaluations of teaching: Teaching quantitative courses can be hazardous to one's career. *PeerJ*, *5*, e3299.

Uttl, B., White, C. A., & Gonzalez, D. W. (2017). Meta-analysis of faculty's teaching effectiveness: Student evaluation of teaching ratings and student learning are not related. *Studies in Educational Evaluation*, *54*, 22–42.

Valcke, M. (2007). *Onderwijskunde als ontwerpwetenschap*. Ghent, Belgium: Academia Press.

Van Den Branden, K. (2011). *Evaluatierapport van Voorrangsbeleid Brussel*. Leuven, Belgium: Centrum voor Taal en Onderwijs.

van der Vleuten, C. (2013). *Taking evidence seriously: What would happen to our training programmes?* Prague: AMEE 2013 (retrieved from www.slideshare.net/roboonya/amee-plenary-cees-without-videos).

Van Lengen, C., & Maddux, C. (1990). Does instruction in computer programming improve problem solving ability? *Journal of Information Systems Education*, *12 (2)*, 23–34.

Vandecandelaere, M., Van den Branden, N., Juchtmans, G., Vandenbroeck, M., & De Fraine, B. (2016). *Flexibele leerwegen in Vlaanderen: Onderzoeksrapport* (p. 42). Leuven, Belgium: KU Leuven.

Veen, M. (2013). *Plenaire reactie op het boek van Wilna A. J. Meijer: Onderwijs, weer weten waarom*. Contribution for the special meeting of the Kohnstamm network. Amsterdam: Free University, 18 April 2013.

Veenman, S. (1995). Cognitive and non-cognitive effects of multigrade and multi-age classes: A best-evidence synthesis. *Review of Educational Research*, *65*, 319–381.

Veenman, S. (1996). Effects of multigrade and multi-age classes reconsidered. *Review of Educational Research*, *66*, 323–340.

Vermeren, P. (2007). *DeHR-ballon*. Ghent, Belgium: Academia Press.

Wagenmakers, E. J., Beek, T., Dijkhoff, L., Gronau, Q. F., Acosta, A., Adams Jr, R. B., & Bulnes, L. C. (2016). Registered Replication Report: Strack, Martin & Stepper (1988). *Perspectives on Psychological Science*, *11*, 917–928.

Wakefield, A. J., Murch, S. H., Anthony, A., Linnell, J., Casson, D. M., Malik, M., & Valentine, A. (1998). RETRACTED: Ileal-lymphoid-nodular hyperplasia, non-specific colitis, and pervasive developmental disorder in children. *The Lancet*, *351*(9103), 637–641.

Walker, S. P., Wachs, T. D., Grantham-McGregor, S., Black, M. M., Nelson, C. A., Huffman, S. L., & Richter, L. (2011). Inequality in early childhood: Risk and protective factors for early child development. *The Lancet*, *378*(9799), 1325–1338.

Wang, M., & Lynn, R. (2018). Intelligence in the People's Republic of China. *Personality and Individual Differences, 134*, 275–277.

Weir, K. (2016). Is homework a necessary evil? *Monitor on Psychology, 47*, 3.

Wetzel, E., Brown, A., Hill, P. L., Chung, J. M., Robins, R. W., & Roberts, B. W. (2017). The narcissism epidemic is dead; long live the narcissism epidemic. *Psychological Science, 28*, 1833–1847.

Wiedemann, H. (1985). *Klavierspiel und das rechte Gehirn. Neue Erkenntnisse der Gehirnforschung als Grundlage einer Klavierdidaktik für erwachsene Anfänger [Piano playing and the right hemisphere: New findings from brain research as a basis for piano didactics for adult beginners]*. Regensburg, Germany: Bosse.

Wigdor, A. K. (1982). Ability testing: Uses, consequences, and controversies. *Educational Measurement: Issues and Practice, 1*(3), 6–8.

Wiliam, D. (2014, June). Randomized control trials in education research. *Research in Education, 6*(1).

Wiliam, D. (2018). *Creating the schools our children need*. West Palm Beach, FL: Learning Sciences International.

Wilkinson, I. A. G., & Hamilton, R. J. (2003). Learning to read in composite (multigrade) classes in New Zealand. *Teaching and Teacher Education, 19*, 221–235.

Willingham, D., & De Bruyckere, P. (2016). *Wat we kinderen echt kunnen leren [translation of When Can You Trust the Experts?]*. Leuven, Belgium: LannooCampus.

Willingham, D. T. (2009). *Why don't students like school? A cognitive scientist answers questions about how the mind works and what it means for the classroom*. Hoboken, NJ: John Wiley & Sons.

Wing, J. M. (2006). Computational thinking. *Communications of the ACM, 49*(3), 33–35.

Winner, E., Goldstein, T., & Vincent-Lancrin, S. (2013). *Educational research and innovation: Art for art's sake? The impact of arts education*. Paris, France: OECD Publishing.

Winters, H., & Velthausz, F. (2014). In een goede stamgroep is het net als thuis. *Mensenkinderen, 30*(143), 5–7.

Wiseman, R., Watt, C., Ten Brinke, L., Porter, S., Couper, S. L., & Rankin, C. (2012). The eyes don't have it: Lie detection and neuro-linguistic programming. *PLoS One, 7*(7), e40259.

Wisman, R. (2018). *Stop de Rekenoorlog*. AOB. https://www.aob.nl/nieuws/stop-de-rekenoorlog/

Witkowski, T. (2010). Thirty-five years of research on Neuro-Linguistic Programming. NLP research data base. State of the art or pseudoscientific decoration? *Polish Psychological Bulletin, 41*(2), 58–66.

Woodley, M. A., te Nijenhuis, J., Must, O., & Must, A. (2014). Controlling for increased guessing enhances the independence of the Flynn effect from g: The return of the Brand effect. *Intelligence, 43*, 27–34.

Woodworth, R. S., & Thorndike, E. L. (1901). The influence of improvement in one mental function upon the efficiency of other functions (I). *Psychological Review, 8*(3), 247.

World Economic Forum (2016a). *The future of jobs* (retrieved from http://reports.weforum.org/future-of-jobs-2016/chapter-1-the-future-of-jobs-and-skills/#view/fn-1).

World Economic Forum (2016b). What are the 21st century skills every student needs? (retrieved from www.weforum.org/agenda/2016/03/21st-century-skills-future-jobs-students/).

Wrulich, M., Brunner, M., Stadler, G., Schalke, D., Keller, U., & Martin, R. (2014). Forty years on: Childhood intelligence predicts health in middle adulthood. *Health Psychology, 33*(3), 292–296.

Xu, D., & Jaggars, S. S. (2013). The impact of online learning on students' course outcomes: Evidence from a large community and technical college system. *Economics of Education Review, 37*, 46–57.

Xu, D., & Jaggars, S. S. (2014). Performance gaps between online and face-to-face courses: Differences across types of students and academic subject areas. *The Journal of Higher Education, 85*, 633–659.

Yeager, D. S., Hanselman, P., Paunesku, D., Hulleman, C., Dweck, C. S., Muller, C., & Duckworth, A. (2018, March 9). *Where and for whom can a brief, scalable mindset intervention improve adolescents' educational trajectories?* (retrieved from https://files.osf.io/v1/resources/r82dw/providers/osfstorage/5a9862261af855000df96541?action=download&version=6&direct&format=pdf).

Index